MW00808756

FINDING THE PIGGLE

FINDING THE PIGGLE
Reconsidering D. W. Winnicott's Most Famous Child Case

Edited by

Corinne Masur

PHOENIX
PUBLISHING HOUSE
firing the mind

The two colour drawings in Chapter One are reproduced with the kind permission of Gabrielle.

First published in 2021 by
Phoenix Publishing House Ltd
62 Bucknell Road
Bicester
Oxfordshire OX26 2DS

Copyright © 2021 to Corinne Masur for the edited collection, and to the individual authors for their contributions.

The rights of the contributors to be identified as the authors of this work have been asserted in accordance with §§ 77 and 78 of the Copyright Design and Patents Act 1988.

All rights reserved. No part of this publication may be reproduced, stored in a retrieval system, or transmitted, in any form or by any means, electronic, mechanical, photocopying, recording, or otherwise, without the prior written permission of the publisher.

British Library Cataloguing in Publication Data

A C.I.P. for this book is available from the British Library

ISBN-13: 978-1-912691-63-0

Typeset by Medlar Publishing Solutions Pvt Ltd, India

www.firingthemind.com

Contents

Acknowledgements

Greatest thanks go to Kate Pearce, my wonderful editor who provided calm, intelligent guidance and help throughout the process of putting this book together during a pandemic.

I would also like to thank Deborah Luepnitz without whom this book would not exist. It was Dr Luepnitz who originally wrote about her discovery of the identity of the adult Gabrielle and whose brilliant paper on this subject inspired me to look further at the case of *The Piggle*. This book was rightfully Dr Luepnitz's to edit but it was my good fortune that she was too busy to do so herself and gracious enough to allow me to do it.

I would also like to thank Salman Akhtar, psychoanalyst and author extraordinaire who has supported all my writing projects and who introduced me to Kate Pearce.

I must also mention my gratitude to the family of the late Christopher Reeves for granting me permission to use his two wonderful articles on *The Piggle* for this volume.

And, of course, I must thank all the chapter authors, Deborah Luepnitz, Laurel Silber, Zack Eleftheriadou, Justine Kalas Reeves, Brett Kahr, and the late Christopher Reeves for all their brilliant work in taking a fresh look at Donald Winnicott's classic child case, *The Piggle*.

About the editor and contributors

Dr Zack Eleftheriadou, MSc, MA, Dip IMH, Dip NCFED, is a chartered counselling psychologist, chartered scientist and a fellow of the British Psychological Society (HCPC reg), a member of The Bowlby Centre, and a founding scholar of the British Psychoanalytic Council (London, UK). She has trained as an integrative and psychoanalytic adult psychotherapist, child and parent–infant psychotherapist (UKCP reg). Since 1990, she has provided training and has published extensively in the following areas: developmental issues, cross-cultural work, and refugees and trauma, including the book *Psychotherapy and Culture* (Karnac, 2010). Currently, she works as a pastoral tutor, infant observation tutor, and clinical supervisor at The Institute for Arts in Therapy and Education. Alongside her teaching work, she runs a consultancy, providing psychotherapy and supervision. She is a visiting external examiner for doctoral level university students and a member of the UKCP Child Faculty subcommittee, Infant–Parent Psychotherapy. Zack feels passionate about promoting early intervention and provides teaching to midwives and paediatric nurses on ways to facilitate the parent–infant relationship.

Angela Joyce, fellow and training and supervising psychoanalyst and child psychoanalyst with the British Psychoanalytical Society. At the Anna Freud Centre she was a member of the pioneering Parent–Infant Project and jointly led the child psychotherapy service. She works in private practice in London. She is currently chair of the Winnicott Trust, a trustee of the Squiggle Foundation, and has been an honorary senior lecturer at University College London. Her publications in Winnicottian studies include *Reading Winnicott* edited with Lesley Caldwell, New Library of Psychoanalysis Teaching Series (Routledge, 2011); 'Introduction to Volume 6', *The Collected Works of D. W. Winnicott* (OUP, 2016); and *Donald Winnicott and the History of the Present* edited (Karnac, 2017).

Professor Brett Kahr has worked in the mental health profession for over forty years. He is Senior Fellow at the Tavistock Institute of Medical Psychology in London and, also, Visiting Professor of Psychoanalysis and Mental Health in the Regent's School of Psychotherapy and Psychology at Regent's University London. He holds additional honorary appointments as Senior Clinical Research Fellow at the Centre for Child Mental Health, as Consultant in Psychology to The Bowlby Centre, and as Consultant Psychotherapist to The Balint Consultancy. He also serves as Visiting Professor in the Faculty of Media and Communication at Bournemouth University, in recognition of his contributions to media psychology, having worked for many years as Resident Psychotherapist on BBC Radio 2. In addition to his roles as a clinician and teacher, Kahr is also a trained historian and has held the position of Trustee at the Freud Museum London and Freud Museum Publications, and has also worked as series co-editor of the "History of Psychoanalysis Series" for the publishers Routledge. Kahr has authored fifteen books and has served as series editor for more than sixty additional titles. His own publications include *D. W. Winnicott: A Biographical Portrait*, which received the Gradiva Award for Biography; *Sex and the Psyche*, which became a Waterstones Non-Fiction Bestseller, serialised in *The Times*; *Tea with Winnicott*; *Coffee with Freud*; *How to Flourish as a Psychotherapist*; *Bombs in the Consulting Room: Surviving Psychological Shrapnel*; and *Dangerous Lunatics: Trauma, Criminality, and Forensic Psychotherapy*.

Kahr has researched the life and work of Donald Winnicott for over thirty years and is currently completing the first part of his multi-volume biography of Winnicott, based on his interviews with more than 900 people who knew the great psychoanalyst personally. A registrant of both the British Psychoanalytic Council and the United Kingdom Council for Psychotherapy, Kahr works with individuals and couples in Central London.

Justine Kalas Reeves is a child, adolescent, and adult psychoanalyst in Washington, DC. She trained at the Anna Freud Centre in London, and the Contemporary Freudian Society in Washington, DC. She teaches at CFS and Howard University. She is currently secretary of the Association for Child Psychoanalysis.

Deborah Anna Luepnitz, PhD, was on the clinical faculty of the Department of Psychiatry at the University of Pennsylvania School of Medicine for over thirty years. In 2007, she joined the teaching faculty of the Institute for Relational Psychoanalysis of Philadelphia. Her books include: *The Family Interpreted: Psychoanalysis, Feminism, and Family Therapy* (1988) and *Schopenhauer's Porcupines: Five Stories of Psychotherapy* (2002), and she is a contributing author to the *Cambridge Companion to Lacan*. In 2005, Dr Luepnitz launched IFA (Insight For All) which connects homeless adults and children with psychoanalysts willing to work pro bono. She received the Distinguished Educator Award from the International Forum for Psychoanalytic Education in 2013, and maintains a private practice in Philadelphia.

Corinne Masur, PsyD, is a child and adult psychoanalyst who has worked with children and adults in a variety of settings for over forty years. She is a co-founder of The Parent Child Center in Philadelphia, The Philadelphia Center for Psychoanalytic Education, and The Philadelphia Declaration of Play. She was the editor of *Flirting With Death: Psychoanalysts Consider Mortality* (Routledge, 2019), and has written on childhood bereavement, the development of trust, the effect of divorce on children, and the denial of mortality, among other topics, and maintains a blog for parents: www.thoughtfulparenting.org.

Christopher Reeves was a child psychotherapist and director of the Squiggle Foundation. Between 1976 and 1990 he was first consultant and later principal of The Mulberry Bush School. He wrote extensively on Winnicott and issues to do with the theory and practice of child psychotherapy and psychoanalysis and he collaborated with Judith Issroff on the book *Donald Winnicott and John Bowlby: Personal and Professional Perspectives.*

Laurel Moldawsky Silber, PsyD, is a clinical psychologist whose training benefitted enormously by Winnicott's writings. She has been working with children and families in Bryn Mawr, PA, for over thirty years. She teaches and supervises at the Institute for Relational Psychoanalysis of Philadelphia. Her publications are in the area of play, intergenerational transmission of trauma, and childism. Her most recent publication was *Locating Ruptures Encrypted in Gender: Developmental and Clinical Considerations,* an original article which appeared in the *Journal of Infant, Child, and Adolescent Psychotherapy.* She co-edited a special issue, "Play for a Change" (Volume 19, Issue 2, 2020) for the same journal.

Foreword

Angela Joyce

The Piggle (1977) is a singular example of Winnicott's actual clinical work. Although his writings are peppered with clinical vignettes and references and there is the full volume of *Therapeutic Consultations in Child Psychiatry* (1971), nevertheless there is only one other extended account of his psychoanalytic clinic: *Holding and Interpretation* (1955). This new book of essays about Winnicott's original work with this young child is also singular. Although over the years since *The Piggle* was first published there have been several articles commenting upon it, there has not been a volume like this, which takes a view of the actual work from the perspective of some fifty-plus years subsequent development of clinical practice. It is a book which is both sympathetic to the original work and also questioning and critical in a creative engagement with it.

Winnicott is renowned as a clinician of rare skill especially with children. He was seen as possessing an extraordinary capacity to "get" children: to establish a connection with them at the deepest level; to discern their needs and wishes in such a way that he could be "used" by them to extend and enrich their selves. Brafman describes the therapeutic consultations as "examples of *communication with children*" (Brafman, 2001, quoting Winnicott, 1971, p. 8; emphasis in the original). Winnicott was interested in the child's experience of his/her problem, their lived experience, rather than any diagnostic category. "He surprised his listeners by his ease, his unaffectedness, his simplicity and his anti-conformity" (C. & P. Geissmann, 1998, p. 219). He frequently referred to his psychoanalytic training as the ground in which these capacities were cultivated.

Psychoanalysis is a living entity and has and is evolving in different directions. Winnicott himself was party to this elaboration during the amazingly creative decades of the mid twentieth century, as he embraced Klein's opening up of the pre-genital, infantile world and then recreated his own, different version of the foundations of early life. While he took Klein's ideas and ran with them, he could be thought of as doing something similar with Freud's. He revolutionised the psychoanalytic understanding of the beginning of life by his insistence on the relational context of the establishment of the self, thus multiplying the complexity of considerations for the psychoanalytic clinician. But he also remained in many respects an avowedly Freudian psychoanalyst, as he considered classical psychoanalysis to have been created for people who had been fortunate to have had a good enough beginning and as a consequence became "whole persons". This meant that they had the privilege of complex mental development through which they were then able to have or were prone to intrapsychic conflict. This in turn gave rise to symptoms whose meanings could be discovered and elucidated within the classical frame. For people who had not been so fortunate, something different was required of psychoanalysis if it was to have any relevance to them. His ability to hold and contain these many, sometimes contradictory threads, not to say tensions, within his identity and practice as a psychoanalyst is reflected in the complexity of his work. Perhaps inevitably, he was coincidentally a man of his time and a pioneer who was able to think outside the box.

Winnicott's treatment of the Piggle took place in the mid 1960s, in the last decade of his life. He remained a pioneer as he sought to integrate these myriad influences on his thinking and practice, in the context of his determination to follow his own ideas authentically. He had been a children's doctor for more than forty years by this time and a psychoanalyst for more than thirty. Before he finished his training as an analyst and then as a child analyst he had already spent more than a decade working with ordinary families with an ill child and a parent or somebody taking responsibility for that child, and this contributed to his concern for health and its dependence on psychosomatic integrity. "He came into it from health, building up health, diagnosing and building up health in children, rather than a lot of people who had to come into it from another angle from adult psychiatry and pathology" (Clare Winnicott, in Kanter, 2004, p. 262).

He had been much influenced by his time at Paddington Green Children's Hospital, at that time a poor area of west London, not only because of the vast numbers of families whom he saw in his clinic, but also because of the richness and variety of work that he was able to do with his team. He had also spent the formative years of World War II as consultant to the hostels in Oxfordshire where evacuated, disturbed children were billeted. By this time in the 1960s he had been married to Claire Britton, whom he had met during that time in Oxfordshire, for nigh on fifteen years, and her social work background was immensely influential in his thinking. She is credited (Kanter) with originating the concept of "holding" in her understanding of the function of social workers in their relationships with their clients.

Winnicott was inclined to a binocular view—holding the tension between inner reality and the external world as central to his understanding of the human predicament. So family life was often the focus of his writings, in all its manifestations of health and pathology, in which each individual person establishes and lives their lives according to how that tension is held, initially for the baby by the mother and father, and ultimately within themselves. This work with the toddler the Piggle, whose difficulties were presented by her parents as related to the birth of her younger sister, is rooted in Winnicott's psychoanalytic understanding of her development through these early years. That understanding was complex and reflected both his sense that her primary relationship with her mother was foundational, and also that as she grew, she was in the grip of "the consequences of instinctual experiences" in the family situation. Here she was working out these instinctual experiences on the interpersonal plane as well as internally. He was of the view that these situations are all the time held by the parents and through this the child is enabled to sort out her coexistent love and hate "so that they are brought under control in a way that is healthy" (Winnicott, 1954).

Several of the papers in this volume (Silber, Kalas Reeves, Eleftheriadou) take up what is seen as Winnicott's insufficient emphasis on the Piggle's family context, an interesting criticism as he is so known to privilege the so-called "environment". Certainly he was mindful of Gabrielle's parents and contrary to practice then current, included them in this "shared" treatment. He was keenly aware of a child's parents as a source of either help or hindrance in ongoing development and he recognised their therapeutic potential in adapting to their children's changing needs. "It is possible for the [psychoanalytic] treatment of a child actually to interfere with a very valuable thing which is the ability of the child's home to tolerate and to cope with the child's clinical states that indicate emotional strain and temporary holdups in emotional development, or even the fact of development itself" (Winnicott, 1977, p. 2).

All this is appreciated in this present book; but with the benefit of decades of development of clinical processes and the extension of knowledge and theory, the authors here bring a set of perspectives which both extend and challenge Winnicott's own understanding of his work. We might claim that his pioneering work within psychoanalysis enabled these later developments to take place. The much quoted aphorism "there is no such thing as a baby without maternal care", apparently needed to be spoken by Winnicott in the midst of the Controversial Discussions at the BPAS in the 1940s, enabled psychoanalysis to some degree to interrogate the relational environment of the nuclear family. Over the decades of the late twentieth century that interrogation became more extensive as the environment over several generations came to be recognised as having a continuing and major if hidden effect. As several authors in this volume point out, when Winnicott was treating the Piggle he seemingly did not investigate her family history over the previous generations. If he had, he would have learnt about the Holocaust history of the mother's family, the father's history of loss and migration, and perhaps extended his understanding of Gabrielle's loss of the exclusive place in her mother's mind.

One trenchant critique of the theoretical paradigm within which Winnicott is working with this child is his apparent ignoring of the thinking coming out of what would become "attachment theory". That he knew about this work is evident in his review of some of the films made by Joyce and James Robertson chronicling the impact of separations on young children in different situations (Winnicott, 1959). There he was fully in agreement with the painful truth of their effects, and even went so far as to say: "for most of us [it] needs no proof" (p. 529). As Masur (Chapter Four) points out, it is interesting therefore that there is no reference to the probable separation that the Piggle had endured when her mother gave birth to her sister. This is all the more interesting in that several of the Robertson films are about such children who had to endure both the separation from their mothers and the subsequent arrival of new siblings. As Masur does, we might speculate about his potential rivalry with John Bowlby, whose work at that time was laying the foundations of attachment theory and with whom Winnicott had a collegial but difficult relationship. Winnicott viewed Bowlby as not taking sufficient cognisance of the inner world and the power of unconscious phantasy in shaping the experience of the external environment.

Winnicott was intent on pursuing his psychoanalytic task of uncovering the unconscious meaning to his patient of her experiences. Here, as a nearly three year old whose early life seemingly had been good enough, he assumed that she was a "whole person", full of conflicting unconscious wishes and anxieties rooted in her instinctual life. His Freudian identity is evident in his focus on her psychosexual development, as his interpretations and indeed his contribution to her play in the transitional space of the work, attend to her oedipal longings as they have now been shaped by the arrival of her little sister. As Masur (this volume) points out, the Kleinian influence is also there: in his references to the inside of the mother's body for instance. He was alert to the presence of health in his patients and privileged the innate tendency towards growth and development. In *The Piggle* he wrote: "It is from the description of the psychoanalytic work, however, that the reader can see the essential health in this child's personality, a quality that was always evident to the analyst even when clinically and at home the child was really ill."

The Piggle was published posthumously, six years after Winnicott's death, and reviewed sympathetically though not regarded as without flaws. Psychoanalyst James Hood (1980) wrote: "Winnicott evidently enjoyed himself immensely in an activity that centrally focuses on play and on the interpretations which make play possible again for an ill child." Hood adds later: "Perhaps even more importantly the vague, chaotic, ill-understood or frankly confusing episodes are also allowed their full measure of description and comment. These have to be tolerated as they are in the treatment process itself." Another review by Ivri M. Kumin (1979) observes that the account is full of "moments of brilliant insight and uncanny clinical judgement, but also instances of misunderstanding, sleepiness, muddle and missed opportunities. In other words this is an honest and human book." Peter Tizard, an eminent paediatric colleague of Winnicott's, wrote to Clare: "The book tells so much about Donald and brings back all sorts of memories of his talking about children and his approach to them in his ordinary outpatients … it said so much about his complete acceptance of other people—adults and children—the one essential basis for good doctoring … there are so many delightful glimpses of Donald's sensitivity to children, for instance to know exactly when to call the child Gabrielle and not Piggle" (unpublished letter, DWW archive).

This book extends our thinking not only about this fascinating case, but also about psychoanalysis, children, history, the external world, inner reality, and the development of theory and practice over time. It demonstrates the aliveness of the psychoanalytic tradition in its myriad iterations.

References

Brafman, A. (2001). *Untying the Knot*. London: Karnac.

Geissmann, C. and Geissmann, P. (1998). *A History of Child Psychoanalysis*. London: Routledge (New Library of Psychoanalysis).

Hood, J. (1980). Review, *The Piggle. Journal of Child Psychology and Psychiatry*, 21(3): 273–279.

Kanter, J. (2004). *Face to Face with Children: The Life and Work of Clare Winnicott*. London: Karnac.

Kumin, I. M. (1979). Review of *The Piggle. Journal of the American Academy of Psychoanalysis*, 7(3): 453–455.

Winnicott, D. W. (1954). The depressive position in normal emotional development. In: L. Caldwell & H. T. Robinson (Eds.), *Collected Works of D. W. Winnicott, Vol 4* (pp. 185–200). Oxford: Oxford University Press, 2016.

Winnicott, D. W. (1955). *Holding and Interpretation*. In: L. Caldwell & H. T. Robinson (Eds.), *Collected Works of D. W. Winnicott, Vol 4* (pp. 303–474). Oxford: Oxford University Press, 2016.

Winnicott, D. W. (1959). Review: *Going to Hospital with Mother*, a film by James Robertson. In: L. Caldwell & H. T. Robinson (Eds.), *Collected Works of D. W. Winnicott, Vol 5* (pp. 529–534). Oxford: Oxford University Press, 2016.

Winnicott, D. W. (1971). *Therapeutic Consultations in Child Psychiatry.* In: L. Caldwell & H. T. Robinson (Eds.), *Collected Works of D. W. Winnicott, Vol 10* (pp. 27–533). Oxford: Oxford University Press, 2016.

Winnicott, D. W. (1977). *The Piggle.* In: L. Caldwell & H. T. Robinson (Eds.), *Collected Works of D. W. Winnicott, Vol 11* (pp. 187–315). Oxford: Oxford University Press, 2016.

Introduction

Corinne Masur

In January 1964, the parents of a little girl named Gabrielle wrote to Dr Donald Winnicott asking whether he could "spare time" to see her. They said, "She has worries, and they keep her awake at night and sometimes they seem to affect the general quality of her life and of her relationship with us, though not always" (Winnicott, *The Piggle*, 1977, p. 5).

Gabrielle's parents contacted Winnicott with a great mixture of feelings, as parents generally have when considering a course of psychotherapy or psychoanalysis for their child. They were worried, of course, and also guilty, fearful that their having had a second child so close in age to Gabrielle might have caused her suffering and necessitated professional intervention.

After reading the parents' letter, Winnicott decided to see Gabrielle, and since the family lived at a significant distance from his London office, and since his schedule was busy he decided to see her "on demand" in what he called "psychoanalysis *partagé*", or shared psychoanalysis in which the parents were an integral part of the treatment, communicating extensively with Winnicott before and after sessions.

Gabrielle was treated over two and a half years and was most often brought to the office by her father.

Winnicott wrote up his notes about this treatment and set them aside for several years until he was asked to supervise a case at the 1969 International Psychoanalytical Congress in Rome in their pre-congress meetings. He was unable to identify a student to supervise for the meeting and thus, in his playful way, suggested to his junior colleague and student, Ishak Ramzy, that Ramzy supervise *him* on the case of *The Piggle* in front of the audience. He said that he would present a child analytic hour and warned Ramzy that he might find it "pretty awful as analysis" (1977, p. xiii). He also threatened Ramzy with the possibility that he would not give him any material to review prior to the meeting—although he ended up giving him the manuscript (which eventually became the book entitled *The Piggle*).

In front of a standing room only crowd, Winnicott and Ramzy presented. Much discussion ensued, concerning, among other things, whether this case represented psychoanalysis or psychotherapy.

The case was later published posthumously in book form in 1977, edited by Ishak Ramzy. As Clare Winnicott (Winnicott's second wife and a child clinician in her own right) said in her preface to the volume, "The book presents the reader with a rare opportunity to be admitted into the intimacy of the consulting room" in order to study the child and the therapist at work (p. vii). Winnicott's notes are provided in order to give the reader insight into his theoretical understanding of what was happening between himself and the child as well as within the child's own mind. The description of Gabrielle's play provides a dramatisation of the child's inner world. As Clare Winnicott said, this work with Winnicott enabled Gabrielle "to experience and play with those fantasies that most disturb[ed] her" (p. viii).

Undoubtedly this treatment, and Winnicott's presence in the life of the Piggle's family were of the utmost importance to both Gabrielle and her parents, providing a powerful cause for hope for the return of this little girl to health and well-being following the onset of her very disturbing symptoms. And for more than five decades since its publication, the written version of the treatment has been read by graduate students, psychiatric hospital doctors, psychoanalytic candidates, social workers, psychologists, psychiatrists, and others interested in childhood psychopathology and the psychotherapeutic treatment of children the world over. It has provided a primer for play therapy with very young children, an art practised successfully by very few. Winnicott's deep listening to Gabrielle has given a model of working with children to practitioners as has his way of entering into and making meaning of the very young child's play.

For years, while this book was read and reread, the identity of the Piggle was unknown to most (although, as you will learn in this volume, some Winnicottian scholars and historians did know). Then, in 2017, Deborah Luepnitz published a paper in the *International Journal of Psychoanalysis* on her discovery of the adult who was the Piggle (reproduced in this volume). In her work with homeless people, Dr Luepnitz had corresponded with another therapist who did similar work. In the course of her second letter to Dr Luepnitz, the other clinician revealed that she was Gabrielle, the child written about by Winnicott in the book entitled *The Piggle*. Dr Luepnitz was fascinated and eventually planned to meet Gabrielle to learn more about her and her recollections and feelings about her treatment.

Dr Luepnitz began to think about the case as it was written by Winnicott in light of the new information she was learning regarding the patient. This led to writing the paper, "The Name of the Piggle" in which Dr Luepnitz investigates new lines of inquiry not regarded as priorities by Donald Winnicott in his treatment of Gabrielle: the transgenerational transmission of pathology/trauma and the ways that language in general and names in particular organise individual subjectivity. Luepnitz states that her goal is not to supplant but to expand Winnicott's—and therefore, our own—understanding of the case.

It is to this same purpose that this volume is dedicated. This book includes Dr Luepniz's wonderful paper and goes further, opening up a large number of new lines of inquiry which are looked at by various authors. This is especially meaningful considering that in Dr Luepnitz's paper she quotes Gabrielle as saying that she hoped at some point the case would be looked at in a new light and areas not covered by Winnicott would be explored. Of course the case has been discussed previously—and in some cases in ways that Gabrielle felt shut down further discussion (see Luepnitz in this volume)—but in this book the case is re-examined with new vigour.

Noted Winnicottian scholars Christopher Reeves and Brett Kahr make contributions to this re-examination as do Laurel Silber, Justine Kalas Reeves, Zack Eleftheradou, and I.

In my chapter, I explore the issue of loss and mourning in the life of Gabrielle and the effect of these upon her inner life and symptomatology. This was an area barely mentioned by Winnicott and only examined or interpreted, in my reading, once or twice—and glancingly so. It is striking to me that both Winnicott and Gabrielle's parents formulated the origin of her distress as coming from sibling and oedipal rivalry rather than from the prolonged loss of her mother during the mother's delivery of the new baby and her recovery. In the 1960s it was common for women to spend ten or more days in the hospital following the birth of an infant. However, that was a long, long time for a toddler to be without her mother. We know now and indeed, it was known at the time of Gabrielle's treatment, how injurious such separation can be for a young child. And the relative absence of interpretation of Gabrielle's sadness, anger, and depressive feelings as related to this loss is particularly notable coming from a man who himself laboured to prevent the separation of children from parents in war-torn London during the Blitz and after.

In Brett Kahr's chapter, new historical information is revealed regarding Winnicott's relationship with Gabrielle's family as is new Winnicottian biographical information, providing a rich context within which to understand Winnicott's work with Gabrielle. Kahr's access to hitherto unexplored historical documents pertaining to the Piggle's family and to Winnicott's life is remarkable and a wonderful contribution to the Winnicottian literature.

In Christopher Reeves' posthumously published chapter he explores the nature and purpose of *The Piggle*'s message. Originally Reeves presented this material in an extended paper published in two parts. In Part I he discussed *The Piggle* in its historical context alongside other contemporary child analyses (Klein's *Narrative of a Child Analysis* and McDougall's *Dialogue with Sammy*) and its ambivalent reception by its contemporary audience. He identified theoretical issues raised by the material; the use of commotional and conjunctional interpretations; the use of time, and analysis on demand; the place of play in therapy and the role of the parents, and he reviewed the dialogue between analyst and child as set out in the text, identifying emerging themes. He attempted to understand what Gabrielle was trying to communicate and reviewed Winnicott's interpretations, identifying areas in which they might have been at odds with what the child was experiencing.

In the second part of the paper, "Discussion and Critique", he reviewed the nature of the messages Winnicott wished to communicate to his audience through the psychoanalytic case of *The Piggle* and reviewed the dialogue which serves as the material for the work. This part provides a discussion and a critical analysis of the case, and an examination of both explicit and less worked-out conclusions which can be drawn from it. Reeves considered the case as evidence that therapy with a child can be intensive without being extensive. He highlighted Winnicott's emphasis on the importance of play for working through internal conflicts, not merely as providing material for interpretation. Whereas Winnicott held firmly to the efficacy of his commotional interpretations, and the notion that Gabrielle's unconscious dispositions were agentive and intentional, Reeves argued for an alternative to Winnicott's interpretation, highlighting the use of make-believe play, the irregular timing of the sessions, and the child's own maturational processes as being important elements in her recovery. He suggested that, for Winnicott, these factors were intuitively, rather than conceptually worked out, and, in so being, contribute to the enigmatic nature of the original work.

In Laurel Silber's chapter entitled "Child analysis is *shared*: holding the child's relational context in mind", she focuses on Winnicott's "psychoanalysis *partagé*". She discusses the way in which Winnicott entered Gabrielle's changing attachment context and helped the family to sort out the grief and fear which they were experiencing around the change brought about by the birth of a new sibling. She examines Winnicott's concept of psychoanalysis *partagé* comparing it to Phillip Bromberg's "standing in the spaces" and Selma Fraiberg's "Ghosts in the Nursery", emphasising as they do the need to consider the subjectivity of all the family members when trying to understand the (child) patient. She goes on to look at the attachment research and the transgenerational transmission process as they apply to the case of *The Piggle*.

In Justine Kalas Reeves' chapter she explores a number of aspects of the case of *The Piggle* including the use of Winnicott as a developmental object for Gabrielle as well as the idea of psychoanalysis *partagé*. She also writes about the theme of sibling rivalry within the case, the idea of intergenerational trauma within the family, and the possible role that the parents' marital troubles may have played in Gabrielle's development of symptoms.

In her chapter, Zack Eleftheradou also looks at the case of *The Piggle* from a contemporary interpersonal perspective. She asks the reader to enter the consulting room and imagine the family asking for help in 2020. She takes into account the concept that the family is a system which needs to be seen in its entirety as well as considering Daniel Stern's and Beatrice Beebe's emphasis on implicit communication within the family and Selma Fraiberg's concept of intergenerational trauma. Importantly, she also discusses cultural and racial issues within the case, a subject which Gabrielle herself reflected on as an adult. As Luepnitz noted in a revised and unpublished version of Chapter One given at the Division 39 Panel in March 2020: "She [Gabrielle] lamented that no one who has written about the case has picked up on its 'massively racist discourse'— by which she means the black mummy and the fears of all things black."

Donald Winnicott has often been described as a non-linear thinker, as courageously original, observant, and insightful, for example, by Judith Issroff. He drew attention to the kinesthetic and motoric ways of communicating (for example, crawling backwards to describe a schizophrenic child's way of lining up his thoughts), he described the importance of the mother–infant relationship in new and revealing ways, he examined the importance of the transitional object and of transitional space as well as developing myriad other new and original ideas and concepts related to human psychic development. His creative genius and sensitivity to children (and to people of all ages) cannot be underestimated and any critique found here is made exclusively in the interest of providing further life for the seminal case of *The Piggle*.

CHAPTER ONE

The name of the Piggle: reconsidering Winnicott's classic case in light of some conversations with the adult Gabrielle*

Deborah Anna Luepnitz

A favourite anecdote has it that a child was sent to Donald Winnicott because her father complained of bad table manners. Winnicott counselled his patient to recite the following to her father:

> I eat my peas with honey,
> I've done so all my life,
> It makes the peas taste funny
> But keeps them on the knife. (Anderson, 2015, p. 37)[1]

The psychoanalyst of play, known for riding his bicycle with feet on the handlebars, would not see pathology in mere peccadilloes. When a child was actually ill, however, Winnicott recommended five treatment sessions per week. The tension between his belief in the healing potential

---

* This chapter is based on a previously published paper: Luepnitz, D. A. (2017). The name of the Piggle: Reconsidering Winnicott's classic case in light of some conversations with the adult 'Gabrielle'. *The International Journal of Psychoanalysis, 98:2*: 343–370. Copyright © Institute of Psychoanalysis, reprinted by permission of Taylor & Francis Ltd, http://www.tandfonline.com on behalf of Institute of Psychoanalysis.

of child analysis, and his trust in things sorting themselves out naturally, is illustrated, par excellence, in the case history known as *The Piggle*. He explains in the book's introduction:

> Once a child has started treatment, what is lost sight of is the rich symptomatology of all children who are being cared for in their own satisfactory homes. It is possible for the treatment of a child actually to interfere with a very valuable thing which is the ability of the child's home to tolerate and to cope with the child's clinical states ... (p. 2)

Published in 1977, *The Piggle* is still taught in courses around the world, and has never gone out of print. Nor are its admirers limited to child analysts. Philosopher Martha Nussbaum (2003) called it "one of the great examples in English literature of an adult entering the wild, conflict-ridden world of a young child" (p. 159; see also Nussbaum, 2018). Best-selling graphic novelist, Alison Bechdel (2012) who introduced Winnicott to lay readers in *Are You My Mother?* sketched herself musing: "I'm curious whether 'Gabrielle' might have written about her analysis with Winnicott ... Maybe his treatment was so effective she didn't need to write about it. She's probably just off living her life somewhere" (p. 156).

Bechdel is not the only reader so captivated by *The Piggle* as to wonder what became of the adult. Forty years after the book's publication, I propose to reconsider the case, in light of my communication from 2015 to the present with the adult Gabrielle, which is her actual name. She has indeed been "off living her life"—as a psychodynamic psychotherapist—in London.

Summary of the case

Winnicott agreed to see Gabrielle, nicknamed "the Piggle", when she was two years, four months old, in response to her parents' description of a bizarre personality change, and night terrors that took two forms. First, she feared a "black mummy" who lived inside her and made her black. Second, she was afraid of trains and "the babacar"—a made-up word her mother thought might combine "baby car" and "black car".

She would cry: "Tell me about the babacar. *All* about the babacar." And: "Mummy, cry about the babacar!" (Winnicott, 1977, pp. 6–7). The night terrors began shortly after the birth of her sister Susan. At a later point, she fears being poisoned (p. 64) and is preoccupied with death (p. 87).

There is discussion at the outset about whether or not a full analysis is needed. The family lived outside London, making five sessions per week nearly impossible. Winnicott reminds the parents that most children outgrow such fears and difficult states, but remains open to seeing her if she doesn't improve on her own. As the child grows more anxious, the mother tells her: "I've written to Dr Winnicott who understands about babacars ..." (p. 7). A distressed Gabrielle reportedly pleads: "Mummy, take me to Dr Winnicott" (p. 7).

The patient is seen on a schedule Winnicott categorises as treatment "on demand". It amounts to sixteen sessions over several years; she is five years, two months old at termination.

During their first meeting, Gabrielle tells of the arrival of her baby sister. She picks up items in the room, asking: "Where did this come from?" Winnicott intervenes: "And where did the baby come from?" (p. 11). He introduces an oedipal theme, asking if she ever gets mad at mummy, given that "they both love the same man" (p. 12). Winnicott saw exceptional ego strength in the Piggle, alongside "elements of madness, e.g. the babacar" (p. 17). After that first consultation, the mother writes to say that she played happily for a bit, but then got worse—insisting openly that she was a baby, and refusing to be called by her own name. The issue, Winnicott tells the reader, is renegotiating a relationship with the mother that can allow for hate. The Piggle remains obsessed with the "babacar", and in the second consultation, Winnicott "takes a risk", interpreting: *"It's the mother's insides where the baby is born from."* She looks relieved and replies: "Yes, the black inside" (p. 24).

In the eleventh consultation, he offers some explanation of the mysteries of reproduction, in clear, Kleinian terms. "The man is a robber. He robs the mother of her breasts. He then uses the stolen breast as a long thing—a wee-wee, which he puts into the girl's baby-hole and in there he plants babies. So he doesn't feel so bad about having been a robber" (pp. 142–143).

On another occasion, she asks about his birthday, and he returns: "What about my death day?" (p. 124), perhaps preparing the child for his own death. Gabrielle invents a game with a rolling pin in which she gets rid of Winnicott—turning helpless fear into playful aggression. Here, he underscores an important truth about therapy with children. Whereas Klein and Anna Freud felt that children's play was important as grist for interpretation, he argued:

> It is not possible for a child of this age to get the meaning out of a game unless, first of all the *game is played and enjoyed*. As a matter of principle, the analyst always allows the enjoyment to become established before the content of the play is used for interpretation. (p. 175)

At the sixteenth and final consultation, Gabrielle, aged five, acts shy. Winnicott says: "I know when you are really shy, and that is when you want to tell me that you love me." He remarks: "She was very positive in her gesture of assent," leaving him with the impression of a "really natural and psychiatrically normal girl of 5 years" (p. 198). In an epilogue written by the parents when Gabrielle is thirteen, they state that, despite normal ups and downs, she is thriving. They cite her strong values, independent judgement and sensitivity to others as possibly related to the experience of "being deeply understood" at a crucial moment in her young life.

Winnicott presented the case at an international conference in 1969, during which he asked a junior colleague to supervise him, instead of vice versa. Publication of the case—made possible through the coordinated efforts of the child's mother and Clare Winnicott—occurred six years after his passing.

The Piggle is a text that can be read in many ways. It is a clinical history, including marginal notes in which Winnicott glosses his interventions, making it a useful primer. It also reads as a kind of epistolary novel, as the treatment sessions are interspersed with letters from the parents describing her progress. When asked, the Piggle says she thought Winnicott was writing his autobiography. Indeed, in addition to being a case study and a novel, it is also something of a memoir, reflecting the last few years of his life as a clinician.

Child psychotherapist and Winnicott scholar, Christopher Reeves (2015a, 2015b), former director of the Squiggle Foundation, in his thorough examination of *The Piggle*, asks what it is that can be considered curative in the case. He calls into question the efficacy of the Kleinian "commotional" interpretations—defined as those that "… intentionally promote the release of anxiety related to conflict …" (p. 162). Moreover, he notes that, like all analysts, Winnicott listens selectively. For example, although the Piggle is afraid of *trains* and the *babacar,* Winnicott pursues the latter only, despite the fact that the word "train" appears three times more often than "babacar". Reeves concludes that *The Piggle* succeeds in demonstrating that positive results may come from a treatment that is *intensive* but not *extensive* in the classical format. However, *The Piggle* cannot be said to represent "on demand" analysis, as claimed. First, says Reeves, it's not clear if a toddler's demand ever can be understood apart from the parents' wishes, and furthermore, there were times the demand was made and not met. Gabrielle had to wait on one occasion for nearly three months, while the parents worried she was on the brink of breakdown.

How words use *us*

Winnicott was a gifted writer with a genius for understanding the nonverbal. Even his greatest admirers, however, have noted something about the area of language that remains undeveloped in his work (e.g. Phillips, 1988). André Green wrote famously:

> After Freud, I see two authors who have pushed their research and coherence very far on the basis of two quite different points of view and which up to a certain point converge. These two authors are Lacan and Winnicott. (1987, p. 121)

Green, who allied himself with the British Middle Group after turning away from Lacan, felt nonetheless compelled to write: "I am not an unconditional Winnicottian … [A]n analyst who really wants to think about practice cannot dispense with a reflection on language, a reflection that is absent in Winnicott" (1987, p. 124).

It is true that Winnicott wrote: "A word like 'self' naturally knows more than we do; it uses us, and can command us" (1960, p. 158). However, he never discussed what words like "self" know, such as how their history and usages shape subjective experience. This is in stark contrast to Freud's collected works where, as Jacques Lacan (2006) points out: "... one out of three pages presents us with philological references" (p. 424). Freud's discovery of the relentless wordplay of the unconscious was used by Lacan (2006) to formulate his own theory of the signifier.

In Winnicott's *oeuvre*, there are very few examples of his pausing to call attention to a patient's turn of phrase, or to underscore a double meaning. The adult patient described in his book-length case, *Holding and Interpretation* (1972) is simply called "the patient" without so much as a pseudonym or initial. (This, in contrast to Freud's considered naming of his patients, e.g. "Dora" and "Rat Man" or Lacan's naming his first patient "Aimée".) Winnicott indicates in the book's introduction that the nickname "Piggle" "is a common term of endearment for a child" (1977, p. 1). In the early sessions, he uses that nickname, but at the sixth consultation, when she is two years, ten months old, he remarks: "This time I knew I must say 'Gabrielle', not 'Piggle'" (p. 77). He doesn't say how he knew or why he wouldn't ask the child her preference. In the tenth consultation, the Piggle, absorbed in play, muses aloud: "My sister's name is Nathalie Susan; it's Italian. I am Deborah Gabrielle" (p. 123). Again, the analyst lets it go—much more interested in providing words for nonverbal gestures. A typical example is in the sixth consultation when she shows off her bare feet: "You are showing me big breasts" (p. 81).

The other category that some contemporary therapists might deem underdeveloped in the case has to do with projective identification and the unconscious transmission of trauma, discussed next.

"Not family therapy—not casework— psychoanalysis *partagé*"

Winnicott's notes on *The Piggle* include these:

> Share material with the parents. Not family therapy—not case-work—psychoanalysis *partagé* (shared). No breach of confidence on their part, and they didn't interfere. (p. viii)

It's not clear if Winnicott had thought about "shared psychoanalysis" before this moment, but obviously such a thing is feasible only with young child patients. (Recall the case of Elisabeth von R. in which Freud famously "shared" with the patient's mother the reason for her daughter's hysterical pains, infuriating Elisabeth who proceeded to terminate treatment (Breuer & Freud, 1895d, p. 160)).

Winnicott felt the need to exchange information in this case so that he could offer direction to two very worried parents. There are generous hints, but no major discussion about how the pathology itself was *partagé*.

The idea of "shared" psychopathology is prefigured in Freud's (1921c) *Group Psychology and the Analysis of the Ego* where, in positing a "group psyche", he explores the phenomenon of scapegoating. (The family, being a special case of a group, can be said to manifest a "family psyche".) Many analysts from the second half of the twentieth century forward insist on a shared-pathology perspective. They have used the work of Klein, Bion, and Winnicott to discuss ways that children hold not only their parents' conscious concerns but also their split-off affects—and illness (Box, Copley, Magagna, & Moustaki, 1981; Sander, 1978; Scharff & Scharff, 1987; Skynner, 1976). Even a very young child can contain anxieties—neurotic or psychotic—for the whole. Moreover, interest appears to be growing in the idea that children can be the unwitting receptacles not only of the pathology of parents and siblings, but also that of grandparents and ancestors as well, in what is called "the trans-generational transmission of psychopathology" (Davoine, 2007; Faimberg, 2005; Volkan, Ast, & Greer, 2002).

Winnicott expressed no interest in a three-generational perspective, neither with child nor adult patients. For example, interviews with his former analysands Marion Milner and Enid Balint revealed that he had explored material about their parents, but not grandparents (Luepnitz, 1992, 2020). Unlike Klein, Winnicott was a strong believer in taking a child's developmental history, and there are hints scattered throughout the text of *The Piggle* that point to the *parents'* unconscious contribution to the child's problem.

For example, the mother, in her first letter to Winnicott, acknowledges the relevance of family dynamics when she writes of the Piggle: "She had a little sister when she was 21 months old which I considered far too early for her. And both this (and I would think also our) anxiety about it seemed to bring about a great change in her" (Winnicott,

1977, p. 6). Winnicott states in a footnote on that page: "I did not know until much later that the mother herself had experienced the birth of a sibling at this very age".

In a letter sent after the first consultation, the mother writes:

> I think that you were right that we had been too "clever" about understanding her distress. We felt very involved and guilty about not having arranged to not have a baby again so soon and, somehow, her nightly desperate pleading, "Tell me about the babacar"—made us feel under pressure to say something meaningful. (p. 20)

After the third consultation, the mother writes to Winnicott saying they, the parents, feel the child is regressing, and may need a full analysis.

Winnicott is still not convinced, and in fact, after the sixth consultation, remarks to the reader: "… I did feel that these parents had some special reason for not relying on the developmental process, which in this child might see her through apart from the provision of treatment" (p. 86).

By the age of four, Gabrielle, to everyone's relief, seems to have resumed developmental strides. The mother writes to Winnicott after the twelfth consultation:

> I would like to tell you—though you may know this—how much writing to you has helped me; somehow to give form to my perplexities and fears, with the knowledge that they would be received with great understanding; and the feeling of being in relation with you. I am sure all of this helped me to work through our anxieties about Gabrielle and again to find our right relationship with her. (p. 161)

Many therapists who find Winnicott immensely useful nonetheless have felt the need to look beyond his two-generational framework. Some arrive at a multigenerational perspective via the work of family therapists such as Bowen (1978) and Boszormenyi-Nagy (1976) who speak of "family legacies" and "unfinished business"—although their understanding of the unconscious is never clear. Others would point out that Freud himself often alluded to grandparents, and that he would have assumed that his readers knew the full story of Oedipus, whose father, Laius—son of Labdacus—had already put the oedipal tragedy in motion when he abducted a young boy. Still others would point to the work of Jacques Lacan—in particular his seminars on the transference (Lacan, 1991) and on the ethics of psychoanalysis (Lacan, 1992) in which he introduces the term: family atè ($\alpha\tau\eta$)—a Greek word probably best translated as the family madness or curse. The analyst may use the preliminary sessions—before the patient lies down on the couch—to ask about two or more generations of family history.

A small but growing number of analysts are attempting to bring Lacan's work into provocative contact with that of Winnicott (Bernstein, 2011; Ireland, 2003; Kirshner, 2011; Luepnitz, 2009; Vanier & Vanier, 2010). These authors vary greatly in their method and purpose for working with both Winnicott and Lacan. Some explore the comparisons and contrasts between them for heuristic reasons only, discouraging any attempt to borrow from both in clinical practice. Others see the two theories as supplementary or even complementary. Ireland (2003) describes her own work as a "Squiggle game" between these two great traditions. Not all are likely to accept the author's term "New Middle Group" to designate those who work with Lacan and Winnicott in any way (Luepnitz, 2009).

How the Piggle came to disclose her identity to the author

In the spring of 2015, I wrote to a therapist in London, commending her on an excellent paper about working in a psychoanalytic way with homeless and other socially excluded adults. I told her about IFA (Insight For All), my group of analysts who work with homeless individuals in Philadelphia (Luepnitz, 2015). She then read my papers, including: "Thinking in the Space between Winnicott and Lacan" (Luepnitz, 2009). That article contained the description of a patient, "Alvareth", who had been named for a Holocaust victim, but whose family couldn't bear to call her by that name. The issues of naming, and of exploring three, not just two generations, were key to that patient's recovery from lifelong depression.

In a letter dated July 11, 2015, the London therapist in question wrote to tell me she appreciated what she called the paper's "Winnicott/Lacan dialogue", and elaborated:

> I hope you don't mind if I add a small personal association to your discussion of the "given name" and the neglect of history in the Middle Group tradition. I was a child patient of Winnicott's nicknamed "the Piggle". My mother's family were refugees—German-speaking Czechs. My mother's background would have been evident to Winnicott because she maintained a very strong "foreign" accent, while also expressing herself beautifully in English. Despite British reserve, people often asked her (or her children) where she was from. As you say, it seems that Winnicott restrained his curiosity in these matters. I was the first post-Holocaust child of my generation. "Gabrielle" is my second name. Esther—my first name—holds the family's Jewish history and trauma. As you describe: "They had dutifully given her the name 'Alvareth' but they couldn't say it." Reading this theme in your paper has crystallized many thoughts that I've had over time about The Piggle text, my family, etc.

We proceeded to correspond throughout the year, and arranged to meet in London. During that year, Gabrielle made available to me roughly 100 unpublished letters between Winnicott and her parents, and drawings he made for her during his post-termination visits to their home. (Two of the drawings are reproduced here on pp. 28–29, with her permission.) Gabrielle's memory of him derives largely from those visits, rather than from the treatment, when she was a toddler. She wrote to me, early on: "… I have rather longed for a time when there could be robust but sympathetic contemporary discussion about some of the issues The Piggle raises" (letter, September 16, 2015). She later added: "… my family were troubled and sought solution by sending one child for treatment—and that didn't resolve all the trouble!" (letter, January 11, 2016). My goal was to find out what she would like future readers to know.

Family history, mother's side

By way of introducing her mother, who died in 2010, Gabrielle sent me the eulogy she herself had delivered. Following are some excerpts:

It is impossible to sum my mother up, but we hope that she will emerge in the things we have chosen to remember her with today ...

Friedl was born in the Czech Republic—on her birth certificate she is Bedriska—the Czech for Frederika—called Friedl. These early days were happy times—by the age of 4, she was a champion skier. At the age of 11, she was sent to school in England—from 1933, crossed Europe every term accompanied only by her younger brother Gerry. At her English girls' school, she was amused to be told off for crossing the road to the playing fields when she had just crossed terrifying Europe, changing trains in Germany. In 1940 she travelled alone to Paris and brought her brother Tom, who was 10 years younger to England. They came in on a fake passport in which he was marked as her son. The Nazis murdered the majority of the Jews in Central Europe including her grandmother Margarethe and her aunt Gerta, whom she much admired. When we celebrate the time we have had with her and those of her generation, we must bear their survival in mind.

... [D]uring the war she volunteered in London shelters for bombed out families. She was also a fire watcher for the London skyline, recounting the experience of walking knee-deep in tea when warehouses on the docks were bombed. At that time she read philosophy at the LSE which had been evacuated to Cambridge.

She moved from London to Oxford when she married a friend of her brother, Tom.

In London, she trained as a child psychotherapist at the Tavistock Clinic. She always loved her work ... She'd been supervised by the great Melanie Klein ... Within the psychoanalytic community, riven with splits and infighting, she was remarkably unpartisan. She engaged Donald Winnicott, an Independent, to work with her troubled toddler [Gabrielle] and the correspondence she had with him forms part of the published account of the case called *The Piggle*. This work with Winnicott was very important to her in the last months of her life ... Winnicott said: "Let me be alive when I die." She quoted this often and intensely alive is how she'll always seem to me, both in body, mind and spirit ...

Meeting Gabrielle

Gabrielle is a slender woman in her late fifties with thick, silvery hair and dark, expressive eyes. She has a clear, resonant voice, a warm, generous laugh, and an unassuming air of self-confidence. After a dinner during which we talked about our work with homeless patients, we met on two subsequent days at her home in South London which she shares with her partner of twenty years, an architect.

I asked when she read *The Piggle* for the first time.

Gabrielle: I was in my twenties ... I can remember feeling profoundly disconnected from it! Not really recognising myself.

  Author: It's about some little girl, but not about you?

    G: Yes.

    A: Do you have even a glimmer of a memory of it?

    G: That's a good way of putting it: a glimmer of a memory. I remember shoes ... and shelves.

In the course of the interview, she acknowledged remembering one important moment of the work, discussed later.

Before training as a psychotherapist, Gabrielle was a social worker, and unlike others in her cohort who rejected psychoanalytic thinking, she was drawn to it. She continues to use Winnicott's ideas in her own clinical work and by no means discounts the notion of "on demand" treatment, particularly with the incarcerated and homeless men and women to whom she has devoted much of her professional life. "My work at the [housing charity] left me feeling that turning up for every session is an over-rated sign of ego strength, probably on the part of both participants!" (letter, August 15, 2016).

She worries a bit that Winnicott's work will be forgotten by the next generation, and was pleased to know that he remains extremely popular in the United States. American students admire the Winnicott who sits cross-legged with the Piggle and pouts, much to her delight: "I want to be the only baby! ... Shall I be cross?" (1977, p. 29). However, those same young therapists are often put off by his Kleinian interpretations, and wonder how children can make use of them. For example, in the twelfth consultation, when she greedily takes the stuffing out of a dog,

Winnicott interprets as follows: "When you love me it makes you want to eat my wee-wee" (p. 156).

I asked Gabrielle if she had a sense that these "commotional" interpretations, as Reeves (2015a) calls them, made it difficult for her to connect with the case on first reading.

G: No, I have no sense of that at all … I already had a strong view that children think a lot about sex and experience sex. So it seemed completely natural for him to be talking about those things. I mean "sex" in the broader sense of: Who am I?, and To whom do I belong?, as well as Who is going to eat me, and whom will I eat?

Gabrielle made it clear in an early letter that she had kept her identity as Winnicott's patient almost completely confidential. She said that being the Piggle had made her the subject of some "reverential attention" over the years on the part of the few who knew. However, she said that it had also caused a certain amount of embarrassment, as many of her fellow students felt that Winnicott's patriarchal attitudes, and his looking the other way with regard to Masud Khan's misconduct (Hopkins, 2006) made it unseemly to have been this man's patient at any time. She raised another source of discomfort with the case—one I did not anticipate.

G: The bit that felt increasingly uncomfortable is something no one has picked up, i.e. that there is a massively racist discourse going on. I don't think I meant "black" as a racial term, but I [as the Piggle] do associate it with everything bad and frightening.

Her parents tell Winnicott that the Piggle is afraid not only of the black mummy, but also of becoming black herself and of black people.

For young children, the absent object is by definition the bad/persecutory object, and a dark room turns presence into absence. Gabrielle agreed that "bad" and "black" might be linked that way at the level of the psyche, but as a young social worker, it was nonetheless a source of discomfort.

G: The memory I *do* have about reading the text in my twenties is worrying about whether I had got the bad meaning of "black" from the racist discourse on race in the UK in the 1960s. I remember then telling myself: It's OK; it's the Queen of the Night from *The Magic Flute* who is a frightening character. And we listened to it a lot when I was little!

Another relevant observation about race is that Jews were not considered to be white, and were often coded as black in Nazi propaganda (Gilman, 1993). All of these associations with racial darkness are belied by the photograph on the cover of the Penguin edition of *The Piggle* with which most readers are familiar. One sees a smartly dressed child with a milky complexion and sad blue eyes the size of ten pence. Gabrielle agreed, and has no idea who that child is, or how the photo was chosen.

No one in the British Middle Group left us any major reflection on race, but Winnicott (1986) himself did raise some excellent questions in a speech he gave in 1965 titled "The Price of Avoiding Psychoanalytical Research". He starts off by arguing that scientific studies should *never* be about *rats, statistics, or parlour games*. His example of what might constitute real research is as follows: "A researcher might ask ten analysts a question such as: 'How has the idea of *black* come into the material of analyses that you have been conducting during the past month?'" This would be based on "... patients' dreams and in children's playing ..." (1986, p. 174). He continues—in a rare bit of social commentary: "One result would be the discovery that much is not yet known about the meaning of black in the unconscious ... What is the price of ignoring this piece of research that could so easily be done? One piece is a serious one in terms of continuing misunderstanding on the part of white-skinned people in relation to black, and of the dark millions in relation to whites" (p. 174). We know that he must have had little Gabrielle in mind because in the ninth consultation—just weeks before he delivered the talk about research—he wrote: "In this setting, the black mother is the good mother who has been lost" (p. 118). Note that for Winnicott, "black" in the unconscious need not mean bad or dangerous, as it is used colloquially. Instead, he maintains that the signifier black refers often to a *lost good thing*—or to the denial of absence. (See also Hogan, 1992.) Here, indeed, is an area ripe for research.

I asked Gabrielle if she had any other associations to the made-up word "babacar".

G: Yes. The Baba Yaga. I think it means "witch". And I would have known about the Baba Yaga at that age—a witch, in Russian.

The Baba Yaga is central to Slavic folklore. Although she can be both helpful and thwarting, she rides in a mortar and wields a pestle, suggesting the phallic mother. This chimes with the Piggle telling her mother, after the tenth consultation, that she imagines mum to have "a long wee". When asked where mother would have got her long wee, she replies: "From the Daddy." And where did *he* get it? "From his students," answers the Piggle (Winnicott, 1977, p. 133). That passage led Lacanian analyst Eric Laurent (1981) to remark that this perceptive child seems to intuit the difference between penis and phallus—the latter being not a biological given, but a signifier that can circulate. (See also Lenormand, 2018.)

Gabrielle stated that she had suffered over the years—in her own estimation—from not fulfilling the potential suggested by the deeply sensitive and precocious girl depicted in the text. The real Gabrielle ended up having learning difficulties in elementary school, particularly around reading. That would, of course, be an apt way of differentiating oneself from two spectacularly learned parents. In any case, it's possible that she felt like a child star who could scarcely live up to adult expectations. This, despite exceptional success on all fronts.

Our interview focused on the family's history—the topic she had introduced in her initial letter. I asked how they were able to flee Eastern Europe. (Note her use of the present tense, below.)

G: Two things are helpful. My mother's father is prescient—and they think him mad. He said, "We must leave." Also, they were very wealthy. It's an uncomfortable fact, because 90% of Czech Jews were killed. However, due to the wool trade, they had connections, and maybe bank accounts here, which was another rule … This is sketchy in my account because it was not talked about. If they did, it was to persuade us that the Nazis were bad, and that the Brits hadn't always been as sympathetic as they portrayed themselves as being.
A: There is a saying that Jewish children are born with tears for the Holocaust. Some families talk about it every day, and others rarely do.

G: It wasn't a taboo. We did talk about it … [In] the early 1930s … the cousins from Brno were moving into a new house. They lived there five years only before they had to flee. No one believed that Hitler's rise to power would affect *their* section of society.

A: Did you say at some point the family moved to France?

G: Yes, but very late—in 1940—they had to leave in a hurry because Hitler is coming. My grandfather has a stroke and comes to England, with my grandmother. My mother had to use a passport that someone made saying her brother, Tom, was her son, on this ship, which is also carrying English soldiers from the front. When she gets to England—this is always told humorously—she doesn't know what to do with him, so she takes him to her [girls' boarding] school, and everyone fusses over him, and he has a nice time.

A: She was eighteen and he, eight. Did she tell that story with a sense of terrible danger?

G: No, humorously.

A: OK—now they are safe in England. And your grandparents came too, because you wrote to me about how their giant poodles were able to come to Scotland. One was called "Bonny"—not *"Bunny"* as the dog is called in *The Piggle*.
[We had discussed that mistake by mail, agreeing that no self-respecting dog would answer to "Bunny!"]

A: The Piggle has a dream of all four grandparents in a swimming pool together. Do you remember?

G: Oh yes! My grandmother had a holiday home in France and we would have gone there—but the other grandparents would not have gone there, and my maternal grandfather died before I was born.

A: What else do you know about your great-grandmother Margarethe and your great-aunt Gerta-Esther? Do you know what year they died at Auschwitz?

G: I don't know. That's quite important, isn't it? I don't know.

A: Have you ever been to Auschwitz?

G: No, I really couldn't, but my sister has … The knowledge I would have had at the time of *The Piggle* is that my grandmother Alice had a brother who was interned in France and survives and married a Hungarian woman who also survived.

A: Have you considered yourself always as the child of survivors?

G: No. Only since I've got older. Just that I've always known my story is a bit different from others'.

A: You said you grew up feeling like a foreigner.

G: Yes, well my Mum kept her accent, and we had foreign ways and also eccentric ways. I was scruffy at school and my white shirts would go in the wash with something pink and come out pink.

This struck the author as yet another worry about whiteness.

Father's history

Gabrielle's father was born in Ireland, and was sent to boarding school in England at the age of eleven.

G: His parents were Irish Protestants; my mother described them as "Anglo-English"! One of the commonalities between my parents was that both knew a country they had lost. My paternal grandfather had worked as an engineer on the big Capetown to Cairo railway project and lived in the Sudan when it was still an English colony. Obviously, at the time of the revolution, the foreign workers were pulled out, during my father's childhood. They came back to a grim and difficult life in Ireland after a privileged colonial life in Africa.

A: Was his father away for long periods of time?

G: He was, and his mother for less protracted periods, and he was cared for by an aunt. He was an only child due to a number of miscarriages, and those separations.

A: Did he talk about his childhood?

G: A bit. My paternal grandparents were extremely formal and rather embarrassed by us as children, especially our compulsive nakedness ... My father, I suspect, walked away from Ireland and his family early on. He lost his Irish accent. Those days, there were signs that said: "No dogs, Blacks or Irish".

A: How did they feel about your Mom?

G: I had a feeling they disapproved of her. I remember things used to go wrong ... Once when they arrived, my mother made a custard with salt instead of sugar... It's important to know that my mother described herself as totally undomesticated. The house was not clean,

the children were covered in mud. Very different from the anal Protestants who cared about decorum!

[Gabrielle had shown me a photograph of her mother's father on his
sixtieth birthday, doing a full handstand, with the family cheering
him on.]

A: Did you say your Dad, like your grandfather, was playful and affec-
tionate with the two of you?

G: Yes!

A: Just as one would imagine from Winnicott's saying in *The Piggle* that
he was impressed at how your father let you climb all over him …
When did they marry?

G: I think 1958 and on their honeymoon there was a motor accident in
France and my father breaks his back, but low down, fortunately. He
was driving. He was in plaster for six months.

A: Did your parents tell the story of falling in love?

G: My father was the friend of my mother's brother, Tom. Tom went
off to play rugby and asked mother to look after his shy friend and
mother was furious because she wanted to read. She said: "He can
come with me on a walk, but I'm going to read my book." That's how
they started! It was the mid fifties. My mother was in her thirties,
and he was twelve years younger, and immature for that. He went
to a boys' boarding school and men's college and I don't know if he'd
ever met a woman!

A: What attracted them, do you imagine?

G: She was fascinated with his mind. He was learned and so was she.
I think he was drawn to her large central European family, very cul-
tured, very at ease.

Another thing Gabrielle mentioned along with the fact that her mother
spoke English with an accent is that her father had a rather significant
stammer, a point not mentioned in the text.

Even in the twenty-first century, a marriage between a woman and
a man twelve years her junior is unusual; in the 1950s, it was all but
unheard of. Gabrielle noted that her mother, although beautiful, was
nearly twice the age of her classmates' mothers. Also, when her parents
would meet her at school, they would hug her, whereas other parents—
the true English—were very reserved, even around their own children.

I commented that while Winnicott is well known for his concept of the *good enough mother*, he never used the term *good enough father*. However, some readers suggest that he offered up an example in *The Piggle*. Both parents attend the first session, and in fact it is the father who accompanies the Piggle on subsequent visits. As one who practised family therapy for many years, this author knows how difficult it can be to convince fathers that therapy is valuable and their own participation important. Gabrielle's father also communicated with Winnicott between sessions in letters and phone calls which reveal him to be a fully involved parent, deeply concerned about his child's night terrors and daytime fears. Gabrielle said that he was often writing in the sitting room, where she and her sister would play and try to snare bits of chocolate. She said she felt loved by both mother and father, and for all their eccentricities and flaws, has no major grievances about their parenting.

I pressed her on the issue of possible neglect or harm because of an article published in 1993 subtitled "The Piggle: A Sexually Abused Girl?" which argues that Winnicott was simply oblivious to what a poor, abused toddler was trying to tell him (Teurnell, 1993). The author contends that the Piggle's symptoms are out of proportion to the birth of a new sibling. She is telling Winnicott, after all, that her body is being invaded, and in her play, begins pushing sticks through openings, and complains to her mother that her "wee" hurts. The Piggle also complains that Dr Winnicott does *not* understand her, and even says: "I ought to make myself dead ..." (Winnicott, 1977, p. 107). Teurnell comments that a victimised child not reporting an assault—even to a sympathetic adult—is commonplace.

> I know that sexual abuse has an explosive effect upon children—mentally and bodily. As a consequence, they develop primitive defenses and functioning: confusion, loss of reality testing, depersonalization in connection with an extremely strong denial ... The assault is not expressed in words ... It is as if it had not happened. (p. 140)

Teurnell goes on to invoke Fairbairn who observed that a child, in order to protect a good object, will identify with the bad one. She argues that the Piggle is doing just that by calling herself "bad" and "black" and scratching her own face. As to why the treatment seems to solve the psychotic terrors, Teurnell writes that "... the treatment could have had a catharsis effect and that Gabrielle's more or less indirect way of telling about the trauma gave her reality back" (p. 144). The author's tone is one of concern for the child, and indignation that Winnicott, "due to his countertransference", could not hear this toddler saying that her body was the target of actual assault.

A response to Teurnell is offered in the same issue of that journal by Jemstadt (1993) who criticises her account as "judicial and closed" and argues that, having reached a conclusion, she simply leaves out material that doesn't fit her case. Teurnell identifies the father as the probable abuser of the child, and Jemstadt remarks that the father must also be then "a cunning traitor, bringing Gabrielle to the sessions, writing letters to Winnicott during the treatment, and writing an afterword to the book" (p. 148).

During our correspondence in 2015, Gabrielle wrote:

> I am relieved that you mention Lena Teurnell's paper, as I think it made "The Piggle" a rather embarrassing subject for subsequent potential writers ... I really don't think Teurnell's speculation about abuse was correct; I think I would have some memory or sense of it. Which is not to say that I wasn't a very Oedipal child, devoted to my father, so probably at pains to give the impression that we were man and wife, etc., but that is different! ... I heard about the paper during a seminar on child protection when I was a social worker—referred to as proof of the collusion of psychoanalysis (in general) with abusive power dynamics (in particular, child abuse)—there was no love lost between the disciplines in those days!

In London, we resumed discussion of that article.

G: Yes. It felt very unfortunate. I had the feeling people saw it and just wanted to keep away from the whole *Piggle* thing. ... Chris Reeves said people just didn't know what to do about it, and stopped looking at the text ...

A: Are you saying that Reeves [who does not cite Teurnell in his own work] claimed people stopped reading *The Piggle* after they read her?

G: Or stopped writing about it. It became an embarrassing thing to engage with.

A: Ah—so she really had an impact!

G: Yes. She had a silencing impact. It may have not been her intention at all.

Winnicott, who is said to have seen tens of thousands of children over a long career, never once mentions a case of actual or even suspected abuse. Some research suggests that roughly 20% of all female children have a sexual encounter with an adult male before puberty (Herman, 1981). Although Winnicott didn't know these statistics, he must have seen many children who had been abused by family members or others. While Klein viewed the domain of psychoanalysis as almost completely intrapsychic, Winnicott believed that what *actual* parents do has an impact. Gabrielle agreed this was the case, but nonetheless emphasised that a preoccupation with trauma became common only after his death. However, even in Freud there is more attention to abuse. In *Studies on Hysteria,* he describes "Katharina" as seduced by an uncle—who turns out to be the patient's father (Breuer & Freud, 1895d). Much later, in the case of the "Wolf Man", he offers another key example of molestation—having admitted earlier to never giving up completely on his trauma theory. In short, criticising the lack of attention to trauma on the part of the British Middle Group is not unwarranted. Nonetheless, the present author agrees with Gabrielle and with Jemstadt (1993) that raising questions, rather than drawing conclusions, would have been more productive.

For people who see sexual trauma everywhere, nothing confirms the suspicion of abuse more readily than the statement: "I was *not* abused." For doctrinaire believers, "No" means "Yes". Of course, denial is an enormous problem as a defence against overstimulating experience. On the other hand, no human being can prove the statement: "I was not sexually abused." Thus, it's not impossible that Gabrielle was molested as a child, not necessarily by a family member, or even an adult. However, as a clinician with thirty-five years' experience, I can say that she didn't remind me of the women I have treated who were abused as children, as she had no experience with cutting, eating disorders, sexual dysfunction, substance abuse, or suicidality. As a psychotherapist herself, she had plenty of analysis during which these issues would have been likely to surface.

People who are able to persevere, despite having been raped or seduced, are called "survivors", the very term used for those who lived through the Holocaust. William Niederland, who coined the term "survivor syndrome", listed among its primary manifestations the following: fears of renewed persecution, sleep disorders, actual or apparent psychosis, and altered personal identity (in Volkan, Ast, & Greer, 2002, p. 12). I would like to suggest that Teurnell was picking up on something very real. The Piggle's family was steeped in trauma—including the imprisonment and murder of the woman for whom the child was named.

The Piggle's names

Lacan's (2006) perspective is helpful again here: "And the subject, while he may appear to be the slave of language, is still more the slave of a discourse in the universal movement of which his place is already inscribed at his birth, if only in the form of his proper name" (p. 414). Many patients are surprised by the insights gained through exploration of both given and surnames. (To protect her privacy, discussion of the family name is not included here.)

A: Your parents named you "Esther", for a relative who died at Auschwitz, but they couldn't *say* it … Any idea how they chose "Gabrielle"?

G: Yes. I was named after Gabrielle D'Estrée—the mistress of Henri *Quatre* of France. There is a risqué painting in the Louvre of one woman holding the other woman's nipple with a baby being bathed in the background. My Mom loved Henri IV.

A: He said: "*Paris vaut bien une messe!*"

G: That's right!

A: Do *you* know who she was?

G: Mother greatly admired Henri *Quatre*. I don't know anything about his mistress.

Henri IV was involved in France's bloody religious wars of Protestants against Catholics, until his assassination in 1610. His beloved mistress, a highly intelligent woman named Gabrielle D'Estrée, is credited with convincing him to convert to Catholicism and promote religious tolerance. She is said to have accompanied him, even while pregnant, to the battlefield. When she died in childbirth at the age of twenty-six, he gave her a queen's funeral. It is of some interest that the Piggle's mother—forced, as a Jew, to flee to a predominantly Christian country—named her firstborn after a famous and famously Catholic woman. At first glance, it's a choice that seems to erase any trace of Jewishness.

A: They ... couldn't bear to *call* you "Esther", but it does seem intriguing that you are named for Gabrielle *D'Estrée*.

It seems plausible that *Estrée* is the return of the repressed "Esther". Esther is also the name of the biblical queen who had to hide her Jewishness from her husband, the Persian king.

Gabrielle seemed intrigued by this connection, and revealed that at the age of eight, she decided to be called "Esther" at school. Apparently, she continued to be called "Gabrielle" at home. I asked later, in a letter, when and why she had reverted to calling herself "Gabrielle" as an adult. She replied:

> I reverted to being Gabrielle both at home and at school when I went to university at 18. One big disadvantage of "Esther" was reading Dickens' *Bleak House* for A-level exams ... The main protagonist of that vast novel is called Esther [Summerson] who is an especially insipid and saintly character, even for that great national treasure of misogyny ... Going to university meant joining a college which had been men-only until the previous year (there were 18 girls, 250 boys when I joined). I think I felt I needed to have my entire identity—home and school/ feminine and feminist—and all my wits about me! (letter, July 7, 2016)

And what about the name by which she is known to psychoanalysts around the world? According to the Oxford English Dictionary, "piggle" is an old spelling of "pickle". "To be in a piggle/ pickle" is to be stuck in a bad situation. Gabrielle herself told me she thought it might have reflected the attempt of a toddler to say "Gabrielle". She imagined it was that, conflated with the nickname of her father.

G: He was "Piggy-Dog".
A: Your Dad?
G: Yes.

He apparently enjoyed drawing cartoons for the children, and she was pleased to share a favourite during the interview. As a child, she had helped bake him a dessert, and he wrote: "Thank you for the lovely cake" with a charming drawing of himself as a very fat pig eating, in great bites, the whole thing.

Gabrielle refers to herself during the treatment as "Pigga" several times, making their nicknames similar.

It is dismaying that Winnicott used her actual name, Gabrielle, in the published text.

G: I don't know why he wouldn't disguise it. It doesn't make much sense to have kept it.

Among the letters Gabrielle made available is one dated March 17, 1967, in which Winnicott explains to the parents his reasons for not disguising her name.

> On Wednesday evening I talked about "the case" at the British Psychoanalytical Society meeting ... One thing I realised was that when we come to publishing this material we will have to use other names ... I could not bring myself to alter the names Piggle and Gabrielle and I said this out loud. It is surprising how one alters one's feelings about a child if one alters the names. I am of course devoted to Gabrielle in a funny sort of way and how could I help it since she gave so much of herself to me in those treatment sessions! It was a very rich experience for me and I lose something very important if I change Gabrielle's name.

Every therapist who has written about patients knows how difficult it is to disguise anything about them. Each name and nickname, every freckle, cowlick, and lisp keeps the person real to us. On the other hand, professional standards require that we use pseudonyms for the people in our care. It should be pointed out, moreover, that, seeing as the book was published six years after Winnicott's death, his widow and the Piggle's mother clearly declined the available option of disguising her name, at least at that point. Were they all being reckless in this matter?

G: When I read *your* work, Deborah, it made me say in my mind to Winnicott: "Yes, you kept my name because you get attached to names, but you don't *do* anything with it. If it's very important to the work that's been done together, then keep it. But just to keep it, sentimentally?"

It does seem to be the worst of both worlds. On the other hand, most readers would surely assume that whatever the Piggle's real name was, it certainly was not "Gabrielle". Some might argue that hiding her name in plain view—as in Poe's *The Purloined Letter*—made it the ideal disguise.

Before our meeting in person, I asked Gabrielle about the tenth consultation in which the Piggle, while busy playing, declares: "I am Deborah Gabrielle." I wrote to ask if "Deborah" were another one of her actual names, or if it was a disguise for "Esther". She replied: "'Deborah' is indeed a pseudonym for Esther, and I have no idea how it would have been chosen."

This seems peculiar indeed, given that "Gabrielle" was *not* disguised, while the name "Esther"—which the family never called her—*was*. In person, we discussed the fact that the family not only couldn't *say* the name of the victim who perished at Auschwitz; they couldn't even *write* it.

One factor may clarify this odd choice. The period during which Gabrielle was being called "Esther" at school corresponds with the publication of *The Piggle*. There was, thus, some practical reason—in addition to unconscious ones—for disguising "Esther".

Before leaving the issue of names, it's important to highlight one transference-related signifier. Masud Khan apparently felt the Piggle's transference to her analyst was not very intense (Reeves, 2015a). Other readers, in contrast, are struck by how early on the Piggle seemed to get down to work, and eventually to express a full range of transferential emotions, from love and envy to cathartic hate. How can we understand what is framed as her own initial "demand" to see him? Clearly, she is troubled by an immense feeling of loss, following the birth of Susan. In the very first consultation, she tries to break this down for her therapist. "I was a baby. I was in a cot. I was asleep" (Winnicott, 1977, p. 10).

And suddenly there is a *new* baby who took over the family—with her own cot! There has been a loss that gets focused on the cot. Mother has proposed seeing someone who can help with this loss. Children know from playing games that one can either *lose* or *win*. Perhaps the signifier helped foster the transference because, having lost her cot, she could go to *Win-a-cot*.

On hearing this suggestion, the grown-up Piggle replied to me with a very enthusiastic: *"I like that!"*

Listening to Winnicott

Gabrielle had never, as an adult, heard Donald Winnicott's voice. I offered to play a CD of his BBC lecture from 1949, titled: "The World in Small Doses".

Although she was delighted to hear him, and her face lit up as she listened, the voice was not familiar. She responded with characteristic humour.

G: I see what people mean by saying his voice was high-pitched. It's slightly nasal. He sounds like the queen.

A: Some say he sounded feminine.

G: "Camp," I would say.

A: Do you mean gay?

G: ... A certain kind of gay. Quentin Crisp ...

Voice of Winnicott: When a child of two or three says: "I want to fly like a bird," we don't say: "Children don't fly!" We pick them up, and swing them around ...

A: What are you thinking?

G: He has an upper class voice, but not upper-upper; it's conversational. I thought he might be more formal.

A: But he is speaking to mothers.

G: Doesn't matter. If you think of the broadcasts during the war: they were patronising. This has a degree of intimacy. It's not [here she imitates the tone of a drill sergeant]: "THE BABY WILL NEED TO BE HELD ABOVE YOUR HEAD TO HAVE THE ILLUSION HE CAN FLY!"

Much laughter.

Winnicott's voice: The mother succeeds not because she is clever— like the philosophers—but because of the devotion she feels for her own baby.

G: [laughs hard] Oh the *yawning* sexism! It immediately makes me think: What about *my* mother who studied philosophy *and* became a mother! ... I guess nowadays he'd be less sexist.

Winnicott was telling women to relax and trust their instincts.

G: Yes, so it's not surprising he would imagine "treatment on demand". "Feeding on demand" was a big debate when I was born, and now it's gone the other way. Now they say: Babies need schedules so you can get them into a crèche.

Winnicott maintained a Rousseauian trust in "nature"—a concept each culture defines according to its needs.

G: And the politics get completely erased, don't they? "TODAY WHAT IS NATURAL IS ..."

More laughter.
Not only her mother, but also her grandmother had intellectual ambitions.

G: Alice started an architecture degree, and apparently, the story is that my grandfather who was twenty years older and just getting to know her, forbade her and said it was not suitable for a woman, which was always told to me with great amusement rather than outrage.
A: Your mother felt no outrage about that?
G: No, the "beloved father" cancelled out the outrage ... My mother was relentlessly envious of her younger brother for another very good

reason. Had they stayed in Czechoslovakia, he would have inherited everything, and she would have been married off.

Gabrielle said that her mother's sibling rivalry was expressed not in fearfulness, as the Piggle's was, but in exceptional "naughtiness". For this, at the age of six or seven, she was sent for treatment to Anna Freud in Vienna for a consultation, while the family was still living in Czechoslovakia.

G: Mother said it was a great disappointment when Anna Freud said there was nothing wrong with her!

Gabrielle was thus the second generation of children in the family sent for analysis—and with another great name.

Having listened to the BBC broadcast both before and after the interview, this author would describe Winnicott's voice as "respectful" and "engaging" but not "*intimate*". Of course, only one of us had had the experience of sitting on the floor and playing with him. It seems possible that Gabrielle's hearing *intimacy* in his recorded voice was based in memory.

It was during this conversation that we had another look at the drawings he had made for her, while sitting on the floor in her family

home when she was seven or eight years old. (She would draw at the same time, but her drawings have not survived.) At least a dozen begin with his writing his last name, and then building a figure on top of it. The one resembling a dragon is captioned "Fierce when hungry only". It is reproduced here along with another that could be a cat. Ironically, the analyst who took little interest in names made good artistic use of his own.

More reflections on the treatment

All the commentaries on *The Piggle* acknowledge that the treatment had a salutary effect on a potentially very disturbed little girl (e.g. Bürgin, 2016; Charles, 1999; Kahr, 2016; Reeves, 2015a, 2015b; Teurnell, 1993).

It seemed important to ask Gabrielle in person about her present-day feelings for Winnicott and about their work together.

A: Do you have any warm feelings for Winnicott?
G: Yes, I think so. That's a good question. I've spent some time wondering what the encounter has to do with *me* … I grew up thinking there was nothing wrong with me, but when I've gone back to the text, I feel I must have been very troubled.

Most troubling was her preoccupation with death—that of her parents (p. 87) and of herself as well. On this question, Gabrielle asked my opinion.

G: Why do *you* think a child says: "I ought to make myself dead"?

Such a comment can be an expression of oedipal guilt, of course. However, those who have treated depressed and suicidal children may have noted that the younger the patient, the more likely it is that he or she is expressing the death-wish of one of the adults.

A: We know from the text that the Piggle quoted mom saying: "Life is difficult" (p. 52). I don't know if you picked up that she was either depressed herself or at least terribly burdened.
G: Well, what you're saying refers back to Esther. We *should* have been dead! The intention *was* to kill the family—to kill all the Jews, and it was almost completely successful ... You could get pulled off a train and shot.

Reeves (2015a, 2015b) does not refer to the family's history, but he does mention that Winnicott ignores the child's stated fear of *trains*. In fact, Winnicott actually admits to *drowsiness* and making only "vague" notes while the Piggle is talking about trains! (1977, p. 115).

Whatever made Gabrielle fall ill, she was herself again by the age of five, and despite the learning difficulties mentioned above, and the normal setbacks of everyday life, has thrived since in love, work, and play.

A: Do you have a sense that those sixteen sessions saved you?
G: [laughs]. It sounds a bit ungrateful but no, I don't! ... It was perhaps owned more by my mother than by me.
A: Do you believe that *she* believed it saved you?
G: Yes! I do—yes!

There is another aspect of *The Piggle* that moved her.

G: What did strike me—maybe not at first but later—was not Winnicott having deep conversations with a child, but a *mother* having deep conversations. For example: "Do you love me?"

The discussion in question is about "liking" rather than "loving", but it shows the mother listening carefully, responding playfully (pp. 49–50).

I asked Gabrielle to talk about the one session she remembers:

A: Do you remember saying goodbye to Winnicott?
G: No. I remember killing him with the rolling pin. I felt quite guilty—the fantasy of killing him. I knew he had been unwell and that I was making him play very hard. I felt something around the sadism involved in that.

Later, with regard to having forgotten so much, she said:

G: You are picking up that I am quite well defended and dissociated.
A: Yes, but you welled up when you spoke of Winnicott's actual death.
G: Yes, you noticed; there was something there.
A: What exactly are you feeling right now?
G: Very sad. You know, we've talked about people leaving and people dying, but this really is the bit that feels sad [she tears up again]. You and I have recently lost our mothers, and I'm in touch with that. I think Winnicott and my mother are very connected as well … Perhaps it's something about how much the therapy of one member, one little member of a family, was supposed to sort everything out.
A: And in her view, it did … Your mother believed Winnicott saved you—and then he was gone.

To add to the sense of loss: her parents separated shortly after Winnicott's death in 1971, and eventually divorced.

"Tell me *all* about the babacar": What the transgenerational adds to a reading of *The Piggle*

Winnicott's interpretation of the babacar as the "mother's insides" seems cogent, but there is more to her "insides" than the womb. The mother's *psyche* is also a vital and mysterious and productive part of her interiority. Indeed, it has been said that the mother's unconscious *is* the baby's mind.

If all first-time mothers are anxious, a forty-year-old woman giving birth to her first child in a new country, separated from her roots, might well experience a heavy mixture of joy, relief, and trepidation. In addition, the Piggle's father who—for better or worse—had also left behind a country, culture, and religious tradition—was an only child, after many miscarriages. Winnicott (1986) argued elsewhere that "only" children have unconscious guilt over the subsequent babies their greedy fantasies have killed off, and actual miscarriages might augment this. In a letter to Winnicott, the father writes that the Piggle "seems to be suffering greatly from what was once called a 'sense of sin'" (p. 36) which might be a projection of his own unconscious guilt over those bested "rivals" and other things left behind.

The Piggle's mother experienced violent jealousy of her younger brother, patently preferred as a boy. She hints at having re-experienced this when "Susan", her younger daughter, was born. The Piggle may have triggered the mother's own bad objects, experienced as persecutory and "black".

This not terribly unusual set of family dynamics took place in the context of flight from actual persecution, where murderous fantasies became real on a scale the world had never before known. The parents' anxieties about the identity of their firstborn, Jewish child became manifest in the naming and unnaming of her as Esther, Gabrielle (i.e. not-Esther), Estrée, etc.

All of this serves to suggest what two-and-a-half-year-old Gabrielle was carrying when she entered Winnicott's consulting room. Despite her tender years, the Piggle—unencumbered by her mother's heavily accented English or her father's stammer—becomes the spokesperson for the family's unspeakable prehistory. She begins separating out a mind of her own in the process of the treatment. Why could the parents themselves not have helped her individuate? In traditional thinking, it is the father—or another adult—who helps the mother and child separate. Lacan (2006) coined the evocative phrase: "*le nom du père*"—the father's *no* or *name*—that fosters the necessary interruption of the child's complete jouissance with the mother. The Piggle's mother described her daughter as "clingy", yet agrees to give her breast to this already weaned child—when she is nearly four years old. Reading their conversations, it is hard not to hear them clinging to each other.

The mother is able to see Winnicott as the expert, the good father, the one who knows. Why was this figure so crucial? One possibility stems from the fact that her husband was twelve years her junior, and might have fallen fatefully into her own intrapsychic category of younger brother. He happened to be a friend of her younger brother, Tom—the one sent with a fake passport listing them as mother and son. The Piggle says out of the blue one night: "I don't know who is Uncle Tom and who is Daddy" (Winnicott, 1977, p. 62). Perhaps this was confusion *partagé*.

It's possible that the only way to thank so salvific an analyst is to help immortalise him through writing. The unpublished letters show Gabrielle's mother not merely cooperating with the preparation of the text, but acting as the driving force behind it.

According to Gabrielle, while her mother lay dying, the doctors announced there was no more medical intervention possible. Friedl asked: "I don't suppose Dr Winnicott is still alive?" Perhaps he served as counterpoint to the titanic evil figure she had fled, Adolf Hitler. Winnicott, who respected individual fathers, was also prone to mocking paternal/phallic protocol, as illustrated in the opening anecdote, where he sides with the child, and the knife is repurposed as a spoon.

With regard to the place of history and history-taking in psychoanalysis, some would argue that, although millions of children were (and are) the daughters and sons of political refugees, each infant psyche is unique. Many children have night terrors, but the "babacar" was hers alone. Bion (1967) aspired to listen to the patient "without memory or desire". In defence of that position, I would add that all analysts—working with adults or children—risk distorting a patient's truth by making too much sense of it. (The present author, accordingly, has chosen not to correct subtle contradictions—or fill in gaps—in the interview.)

Other clinicians believe that psychoanalytic treatment *begins* with history. Freud and most contemporary Freudians fall into this category. A good example comes from Ira Brenner's (2002) foreword to *The Third Reich in the Unconscious*. Brenner describes a patient who "repeatedly provoked and narrowly escaped entanglements with the law and was eventually jailed at the very age his father had been during his capture by the Gestapo … I felt it imperative to help the analysand reconstruct in great detail his parent's Holocaust experience as well as his own childhood fantasy life" (in Volkan, Ast, & Greer, 2002, p. xiii). Some who value Winnicott's insight that "There is no such thing as a baby"—only what he called "nursing couples"—contend that there are likewise no "nursing couples" outside a social/temporal order (Eichenbaum & Orbach, 1983). Genealogical facts do not take the place of evenly hovering attention and analytic reverie. However, history—as rendered by the patient—becomes part of that reverie.

One aspect of unconscious transmission across generations that is difficult to teach is precisely *how* it occurs. How do parental anxieties become the child's?

A glimpse into that process is offered by the matter of the mother's *singing*. Winnicott comments to the reader:

> There was a song that was associated with the Piggle's babyhood, but when the parents sang this recently she cried bitterly and said: "Stop. Don't sing this song." ... The song she didn't like was a German parting song and was evidently closely related to the mother's intimate relationship with her baby. (1977, p. 13)

In a footnote, he quotes the mother saying: "For a long time she had tears in her eyes when someone hummed the tune. We have now given it new words ... Sometimes she likes it now, sometimes she calls 'Stop!' when someone sings it" (p. 13).

Winnicott seems to imply that the Piggle—whose place has been usurped by the new baby—is finding unbearable a song she heard when she was the only one.

It's difficult to imagine that someone who had fled Eastern Europe in the 1930s, having given up her mother tongue, could sing this tune without communicating abject sorrow. It is arch, but irresistible to ask if, faced with a child with psychotic night terrors, singing a *non*-parting, *non*-German song wouldn't have been the better choice, since a frightened parent can unconsciously *coach* a child's fear.

(The song, *"Muss ich denn"* with the motif: "Must I go?" was played at her mother's funeral.)

A signature characteristic of trauma is the inability to mourn, because survival becomes all. The task of grieving is often passed on to the next generation, and children become the designated mourners (sometimes referred to as "memorial candles"). The very young have no ability to reject this function—although the more perceptive child may try to hand it back to the adults. ("*Cry, Mummy* ... because of the babacar!" p. 18.)

This is not to criticise the parents. One wonders what it might mean to cope perfectly with one's Holocaust history. The point is simply that among the curative factors, Winnicott's treating the split-off anxieties of the parents, stored in the child through projective identification, might rank higher than has been acknowledged. Furthermore, the unpublished letters show that Winnicott closed many of his letters to the family with: "Love, DWW" or "Love to all 4". Perhaps, in addition to the brilliant analytic play therapy, a positive outcome was fostered by four years of love letters to a family in pain.

It's easy for contemporary readers to say: "Had this been my patient, I would have done analytic couple therapy, and let the two-year-old play." According to Gabrielle, both adults had already had individual analysis (by someone other than Winnicott). Nonetheless, addressing psychotic anxiety directly, once they had become parents themselves, might have been literally unbearable.

It seemed relevant to ask whether Gabrielle's second (i.e. adult) analyst hadn't come to a similar conclusion. Apparently, the topic was not much discussed. She did mention having given that analyst a copy of *The Piggle*, on saying goodbye—a gesture certainly open to interpretation.

Reeves (2015b) argues that Gabrielle influenced Winnicott as much as he did her, noting that he turns further away from interpretation, insisting in his final writings that psychotherapy is, above all, about therapist and patient *playing together*. (See also Anderson, 2014.) Gabrielle let me know she appreciated that insight, enjoyed her conversations with Reeves, and felt his close reading of the case made an important contribution. This led me ultimately to the question of why, then, she wouldn't have turned over the scores of drawings and letters to *him*, or spoken to him about the family's Holocaust history. Why, in short, did she choose an American—and someone who is not a child analyst—as interlocutor? Gabrielle reminded me that it was only after her mother's death that she began to feel ready to speak about the family dynamics. She mentioned also that it was important to choose someone who identified as feminist. There is at least one additional factor, we agreed, and it has to do with names.

Despite having read the case many times, this author did not, until last year, react consciously to the fact that my first name and hers meet in the text. (Recall that in the tenth consultation she tells Winnicott: "I am Deborah Gabrielle.") Winnicott didn't make much of such things, but in a Lacanian light, one sees how letters and words *insist*. We are guided, ruled, hounded, and enchanted by them, often all unawares. One cannot rule out a connection between the repeated experience of seeing our names juxtaposed and the fact that we ultimately met, in what seemed like pure serendipity.

At dinner, we toasted our parents' good judgement in giving us beautiful, if contested, names.

In a letter dated July 24, 2016—after our meeting in London—Gabrielle, encouraging me to write about the case and our interview, added: "I certainly love the fact that you and I meet in the [*Piggle*] text: Deborah Gabrielle."

We meet again in print here, forty years on, thanks to our shared commitment to the homeless.

Repetition with a difference.

Acknowledgements

The author is grateful to Drs Margaret Boyle Spelman, Vera Camden, Murray M. Schwartz, Leone McDermott—and above all, to Gabrielle—for their comments on an early draft.

Note

1. The "peas with honey" anecdote, recounted by Marion Milner, was discovered by Dr Margaret Boyle Spelman in the Enid Balint archive, as described in the following podcast: Boyle Spelman, Margaret, "The Work of Donald W. Winnicott", interviewed by Berna O'Brien. Irish Forum for Psychoanalytic Psychotherapy (Podcast, Real Smart Media, Dublin, April 23, 2016). https://m.soundcloud.com/real-smart-media/ifpp-donald-winnicott-margaret-boyle-spelman-berna-obrien.

References

Anderson, J. (2014). How D. W. Winnicott conducted psychoanalysis. *Psychoanalytic Psychology, 31*(3): 375–395.

Anderson, J. (2015). Unpublished interview with Marion Milner, October, 1981, cited in: Winnicott's constant search for the life that feel's real. In: M. Boyle Spelman & F. Thomson-Salo (Eds.), *The Winnicott Tradition: Lines of Development* (pp. 19–38). London: Karnac.

Bechdel, A. (2012). *Are You My Mother? A Comic Drama*. New York: Houghton Mifflin.

Bernstein, J. W. (2011). The space of transition between Winnicott and Lacan. In: L. Kirshner (Ed.), *Between Winnicott and Lacan: A Clinical Engagement* (pp. 119–132). New York: Routledge.

Bion, W. R. (1967). Notes on memory and desire. *The Psychoanalytic Forum, 2*(3).

Boszormenyi-Nagy, I., & Spark, G. (1976). *Invisible Loyalties.* New York: Harper & Row.

Bowen, M. (1978). *Family Therapy in Clinical Practice.* New York: Jason Aronson.

Box, S., Copley, B., Magagna, J., & Moustaki, E. (1981). *Psychotherapy with Families: An Analytic Approach.* London: Routledge & Kegan Paul.

Boyle Spelman, M., & Thomson-Salo, F. (Eds.) (2015). *The Winnicott Tradition: Lines of Development.* London: Karnac.

Brenner, I. (2002). Foreword. In: Volkan, V., Ast, G., & Greer, W., *The Third Reich in the Unconscious: Transgenerational Transmission and Its Consequences* (pp. xi–xvii). New York: Brunner/Routledge.

Breuer, J., & Freud, S. (1895d). *Studies on Hysteria.* New York: Basic Books.

Bürgin, D. (2016). Analysis on demand. *British Journal of Psychotherapy, 32*(3): 347–358.

Charles, M. (1999). *The Piggle*: Confrontations with non-existence in childhood. *International Journal of Psychoanalysis, 80*(6): 783–795.

Clancier, A., & Kalmanovitch, J. (1987). *Winnicott and Paradox: From Birth to Creation.* A. Sheridan (Trans.). London: Tavistock.

Davoine, F. (2007). The characters of madness in the talking cure. *Psychoanalytic Dialogues, 17*: 627–638.

Eichenbaum, L., & Orbach, S. (1983). *Understanding Women: A Feminist Psychoanalytic View.* New York: Basic Books.

Faimberg, H. (2005). *The Telescoping of Generations.* London: Routledge.

Freud, S. (1921c). *Group Psychology and the Analysis of the Ego. S. E., 18*: 69–134.

Gilman, S. (1993). *Freud, Race, and Gender.* Princeton, NJ: Princeton University Press.

Green, A. (1987). Interview with Anne Clancier. In: Clancier, A., & Kalmanovitch, J., *Winnicott and Paradox.* A. Sheridan (Trans.). London: Tavistock.

Herman, J. (1981). *Father–Daughter Incest.* Cambridge, MA: Harvard University Press.

Hogan, P. (1992). The politics of otherness in clinical psychoanalysis: Racism as pathogen in a case of D. W. Winnicott. *Literature and Psychology, 38*(4): 36–43.

Hopkins, L. (2006). *False Self: The Life of Masud Khan*. New York: Other Press.

Ireland, M. (2003). *The Art of the Subject*. New York: Other Press.

Jemstadt, A. (1993). A comment on Teurnell's "The Piggle—A sexually abused girl?" *International Forum of Psychoanalysis, 2*: 145–148.

Kahr, B. (2016). *Tea with Winnicott*. London: Karnac.

Kirshner, L. (Ed.) (2011). *Between Winnicott and Lacan: A Clinical Engagement*. New York: Routledge.

Lacan, J. (1991). *Le séminaire, Livre VIII. Le transfert*, 1960–61. Paris: Seuil.

Lacan, J. (1992). *The Seminar of Jacques Lacan, Book VII. The Ethics of Psychoanalysis, 1959–60*. First American edition. New York: W. W. Norton.

Lacan, J. (2006). *Écrits*. B. Fink (Trans.). New York: W. W. Norton.

Laurent, E. (1981). Lire Gabrielle et Richard à partir du petit Hans. *Quarto, 1*: 3–20.

Lenormand, M. (2018). Psychoanalysis *partagé*: Winnicott, *The Piggle*, and the set-up of child analysis. *International Journal of Psychoanalysis, 99*(5): 1107–1128.

Luepnitz, D. (1992). Unpublished interviews with Charles Rycroft and with Enid Balint. London.

Luepnitz, D. (2009). Thinking in the space between Winnicott and Lacan. *International Journal of Psychoanalysis, 90*(5): 957–981.

Luepnitz, D. (2015). "Where we start from": Thinking with Winnicott and Lacan about the care of homeless adults. In: M. Boyle Spelman & F. Thomson-Salo (Eds.), *The Winnicott Tradition* (pp. 149–162). London: Karnac.

Luepnitz, D. (2021). Interview with Marion Milner. In: M. Boyle Spelman & J. Raphael-Leff (Eds.), *The Marion Milner Tradition*. London: Routledge.

Nussbaum, M. (2003). Dr. True Self: A review of F. Robert Rodman's *Winnicott: Life and Work*. In: *Philosophical Interventions: Reviews: 1986–2011*. Oxford: Oxford University Press, 2012.

Nussbaum, M. (2018). *The Monarchy of Fear: A Philosopher Looks at Our Political Crisis*. New York: Simon & Schuster.

Phillips, A. (1988). *Winnicott*. Cambridge, MA: Harvard University Press.

Reeves, C. (2015a). Reappraising Winnicott's *The Piggle*: A critical commentary. Part I. *British Journal of Psychotherapy, 31*(2): 156–190.

Reeves, C. (2015b). Reappraising Winnicott's *The Piggle*: A critical commentary. Part II. *British Journal of Psychotherapy, 31*(3): 285–297.

Sander, F. (1978). Marriage in the family in Freud's writings. *Journal of the American Academy of Psychoanalysis, 6*(2): 157–174.

Scharff, D., & Scharff, J. (1987). *Object Relations Family Therapy*. Northvale, NJ: Jason Aronson.

Skynner, A. C. R. (1976). *Systems of Family and Marital Psychotherapy*. New York: Brunner/Mazel.

Teurnell, L. (1993). An alternative reading of Winnicott: The Piggle—A sexually abused girl? *International Forum of Psychoanalysis, 2*: 139–144.

Vanier, A., & Vanier C. (2010). *Winnicott avec Lacan*. Paris: Hermann Editeurs.

Volkan, V., Ast, G., & Greer, W. (2002). *The Third Reich in the Unconscious: Transgenerational Transmission and Its Consequences*. New York: Brunner/Routledge.

Winnicott, D. W. (1960). Counter-transference. In: *The Maturational Processes and the Facilitating Environment*. New York: International Universities Press, 1965.

Winnicott, D. W. (1972). *Holding and Interpretation: Fragment of an Analysis*. New York: Grove.

Winnicott, D. W. (1977). *The Piggle: An Account of the Psychoanalytic Treatment of a Little Girl*. London: Penguin.

Winnicott, D. W. (1986). *Home Is Where We Start from*. New York: W. W. Norton.

CHAPTER TWO

"The Piggle Papers": an archival investigation, 1961–1977

Brett Kahr

PART ONE: DINNER WITH "THE PIGGLE" AT KETTNER'S

One afternoon in March, 1996, long before the omnipresence of cell phones, I picked up the receiver of my old-fashioned plastic telephone, placed squarely on the desk of my office in London's Regent's Park, and I dialled the home number of a young woman, once known as "the Piggle"—certainly one of the most famous patients in the entire history of psychoanalysis.

I must confess that, never having spoken to this person before, I reached out to this iconic psychoanalytical celebrity with more than a bit of trepidation.

The Piggle answered my call and we spoke directly, and I introduced myself as the biographer of Dr Donald Winnicott. I found the Piggle to be both sweet and straightforward, and she expressed an interest in my research and agreed to be of assistance with any childhood reminiscences of her former psychoanalyst. Towards the end of our short telephone conversation, I invited her to join me for supper, at her convenience; and to my delight, the Piggle agreed to the plan.

As I intended to take the Piggle for a meal at a lovely restaurant tucked away down a little side street, I suggested that we might meet in front of the more visible Shaftesbury Theatre nearby, in the very heart of London's West End, then home to the long-running musical *Les Misérables*, at 7.00 p.m. on Tuesday, 2nd April, 1996. I explained to the Piggle that, for ease of identification, I would be standing outside the theatre, clutching a copy of one of Donald Winnicott's classic tomes.

At the appropriate time, the Piggle arrived, recognised the book in question, and we greeted one another warmly. I then walked with her to Kettner's, one of my very favourite restaurants, located on Romilly Street, not far from the theatre. I chose this particular venue not only for its excellent food and friendly, convivial atmosphere but, also, for its psychoanalytical significance, because, some forty-four years previously, on 30th March, 1952, the noted psychoanalyst, Mrs Melanie Klein, had celebrated her seventieth birthday at this restaurant in the presence of a handful of carefully curated guests, including such distinguished clinical colleagues as Dr Michael Balint, Dr Paula Heimann, Dr Ernest Jones, Mrs Marion Milner, Dr Sylvia Payne, Mrs Joan Riviere, Dr Herbert Rosenfeld, Mr James Strachey, and none other than the paradigm-shifting genius Dr Donald Winnicott (Grosskurth, 1986).

Only after I put down the receiver of the telephone did I appreciate fully that I had arranged to meet with the Piggle on 2nd April, 1996, literally five days in advance of Donald Winnicott's centenary on 7th April of that year.

But how on earth did I manage to obtain the home telephone number for the Piggle? And how, indeed, did I discover her real name?

Merely a few weeks before meeting the Piggle in person, I had published my very first book (Kahr, 1996a)—a biography of Dr Donald Woods Winnicott, upon which I had first embarked in 1990, some six years previously.

As part of my research for the Winnicott biography, designed to appear in print in time for the great man's one hundredth birthday, I had the privilege of studying many of his unpublished manuscripts and much of his private correspondence, buried in various archives on both sides of the Atlantic Ocean; and, additionally, I had undertaken a very extensive series of oral history interviews with literally hundreds of elderly colleagues and family members who had known Winnicott personally.

As a young clinician and historian, I took tea with Mrs Marion Milner; I lunched with Dr Hanna Segal; and I enjoyed a memorable supper with Dr John Bowlby. I corresponded with Mrs Francesca Bion (the widow of Dr Wilfred Bion); I had the privilege of spending a morning in the company of Mrs Enid Balint; I lingered for hours on the telephone with Professor Elliott Jaques; and, moreover, I even took a train to the wilds of Kent, in the South-East of England, to meet Dr Margaret Little. Additionally, I interviewed quite a number of Winnicott's nephews and nieces and cousins, not to mention his long-standing secretary, Mrs Joyce Coles, as well as his cardiologist, Dr Michael Rosenblüth, and, even, his bespoke tailor, Mr Cyril Rosenberg.

I got rather carried away by my overly enthusiastic attempt to meet every single surviving person who had ever encountered Winnicott (however briefly); and, over many years, I succeeded in interviewing more than 900 people who knew Donald Winnicott personally, including approximately fifty of his former patients.

Sadly, as the years have unfolded, all of these great figures from the history of psychoanalysis have since passed away, with only *one* exception, namely, the Piggle, born in 1961. At the time of this writing, she remains a mere stripling in her late fifties.

I had certainly never suspected that I would ever meet the Piggle in person, as I did not know her true identity. Moreover, even if I had access to her contact details, I doubt that I would have written to her out of the blue, because, as a clinician, I would have considered such a request as potentially quite intrusive. As a one-time patient of Dr. Winnicott, the Piggle had previously enjoyed a private, confidential experience in his consulting room at 87, Chester Square, in Belgravia, London. Although I had met many of Winnicott's other patients, in virtually all instances *they* had contacted *me* first, through various channels, offering assistance with my research, once they had discovered that I had begun to write Winnicott's biography, or, in certain cases, mutual colleagues or acquaintances had thoughtfully facilitated an introduction. I never reached out to any of Winnicott's former patients directly.

I did strongly suspect that the Piggle might still be alive and well and, at that time, in the 1990s, a woman in her mid-thirties, but I had absolutely no means of engaging her, and I presumed that we would, therefore, never meet in person.

However, towards the latter part of 1995, one of my interviewees—a kind and helpful elderly lady who still worked in the mental health profession and who had, during the 1960s, come to know Winnicott reasonably well—told me, quite unexpectedly, that she had once enjoyed an acquaintance with none other than the *mother* of Winnicott's famous child patient and asked whether I might wish to meet the woman to whom I shall refer, hereafter, as "Mrs Piggle". Naturally, I expressed great interest, subject, of course, to Mrs Piggle's agreement. Thankfully, within a mere matter of days, my interviewee provided me with a postal address for Mrs Piggle, whereupon I wrote her a formal letter of introduction on 7th November, 1995, describing my credentials and the nature of my research project (Kahr, 1995a).

Shortly thereafter, I received a handwritten letter in the post from Mrs Piggle, explaining that she would be very pleased to speak to me and suggested that I should telephone her at her home in Oxfordshire. Mrs Piggle's penmanship struck me as Continental, rather than as traditionally British in handwriting style, and I sensed that she had probably grown up and learned her letters in a foreign country.

Cheered by Mrs Piggle's willingness to be interviewed, I then rang her directly and we talked on the telephone at great length (Kahr, 1995c).

I found Mrs Piggle to be a delightfully friendly person—very open-hearted, very generous with her time, and very eager to talk. She spoke with a distinctly German accent.

As an interviewer, I did not have to do very much at all on that occasion. Mrs Piggle needed little prompting and she communicated in a fluid manner, having absolutely no difficulty articulating the entire story of how and why she had arranged for her daughter to undergo child analysis with Dr Winnicott more than three decades previously. I sat quietly in my office, holding the receiver of my landline telephone in my left hand, with a pen in my right hand, and, with the blessing of Mrs Piggle, I took detailed notes of the entire conversation.

I had assumed—incorrectly, in fact—that Mrs Piggle had first discovered Dr Winnicott through his writings or radio broadcasts and that, as a mother in Oxfordshire, she had reached out for professional help when she discovered that her daughter suffered from various anxieties and symptoms in the wake of the birth of her younger sister, Susan. But, to my surprise, I learned that Mrs Piggle had actually known Winnicott personally for many, *many* years, and that she had worked in the mental health profession and had even attended Winnicott's famous child psychiatric clinic at the Paddington Green Children's Hospital in West London and had watched him in action, interviewing young people and their families. (I subsequently discovered that not only had Mrs Piggle met Winnicott on many occasions, but so, too, had her own mother—the *grandmother* of the Piggle—who had visited the Paddington Green Children's Hospital not long after the Second World War.)[1]

In fact, at some point during the 1950s, Mrs Piggle had even arranged for Winnicott to deliver a lecture at her workplace. She recalled that Winnicott had, alas, received rather a frosty reception from her colleagues, some of whom regarded his ideas with suspicion as he, unlike many of his other London colleagues, did not insist that each child must undergo *five-times-weekly* psychoanalysis. Many of the stodgier child mental health professionals, steeped in the work of both Miss Anna Freud and Mrs Melanie Klein, considered Donald Winnicott somewhat heretical for having adopted a more open-minded and creative stance, which included the fact that he offered to treat children according to their needs, rather than subscribing to a predetermined protocol of frequency. Mrs Piggle herself had trained in the Kleinian tradition and remained a dedicated supporter of the work of Melanie Klein throughout her career; nevertheless, she admired Winnicott and chose him, rather than a Kleinian child psychoanalyst, to consult to her daughter ("The Piggle", 2020).

Mrs Piggle explained that, over time, she and Donald Winnicott developed a warm association and that he often visited her at her home in Oxford, a city to which Winnicott travelled from time to time, particularly as he and his wife, Mrs Clare Winnicott, enjoyed a warm friendship with Miss Lucy Faithfull—a noted social worker and child advocate (and, subsequently, a baroness), who happened to live quite close by.

Thus, although it will not be widely known, Winnicott first met the Piggle at the family home in Oxfordshire, rather than in his consulting room in Chester Square. In fact, Winnicott enjoyed a long-standing association not only with Mrs Piggle—a fellow mental health colleague—but also with her husband, whom I shall call "Mr Piggle", and with the Piggle and her younger sister as well.

Mrs Piggle spoke entrancingly about her early association with Winnicott and then told me that she found him to be a most charming man, so much so that he conquered the hearts of many of those whom he had encountered. She also stressed that Winnicott enjoyed the capacity to help people discover parts of themselves that they had not known about previously. Consequently, in view of her high regard for this distinguished psychoanalyst, then in his late sixties, she had no hesitation in writing to him to arrange an appointment for her daughter, the Piggle, having become concerned for her child's well-being in the wake of the birth of her second baby, Susan.

I talked at great length with Mrs Piggle on several occasions thereafter and we engaged in further written correspondence as well. With extreme generosity, she even sent me one of the Christmas cards that Winnicott had hand-painted for her family decades previously. Eventually, having come to appreciate my very serious and respectful passion for Winnicott's work, Mrs Piggle asked me, "Would you like to meet my daughter?" I replied that I would be delighted and honoured to do so, but only if the Piggle had no objections. Mrs Piggle assured me that her daughter would be happy to speak to me. And thus, I rang the Piggle and arranged our supper at Kettner's restaurant.

On that Tuesday evening in April, 1996, the Piggle and I enjoyed a very delicious meal. Although she seemed a bit nervous at first, she soon relaxed and began to talk and to reminisce. Rather like her mother, she seemed quite keen to help me with my biographical research (Kahr, 1996d). I warmed to the Piggle immediately and I found her to be a very pleasant person.

Because the Piggle had attended Chester Square for a small number of consultations throughout 1964, 1965, and 1966, between the ages of two years and five months and five years and two-and-three-quarter months, she could remember very little of the content of these psychoanalytical sessions, not least as she found it somewhat difficult to differentiate her direct memories from what she had subsequently read about the experience in the published version of Winnicott's now legendary book, *The Piggle: An Account of the Psychoanalytic Treatment of a Little Girl*, first published in 1977, some nineteen years prior to our supper at Kettner's. But although she could not recall many of the intricate details of her child analysis as such, she did, however, remember some seemingly insignificant pieces of information about the physicality of Winnicott's consulting room, and continued to do so across the years, including the fact that his office boasted brown Bakelite-covered electrical plugs—a piece of data that one will not find in any published accounts ("The Piggle", 2017).

I felt very blessed to be in the presence of such a friendly and helpful young person and one who had enjoyed such a psychologically intimate experience with one of the great heroes of world mental health.

As our supper unfolded, the Piggle reminisced further about the pleasant atmosphere that Dr Winnicott had created in his office, and she described him as a kindly and decent soul towards whom she had developed a great affection.

Although the Piggle did not remember much of the actual dialogue and playfulness that she had experienced with Winnicott between the ages of two and five, she reminisced far more clearly that, as a nine-year-old girl, she burst into tears after her mother told her the sad news of Winnicott's death on 25th January, 1971, at the age of seventy-four years.

The Piggle proved most gracious and generous with her memories. She also put me in touch with her father, Mr Piggle, with whom I then embarked upon a correspondence. Over the intervening years, the Piggle and I developed a warm association and we have continued to meet for supper from time to time. I would describe her as a most engaging and convivial dinner companion.

Even though the Piggle did not remember Donald Winnicott in the same detailed way in which Mrs Piggle had done—owing to their age differences at the time of their association with the great psychoanalyst—I nevertheless had a strong sense that Winnicott had helped the Piggle tremendously. Certainly, the woman with whom I dined at Kettner's on that memorable evening struck me as a person of considerable mental sturdiness, warmth, compassion, and intelligence. And while we cannot attribute all of these qualities solely to the Piggle's handful of consultations with Winnicott, I had suspected that her extraordinary experience at Chester Square might well have contributed greatly to the development of her impressive personality structure and the socially minded professional career in which she has flourished.

Many years later, in 2011, while dining with the Piggle, she told me that she and her sister had recently discovered a large collection of old letters and photographs from their childhood, which contained much correspondence between her parents and Donald Winnicott. The Piggle had also unearthed the very first unpublished draft of the book, encased in an ageing and slightly crumpled binding, which ultimately became enshrined in psychoanalytical history as Winnicott's most celebrated case study.

With great trust and generosity, the Piggle, knowing of my interest in pursuing further research on Donald Winnicott, kindly loaned me a very large and weighty box, which I studied carefully over several years. I returned this box to the Piggle in 2017 with tremendous gratitude.

In the pages which follow, I shall endeavour to draw upon this unique archive of family papers, which I have come to call "'The Piggle' Papers", as well as my several decades of research in the various Winnicott archives, to offer a more comprehensive and more fully contextualised account of this landmark case in the history of child psychoanalysis and to explore at greater length the nature of Winnicott's remarkable achievement.

PART TWO: DONALD WINNICOTT
AT SIXTY-SEVEN YEARS OF AGE

The Piggle attended for her very first formal consultation with Donald Winnicott on Monday, 3rd February, 1964.

What did Donald Winnicott look like, physically, at that point, in the early months of 1964? What sort of life did he lead at that time? And what, if anything, do we know about his state of mind and about his preoccupations, whether professional or, indeed, personal?

In 1964, Winnicott had every reason to be utterly exhausted, having worked tirelessly and unrelentingly in the health professions since the Great War. Throughout the 1920s and beyond, he always toiled full-time as a clinician and made a considerable contribution by having introduced dynamic psychology into the field of children's medicine (e.g. Winnicott, 1931a, 1931b, 1932, 1933, 1939); moreover, he helped to pioneer the new disciplines of both child psychiatry and child psychoanalysis in Great Britain (e.g. Winnicott, 1940, 1942, 1945, 1948a, 1948b, 1953, 1963c, 1963h, 1965c, 1966a, 1967a, 1968a; cf. Kahr, 2015, 2019b). Not only did he engage in psychoanalytical work with children and their parents, he also maintained a thriving practice with adult patients as well. Additionally, he distinguished himself as a lecturer, a supervisor, a teacher, an administrator, a writer, and a broadcaster—a behemoth set of achievements which might rival those of Professor Sigmund Freud.

Unsurprisingly, such unrelenting workaholism exerted a heavy toll upon both his marriage to Miss Alice Buxton Taylor, whom he had wed in 1923, and, also, upon his physical health. In 1949, both his marital relationship and his heart suffered dangerous explosions, and after a perilous coronary episode—the first of many more to come—he nearly died (Kahr, 2019a, 2021). By 1951, he had divorced his first wife, and then he married Miss Clare Britton, a talented and engaging social worker who trained, subsequently, as a psychoanalyst in her own right, and, moreover, he moved from his long-standing home in Hampstead, North London, to a large, rented house in a luxurious section of Belgravia, not far from Buckingham Palace (Kahr, 1996a).

The love and care and affection that Winnicott received from his second wife certainly helped to fortify him and, also, to re-energise him. And throughout the 1950s, he became even more creative than ever before, publishing several landmark books (e.g. Winnicott, 1957a, 1957b, 1958), and serving as President of the British Psycho-Analytical Society.

Throughout this time, Winnicott maintained his long-standing post as a physician at the Paddington Green Children's Hospital in West London, which became his principal clinical laboratory. Although Winnicott had trained as a child psychoanalyst and had treated quite a number of young people on a five-times-weekly basis in traditional Freudian style, he certainly could not offer such regular and intensive treatment to the many thousands of troubled children and families who attended his specialist clinic at Paddington Green; hence, he had to develop a capacity for offering one or two therapeutic consultations only, during which he would endeavour to identify a core anxiety within the child or family which could then be interpreted, rendered conscious, and, in many instances, even allayed or cured (e.g. Winnicott, 1968b, 1971).

Donald Winnicott remained passionately devoted to Paddington Green since he had begun to work there in 1923. But shortly after his sixty-fifth birthday, on 7th April, 1961, he knew that he needed to retire. Indeed, on 3rd July, 1961, Winnicott (1961f) wrote to his younger colleague, the child psychiatrist Dr Gordon Levinson, "At the present minute I feel that if I survive till the middle of September it will be quite a feat."

To mark his retirement, Winnicott wrote a very short essay for the *St. Mary's Hospital Gazette*, the newsletter of St Mary's Hospital, London, which served as the umbrella body of several local health care facilities, including the Paddington Green Children's Hospital. In this communication, Winnicott reflected upon the establishment of his very specialist unit, which he named "The Paediatric Department of Psychology", where he had, over the decades, deployed psychoanalytical concepts in order to treat both paediatric and child psychiatric cases. In the unpublished draft of his article, Winnicott (1961e) took a swipe at some of his more orthodox medical colleagues who would, occasionally, perform leucotomies upon patients, but, on further reflection, he removed this potentially inflammatory criticism from the final, published version of the piece (Winnicott, 1961b), eager, perhaps, to avoid being provocative after so many years of gratitude towards the institution.

The *St. Mary's Hospital Gazette* published not only Winnicott's essay about his unique paediatric department but, also, a special tribute to him, designed to commemorate his many decades of dedicated service to the institution. Mr Gershon Hepner (known to all as "Gershy"), a Leipzig-born refugee to England and, subsequently, a senior medical student who had worked at Paddington Green, conducted a bespoke interview with Winnicott in preparation for this article. Nearly half a century later, I had the privilege of interviewing Dr Gershy Hepner, then a retired physician in his own right, who still recalled his visit to Chester Square nearly fifty years earlier, and who remembered Dr Winnicott as "very engaging" (quoted in Kahr, 2009b) with a "winning personality" (quoted in Kahr, 2009b), explaining that he could happily have talked to him for hours. Hepner summarised his encounter with Winnicott thus: "I cannot think of anyone whom it was more pleasant to interview" (quoted in Kahr, 2009b).

In his article, published anonymously, Hepner described Winnicott as "one of the greatest living child psychiatrists" (Anonymous [Gershy Hepner], 1961, p. 137). Unsurprisingly, Winnicott deeply enjoyed this public praise, so much so that he then ordered six copies of the magazine at the cost of one shilling and three pence each (Hepner, 1961).

To mark his retirement, the hospital organised a special leaving party for Donald Winnicott and, also, for a fellow medical colleague, a noted paediatric surgeon, Mr Frederick William Markham Pratt, who had worked at Paddington Green since 1933. As a gesture of the institution's deep appreciation, Winnicott (1961g) received what he described as an "astonishingly fat" voucher from Harrods department store.

Needless to say, like many hard-working, creative people, Winnicott discovered that "retirement" from his part-time post at the Paddington Green Children's Hospital simply afforded him more opportunities to undertake *additional* work. In September 1961, he flew to Helsinki in Finland to present a paper on "Psycho-Neurosis in Childhood" to the Scandinavian Orthopsychiatric Congress; then, in November of that year, he delivered a talk on "A Child Psychiatry Case" to the Oxford University Mental Health Association, and, in that same month, he spoke to the Royal Medical-Psychological Association on "Example of a Therapeutic Consultation with a Child". He also published numerous pieces in professional journals (e.g. Winnicott, 1961a, 1961c) and in popular magazines (e.g. Winnicott, 1961d).

In 1962, Donald Winnicott immersed himself even more fully into the professional mental health community, both nationally and inter-nationally. For instance, he maintained his long-standing commitment as a lecturer for students at both the Institute of Education in the University of London, and, moreover, at its sister organisation, the London School of Economics and Political Science, also part of the University of London. Additionally, he continued to undertake committee work for the British Psycho-Analytical Society, and he persevered as a speaker at conferences, not only in the United Kingdom, but, also, overseas. For instance, in May 1962, he flew to Paris, France, in order to address the Société Psychanalytique de Paris about regression in clinical work; and in the autumn, he flew to Los Angeles, California, for a multi-week American lecture tour, during which time he spoke to numerous organisations, including, inter alia, the Los Angeles Psychoanalytic Society, the San Francisco Psychoanalytic Institute, the Topeka Psychoanalytic Society, the Menninger School of Psychiatry (also in Topeka, Kansas), the Beth Israel Hospital, in Boston, Massachusetts, as well as the Boston Psychoanalytic Society and, additionally, the Division of Psychoanalytic Education at the State University of New York in the Bronx, New York.

Throughout 1962, he not only lectured, supervised, attended conferences, and composed professional papers (e.g. Winnicott, 1962a, 1962b, 1962c, 1962d, 1962e), but he also persevered with his treatment of private patients in his consulting room at Chester Square. Moreover, in spite of his official retirement, Winnicott refused to leave Paddington Green entirely and still made regular visits as a Consulting Physician to that institution virtually every Monday afternoon, during which time he continued to conduct clinics.

In view of Winnicott's long-standing attachment to the Paddington Green Children's Hospital and to his unique expertise in psychoanalytical child psychiatry, one can readily appreciate his reluctance to remove himself from the institution completely. We can only begin to imagine the sadness that he must have felt when, one day, circa 1963, he pitched up at the hospital for a visit, and the new receptionist, who did not recognise him, announced to his successor, Dr Susanna Isaacs, "There is a Dr Winnicott to see you" (quoted in Kahr, 1994b).

Eventually, Winnicott ceased his visits to the Paddington Green Children's Hospital entirely and devoted most of 1963 to other professional pursuits, including numerous lectures, not only throughout England and Scotland but, also, in Rome, and in Stockholm, as well as overseas, visiting various American states, such as Connecticut, Georgia, Maryland, Massachusetts, New York, and Pennsylvania. Naturally, he persevered with writing and publication (e.g. Winnicott, 1963a, 1963b, 1963c, 1963d, 1963e, 1963f, 1963g), and, furthermore, he received honorary membership in the British Paediatric Association (Hart, 1963), an organisation whose annual conferences he had attended quite regularly over several decades.

Fortunately, Winnicott seemed to manage his ongoing cardiac illness quite well across the early 1960s and he remained in reasonably good health, aided, perhaps, by his more complete retirement from the British National Health Service in 1963.

Although Donald Winnicott did enjoy a respite from his near-deadly coronary crises of the late 1940s and early 1950s, he did, however, navigate a serious health scare at some point during the 1960s, namely, a significant injury to one of his eyes.

In 1997, not long after my first meeting with the Piggle, a colleague introduced me to a gentleman to whom I shall refer as "Edmund

Fothergill" (a pseudonym), one of Winnicott's patients in the 1960s. Mr Fothergill—a generous person—very kindly agreed to speak to me about his sessions with Dr Winnicott. Blessed with a very vivid memory, Fothergill shared many useful details about Winnicott, including the fact that, during one of his consultations, the two men spoke at length about Fothergill's complex relationship to violence. In the midst of their discussions, Winnicott revealed to his patient that, sometime previously, during a psychotherapeutic consultation with an autistic child, he had focused too much attention on the child's mother, at which point this angry autistic youngster grabbed a sharp instrument, possibly a pencil, used for drawing squiggles, and stabbed Winnicott in the eye! Fortunately, Winnicott did not lose his vision in that eye, but he told Fothergill that his eye continued to cause him great pain (Kahr, 1997; cf. Kahr, 2020).

To the best of my knowledge, no one has ever written about this physically burdensome and, indeed, truly horrifying episode in Winnicott's life; indeed, I came to know about this injury solely from my interview with Edmund Fothergill. I have strong reason to believe this reminiscence to be completely true, because we do have independent evidence that, in 1963, shortly before Winnicott first met the Piggle, he did visit the noted London ophthalmological surgeon, Mr Frank Law (1963), who maintained a private office at 36, Devonshire Place, in the heart of London's elite medical district.

Moreover, I subsequently discovered another unpublished source, written in 1965, in which Winnicott revealed that a very long-standing female patient—an adult—also poked him in the eye. For reasons of confidentiality, I cannot provide a precise bibliographical reference to this paper, contained within public archives, as that would breach the patient's name, but I can confirm the truthfulness of this episode.

Thus, in view of these two separate instances of ocular injury, one of which occurred just prior to the meeting with the Piggle and the other which may have occurred at roughly the same period of time, we can acquire a much greater understanding of why Winnicott kept bottles of Optrex in his consulting room and why he made so many references to these objects throughout the text of *The Piggle: An Account of the Psychoanalytic Treatment of a Little Girl.*

Donald Winnicott's full retirement from the Paddington Green Children's Hospital, after some forty years of service, created much more physical space in his diary and, no doubt, much more mental space as well, which allowed him to provide an opportunity to work with the Piggle at the very start of 1964. But these tragic and no doubt highly frightening injuries to his eye—a little known, indeed *unknown*, fact of Winnicott's biography—peppered their various meetings across the years.

Let us now explore the interweaving lives of Donald Woods Winnicott and the Piggle throughout the time of their occasional consultations and beyond, drawing predominantly upon unpublished archival materials and unpublished oral history interviews.

PART THREE: TWO INTERWEAVING BIOGRAPHIES, 1964–1971

Section one: 1964

Born on Friday, 18th August, 1961, the Piggle grew up in the English county of Oxfordshire, the eldest child of two intelligent, concerned, and reliable parents. But her life changed dramatically when, during her twenty-first month—not quite two years of age—Mrs Piggle gave birth to a second baby, Susan, and, in consequence, the Piggle (also referred to in the published version of the case history as "Gabrielle"), like many youngsters, struggled with profound sibling rivalry. Indeed, the Piggle began to scratch her own face and she became preoccupied with blackness and often struggled to sleep. Moreover, the Piggle experienced significant distress and boredom, and she would often fall down, cry, and feel hurt. In consequence of these regressive behaviours and these strong psychological concerns, the parents decided to seek the assistance of Donald Winnicott, whom Mrs Piggle had already met on several occasions as part of her work in the mental health field (as we have noted previously). When the mother spoke to her elder daughter about the possibility of meeting with Winnicott, the Piggle replied, "Mummy take me to Dr Winnicott" (quoted in Winnicott, 1977, p. 7), whereupon the parents wrote to the great doctor at his home-office in Chester Square on 4th January, 1964, requesting a consultation ("Mr Piggle" and "Mrs Piggle", 1964a).

At the start of that New Year, Donald Winnicott had quite a lot on his mind. On 3rd January, 1964, the day before Mrs Piggle penned her note, hoping for an appointment, Dr Winnicott had paid a final visit to his very elderly medical mentor, Professor Sir Francis Fraser, a physician under whom he had worked at St Bartholomew's Hospital in London, during the early 1920s, and who now suffered from a serious illness and who would die several months thereafter. Additionally, Clare Winnicott—his second wife—had received an invitation to attend a very important interview on 8th January, 1964, at the Home Office—a seminal ministerial department of the government of Her Majesty the Queen, Elizabeth II—to determine whether she would assume the hugely responsible post as head of the Central Training Council in Child Care.

Also, during this same month, one of Winnicott's long-standing analysands, Mrs Jane Shore Khan, the former wife of yet another one of his sometime patients, fellow psychoanalyst Mr Masud Khan, married for the second time. Winnicott proved quite instrumental in helping Jane Khan to recover from her complex and painful marriage to the ever controversial Masud Khan (Hopkins, 2006; cf. Kahr, 2009c).[2] But in spite of the success of his work with Jane Khan, Winnicott may have experienced considerable guilt that his analysand and colleague—the infamous Masud Khan—had treated his wife so unfaithfully (cf. Kahr, 2003).

In addition to these potentially emotionally evocative encounters—bidding goodbye to one of his most crucial medical teachers; supporting his wife during a stressful job interview; and having to dwell upon the complex marital woes of not one, but two, of his analysands—Winnicott also attended to other more regular tasks during January, 1964, including delivering several lectures to child care students at the London School of Economics and Political Science, participating in meetings of both the British Psycho-Analytical Society and, also, the Medical Section of the British Psychological Society, as well as travelling to Oxford on 29th January, 1964, to dine with members of the Oxford Union Society, and to present a paper on "The Concept of the False Self" as part of a conference on "Crime: A Challenge", held at the university's distinguished All Souls College (Winnicott, 1964c).

On Saturday, 1st February, 1964—only two days before his first official professional in-person encounter with the Piggle—Winnicott met up with two of his nieces by marriage, Miss Alison Britton and Miss Celia Britton, at Peter Jones—a large department store in Chelsea, London—at 11.00 a.m.; and then, at 4.00 p.m., he spent the late afternoon with two of his long-standing producers at the British Broadcasting Corporation, Mrs Isa Benzie and Miss Janet Quigley, each of whom had facilitated his career as a psychological expert on the radio (e.g. Kahr, 1996a, 2018; Karpf, 2014). Alas, on Sunday, 2nd February, 1964, Winnicott could not even permit himself a day of rest because he had to conduct an emergency session with a very psychiatrically ill private patient. The ageing psychoanalyst often filled his weekends in this way.

Thus, Winnicott may well have felt somewhat fatigued by Monday, 3rd February, 1964—the day on which he facilitated his very first consultation with the Piggle.

According to his unpublished diaries, carefully preserved in the Archives and Manuscripts division of the Wellcome Library, part of the Wellcome Collection in London, Winnicott met with the Piggle and her parents at 4.00 p.m. on that very afternoon.

What would the Piggle have experienced upon walking into the large and stately house at 87, Chester Square, in London's Belgravia? Fortunately, we know a great deal not only about Winnicott's physical appearance at the time but, also, about the details of his consulting room.

In all likelihood, Winnicott answered the front door himself. Although he employed a conscientious and devoted full-time secretary, Mrs Joyce Coles, to attend to his correspondence and typing and other administrative chores, including household tasks, and although she did answer the door from time to time (Anonymous, 2000), on the basis of my interviews with many of Winnicott's former patients, I can confirm that, on most occasions, he greeted the patients by himself in the foyer and then ushered them into his office.

Upon entering Chester Square, accompanied by both her mother and her father, the Piggle would have encountered a somewhat balding psychoanalyst, some 5'6" or 5'7" in height (Kahr, 1995b), with a rather wizened face marked by prominent crow's feet around his eyes (e.g. Kahr, 1994a, 1994c, 2009a, 2010a). Winnicott always wore finely tailored suits of clothing, which often became quite worn around the knees. As his wife, Clare Winnicott (1982) explained, her husband "had exceptionally strong powers of concentration when he was with patients. In analytic sessions he sat forward on a low straight chair with his elbows on his knees. (For a long time I could never understand why his trousers split across at the knees.)" Thus, Winnicott may well have appeared both elegant and a bit ragged at the same time.

After a brief conversation in the consulting room among Winnicott and all three members of the family, the parents—Mr Piggle and Mrs Piggle—then returned to the nearby waiting room, while Winnicott invited his somewhat reluctant new child patient back into the ground-floor double-length office for what would prove to be the first of sixteen clinical consultations.

Donald Winnicott maintained a beautiful, carpeted office, heated by a gas fire, which contained a psychoanalytical couch, several chairs (one blue in colour), a desk, a small table for taking notes, as well as several bookshelves, which boasted a smattering of titles on psychology as well as various volumes devoted to art and literature (Guntrip, n.d.). The consulting room overlooked Chester Square itself, with curtains draped across the windows, not to mention many plants, including a box of crocuses. Winnicott adored plants, and one could actually see his blessed roof garden through the back window of his office. He also hung pictures on his office walls, including a portrait of a little girl aged six or seven years, who looked rather serious. As a child psychoanalyst, Winnicott kept a generous stash of toys in his office, often secreted underneath one of his bookshelves. His collection consisted of numerous delights, including little cars and boats, a train, a box, a tractor, some houses, pieces of wood, crayons, a small electric light bulb, soft toys, such as a lamb and a faun, as well as more complex toys which included a donkey and cart, not to mention a figure of a little boy pulling a little girl on a sleigh. He also carried a pair of scissors in his pocket, no doubt used for cutting paper or string (Winnicott, 1977).

Thus, the Piggle met Donald Winnicott at the height of his career, as a senior clinician with vast experience, safely lodged in the secure space of his pleasantly furnished, familiar consulting room in his home of long standing, tucked away in an elegant and expensive part of London.

During the first of these encounters, the Piggle inspected Winnicott's consulting room; she played with some toys; and she began to become familiar with this important new setting. In his published account, Winnicott (1977) noted that some of the regressed behaviour of this little girl might well be indicative of her own wish to be a baby and thus take the place of her little sister, towards whom she experienced a strong sense of rivalry.

The Piggle felt quite safe in Winnicott's presence, and, after the first consultation, she agreed to return for a second meeting, held several weeks later, on Wednesday, 11th March, 1964, followed by a third con-sultation on Friday, 10th April, 1964, and, then, a fourth consultation on Tuesday, 26th May, 1964.

Throughout these subsequent encounters, Winnicott became increasingly aware of the extent of the little girl's hatred for her annoy-ing new sister Susan. In fact, in the midst of the second consultation, the Piggle announced, "Put the baby in the dustbin" (quoted in Winnicott, 1977, p. 29). After the third meeting, Winnicott (1977, p. 39) had engaged in such significant contact with his new child patient that he could already begin to see improvements, noting that the Piggle had begun to appear "less tense than before" and, moreover, that she had developed a "new ability to *play at* (thus coping with) rather than *to be in* the frightening fantasy" (Winnicott, 1977, p. 47). Treatment seemed to be working.

After several months, Winnicott and the Piggle had established a deeply engaged relationship, so much so that Mrs Piggle (1964, p. 63) wrote to Winnicott, "The Piggle has asked several times to see you."

In response to the mother's request, Winnicott then facilitated a fifth encounter with the Piggle, exactly one week later, on Tuesday, 9th June, 1964.

Reading through the published version of Winnicott's text, one would cheerfully assume that, having met the Piggle on five occasions, and having worked with her so intensively, analysing the meaning of her play and her many communications in such detail, he had become her definitive psychoanalyst, and that he would remain her chosen physi-cian. However, owing to the fact that the child lived in Oxford, some fifty miles north-west of London, he had already agreed to the plan that the Piggle might visit him only as needed, on a so-called "on demand" (Winnicott, 1977, p. 2) basis.

But reading through the unpublished correspondence in "'The Piggle' Papers", one finds a letter written by Winnicott (1964d) to Mrs Piggle on 25th June, 1964, not long after the fifth consultation, indicating that he had thought seriously about the real challenge posed by geographical distance, which prevented the child from visiting him on a more frequent basis. In consequence, Winnicott had considered the possibility of referring his new, young child patient to a colleague, Dr Donald Meltzer, an American-born physician who had emigrated to Great Britain in order to undertake a training analysis with Mrs Melanie Klein (Grosskurth, 1986). During the early years of Meltzer's career as a psychoanalytical practitioner, Winnicott rated him highly, in part because of his willingness to work with psychotic patients. As time progressed, however, the relationship between these two men became increasingly strained. Meltzer created quite a stir among his colleagues in the British Psycho-Analytical Society by having become possibly the first practitioner to work part-time in London and part-time in Oxford, before moving his office to Oxford on a full-time basis, and this raised many eyebrows (owing to rumours that he encouraged his patients to undergo psychoanalysis by dividing their time between these two separate cities). Nevertheless, in view of Meltzer's proximity to the Piggle and her family in Oxfordshire, it made great sense for Winnicott to have considered this option. In the end, he decided against facilitating such a referral.

Winnicott and Mrs Piggle also discussed the possibility that he might attempt to engage the Piggle by telephone—perhaps an early precursor to "Skype therapy" or "Zoom therapy" (!)—but, in the end, Winnicott (1964d) dismissed this suggestion, having noted, "I too think that conversations by telephone are liable to go awry." Thus, in the end, Winnicott (1964d) opted for in-person, London-based sessions at Chester Square, recommending that, "It is much better to think in terms of natural recovery with an occasional visit to me helping things along a bit."

In his letter of 25th June, 1964—only part of which appears in the published version (cf. Winnicott, 1964d)—Donald Winnicott (1977, p. 74) concluded that a "full-scale analysis" of five sessions weekly would not be possible, but that the Piggle could see him for "an occasional visit" (Winnicott, 1977, p. 74). Thus, after five consultations, spaced over several months, the so-called "on demand" treatment contract became established more formally between Winnicott and the parents.

Throughout 1964—the first year of Winnicott's work with the Piggle—the ageing psychoanalyst remained characteristically busy, leading a full professional life. He continued to deliver lectures at both the Institute of Education and, also, at the London School of Economics and Political Science, which had become a regular feature of his working week for many years. He also devoted considerable energy to the British Psycho-Analytical Society, attending Wednesday night Scientific Meetings and serving on committees. Additionally, Winnicott contributed to other professional organisations such as the Child Psychiatric Section of the Royal Medico-Psychological Association (the precursor to the Royal College of Psychiatrists).

On 27th March, 1964—Good Friday—between his second and third assessment sessions with the Piggle, Winnicott flew to Rome in order to present a paper on "The Neonate and His Mother" to a symposium on "Problemi neurofisiologici, neuroclinici e psicologici del neonata a termine e prematuro" ["Neurophysiological, Neuroclinical and Psychological Problems of the Full-Term and Premature Neonate"], organised by a distinguished Italian psychoanalyst, Professoressa Renata Gaddini (1996)—a woman whom he admired greatly. In his paper, eventually published in the periodical *Acta Paediatrica Latina*, Winnicott (1964b) described a very psychiatrically ill patient with whom he had worked for an extremely long period of time. Quite independently of my research on the Piggle, I have come to learn the identity of this particular patient, in part through one of my many interviews with Winnicott's secretary, Joyce Coles (Kahr, 1994d), and in part through having studied much of Winnicott's unpublished correspondence; and I know that this highly troubled woman caused Winnicott immense stress, anxiety, and concern.

Not only did Winnicott preoccupy himself with that particularly challenging psychotic patient, but, also, he had to treat at least one *other* psychotic patient during the early months of 1964, who required institutionalisation, and whom Winnicott visited in hospital on *at least* one occasion, if not several times. Although psychoanalytical work with small children can often be quite taxing and physically demanding, especially for the nearly seventy-year-old clinician, one suspects that Dr Winnicott might well have experienced his intermittent sessions with the Piggle— an ordinarily troubled though essentially highly sweet and eminently helpable young person—as rather relaxing by comparison to his other much more burdensome and worrisome patients.

After his return to London from Rome, Winnicott delivered a range of further talks, including a speech on "The Origins of Violence" to the Cambridge University Campaign for Nuclear Disarmament, as well as a presentation on "The Psycho-Somatic Dilemma" before the Society for Psychosomatic Research.

Perhaps of greatest importance, the distinguished British publishers, Penguin Books, produced an omnibus edition of Winnicott's talks and broadcasts for members of the general public, which had originally appeared in two volumes back in 1957 as *The Child and the Family: First Relationships* (Winnicott, 1957a) and *The Child and the Outside World: Studies in Developing Relationships* (Winnicott, 1957b). The new collection—an amalgamation of these texts—bore the now famous title *The Child, the Family, and the Outside World* (Winnicott, 1964a), and this paperback volume soon became the largest-selling of all Winnicott's many publications. Priced initially at four shillings and six pence, this book actually sold an impressive 12,939 copies in the first year alone (Palmer, 1967).

Also, in 1964, Winnicott offered much assistance to the budding psychoanalytical society in Finland. Dr Maxwell Gitelson (1963), the president of the International Psycho-Analytical Association, invited Winnicott to meet the growing community of Finnish psychoanalysts, in order to ensure that their training conformed to the exacting standards of other institutions worldwide. Winnicott made several trips to Finland and Sweden during the 1960s to supervise this process; and, to his delight, he helped the Finns to receive official recognition (Zetzel, 1964; King, 1997). It will not be widely known that Winnicott undertook this task of vetting the Finns, not only with characteristic generosity, but, also, with tremendous vigilance; and when he discovered that one of the Scandinavian psychoanalysts went on holiday with a patient, Winnicott recommended that this person's membership should be revoked (Kahr, 2005).

Furthermore, in 1964, Winnicott became a Patron of the Peredur Appeal—a pioneer scheme for emotionally insecure school-leavers. In this honorary role, he sat alongside such distinguished fellow patrons as His Grace the Duke of Norfolk (Bernard Fitzalan-Howard)—Earl Marshal to Her Majesty Queen Elizabeth II—as well as the actor Sir Laurence Olivier and the musician Yehudi Menuhin (Birt, 1964). Although Winnicott accepted this position as a Patron, he turned down numerous other opportunities and he refused lecture invitations from such distinguished organisations as the Howard League for

Penal Reform, the Board of Extra-Mural Studies at the University of Cambridge, the Institute of Youth Employment Officers, the Association of Workers for Maladjusted Children, the Northern New England District Branch of the American Psychiatric Association, the Massachusetts Society for Research in Psychiatry, the Boston Society for Psychiatry and Neurology, and many others besides.

In spite of having retired from four decades of service at the Paddington Green Children's Hospital, Donald Winnicott still had little time to spare during the 1964 calendar year. Indeed, Winnicott often could not see all the potential patients who had requested consultations; and, owing to his crowded timetable, he had to turn down innumerable clinical referrals. We know from his unpublished correspondence that he maintained a list of some trusted junior psychoanalytical colleagues, including, inter alia, Dr Herman Hardenberg, Dr James Armstrong Harris, Mr Masud Khan, Dr Margaret Little, Dr Peter Lomas, and Dr Barbara Woodhead, and he would recommend these individuals to prospective patients, many of whom no doubt experienced a deep sense of disappointment that they would not be able to work with the great man himself.

Thus, the parents of the Piggle, and the little girl too, might have felt very pleased that Winnicott had actually agreed to approximately monthly consultations, especially in view of his packed schedule.

Certainly, without his embrace of "on demand" therapy, Winnicott would not, in all likelihood, have had the capacity at this point in his career to provide ongoing treatment for his new child patient. Fortunately, "on demand" treatment proved particularly attractive to Winnicott, not only in view of his appreciation of the Piggle's geographical location but, also, her clinical needs, and, moreover, his reality-oriented recognition of what he could or could not manage from a straightforward, practical, timetabling point of view.

Contemporaneously, Mrs Clare Winnicott, did, in fact, receive the appointment as Director of Child Care Studies in the Children's Department of the Home Office—a very important government position which she would hold until 1971. Thus, not only did Donald Winnicott struggle with a hugely overburdened timetable in 1964, but so too did his wife. In consequence, the Winnicotts had to refuse many social invitations. Indeed, in 1964, he wrote to Mr Michael Duane, the Head of the

Risinghill School in North London, describing himself as "frantically overloaded" (Winnicott, 1964e).

As 1964 unfolded, the Piggle continued to make great progress in her very unique form of psychoanalysis, so much so that Mr Piggle and Mrs Piggle wrote to Winnicott, that, "on the occasions that Gabrielle is well, she is very well indeed" ("Mr Piggle" and "Mrs Piggle", 1964b, p. 97).

By the end of that first calendar year, the Piggle had visited Chester Square on fully eight occasions. During this time, Winnicott facilitated much play therapy with the Piggle and also encouraged conversation about a whole range of matters. Among the many striking themes discussed by Winnicott and the Piggle, one appreciates the focus on the little girl's sense of her own vulnerability. Indeed, in the eighth consultation, held on Tuesday, 1st December, 1964, the Piggle expressed her wish that one day she would be powerful, so much so that, "When I am big I will get old before Mummy's old, before she is old" (quoted in Winnicott, 1977, p. 103). The Piggle also acquired the ability to speak directly about her complex feelings towards her baby sister. She admitted, "I'm scared of the black Susan; so I play with your toys. I hate Susan. Yes I hate her very much" (quoted in Winnicott, 1977, p. 103). Through play and through verbalisation, Winnicott helped the Piggle to experience a growing sense of catharsis and to develop a greater sense of robustness.

Winnicott capped the calendar year by sending a special Christmas card to the Piggle with a hand-drawn picture of a donkey inside!

Section two: 1965

Throughout 1965, the Piggle attended for only five consultations. Although Winnicott did not elaborate upon his reasons for having offered three fewer appointments than he had done during the previous year, one imagines that a combination of extraordinary work pressures and physical ageing contributed to the difficulties of arranging psychoanalytical sessions. But, moreover, we might suppose that the Piggle had begun to develop successfully and, thus, had become better able to manage her sibling rivalry and other ordinary challenges of childhood, and, hence, may not have required as many consultations.

Although Winnicott maintained contact with the Piggle, now three years of age, he also enjoyed an extensive correspondence with each of the parents, who wrote to him frequently. We know from an inspection of the family archive that Mrs Piggle, in particular, would prepare numerous handwritten drafts of her letters before sending a more polished version to Dr Winnicott. By studying the original documents, including these multiple drafts with many crossings-out, one can readily see how much energy Mrs Piggle devoted to her correspondence with Winnicott, and one can certainly imagine the important "holding" function that Dr Winnicott offered not only to the Piggle but, *also*, to the parents. After all, Mrs Piggle had known Winnicott over many decades; hence, he occupied a vital position in her mind, and he may also have served as an honorary psychoanalyst of sorts to her as well.

In terms of Donald Winnicott's wider professional commitments, 1965 proved to be an even more crowded year than 1964. Of greatest importance, he published two of his most impressive books—each a volume of carefully curated collected papers—namely, *The Family and Individual Development* (Winnicott, 1965a) and, also, *The Maturational Processes and the Facilitating Environment: Studies in the Theory of Emotional Development* (Winnicott, 1965b), which has since become a classic in the history of psychoanalysis. The first of these books, *The Family and Individual Development*, produced by Tavistock Publications, appeared in the early part of 1965 and sold for thirty shillings. Its even more substantial successor, *The Maturational Processes and the Facilitating Environment: Studies in the Theory of Emotional Development*—released by the Hogarth Press in collaboration with the Institute of Psycho-Analysis of London, as part of "The International Psycho-Analytical Library" series—became available for purchase in the summer of 1965 at the cost of forty-two shillings.

Winnicott worked extremely hard to prepare these two significant volumes for publication. In consequence, he had little time for social encounters or for meetings with colleagues, lamenting to his long-standing psychoanalytical contemporary, Dr Roger Money-Kyrle, "It is sad that we meet so seldom, and life slips away, but somehow it can't be helped—this job we are in takes so much of our time and emotional energy" (Winnicott, 1965e).

Amid this flurry of creative activity, Winnicott's fame continued to spread, even to Africa. Indeed, a student from Rhodesia, Miss Pam Gabriel (1965a), wrote to him asking for references about the psychology of the only child. Winnicott (1965h), overwhelmed by work, took two months to reply to Miss Gabriel but, eventually, he did so, prompting the young woman to enthuse, "I was honoured to receive a letter from such a distinguished person" (Gabriel, 1965b). By the mid-1960s, Winnicott's reputation had become so potent that one of his London colleagues, Dr Martin James (1965), enthused, "You see, you have become a commercial proposition like the Beatles ("let me be your Brian Epstein" etc.)." One cannot help but wonder whether the parents of the Piggle considered themselves quite fortunate that Great Britain's most distinguished psychoanalyst had carved out any time for them at all.

Throughout 1965, Winnicott persevered with his teaching and lecturing. On 25th February, 1965, he delivered a talk on "The Price of Disregarding Research Findings" at a distinguished conference on "The Price of Mental Health", sponsored by the National Association for Mental Health. Winnicott (1965d) took to the stage immediately after The Right Honourable Kenneth Robinson (1965), the Minister of Health, who discussed the heavy financial cost of mental illness.

In May, 1965, Winnicott travelled to Copenhagen, in Denmark, to continue his work as one of the sponsors of the developing Scandinavian psychoanalytical community. And in July of that year, he spoke to his colleagues in the British Psycho-Analytical Society on "The Therapeutic Consultation in Child Psychiatry", before travelling to Amsterdam, in The Netherlands, in order to participate in the International Psycho-Analytical Congress, hosted by the International Psycho-Analytical Association, at which he not only chaired a session of talks about child psychoanalysis but, also, presented his own thoughts on obsessional neurosis (Winnicott, 1966b).

Of greatest importance, Winnicott stood for election as President of the British Psycho-Analytical Society, a post of enormous responsibility, having already occupied this seminal role once before, between 1956 and 1959. In 1965, Donald Winnicott ran against colleagues Dr Paula Heimann, Dr Herbert Rosenfeld, and Dr Lothair Rubinstein, and he beat all three of them. Miss Pearl King, Winnicott's sometime supervisee, became his Deputy President, having served previously as Secretary during his prior term of office. A woman of immense administrative reliability and capability, Miss King (2001) undertook a vast amount of the tedious paperwork on behalf of this professional organisation, thus permitting Winnicott to attend to the more ceremonial tasks.

Throughout this time, Winnicott continued to treat the Piggle successfully and he maintained his vital correspondence with Mr Piggle and Mrs Piggle, especially the latter, who continued to rely upon the great psychoanalyst for her own containment and reassurance. On 12th July, 1965, not long after his eleventh consultation with the young girl, Winnicott (1965f, p. 145) wrote to Mr Piggle and Mrs Piggle, "Children do have to work through their problems at home and I would not be surprised if Gabrielle is able to find a way through the present phase" (cf. Winnicott, 1965f).[3]

The Piggle continued to engage with the safe-making and delightful elderly psychoanalyst, and one senses that she paid very close attention to his every movement. As I indicated earlier, at some point during the early 1960s—very probably in 1963—Winnicott endured one or more injuries to his eyes and had to consult an ophthalmologist. He suffered considerable pain, and, in consequence, he kept a bottle of Optrex eyebath in his consulting room at Chester Square. Whereas most psychoanalysts would secrete their medications in a drawer, Winnicott needed to soak his eyes on such a regular basis and, consequently, the Piggle became quite drawn to this very visible and most unusual object. As early as 11th March, 1964—the second of her consultations—the child picked up this blue bottle and enquired, "What's this?" (quoted in Winnicott, 1977, p. 23). Before Winnicott had a chance to reply, the Piggle had already begun to preoccupy herself with a toy train. But later in this same session, the Piggle began to speak about eyes and, after handing Winnicott an electric light bulb, she chirped, "Put in more eyes and more eyebrows" (quoted in Winnicott, 1977, p. 26).

References to eyes and to Optrex would continue to punctuate the treatment. On Saturday, 10th October, 1964—the seventh consultation—Winnicott noted that the Piggle played with the bottle of Optrex once again. And during the following meeting on Tuesday, 1st December, 1964—the eighth consultation—the Piggle played with the Optrex for at least the third time and asked her psychoanalyst directly, "What is this for?" (quoted in Winnicott, 1977, p. 103). Immediately thereafter, she began to speak about her mother becoming older. One cannot help but wonder whether the Piggle sensed that Dr Winnicott used the Optrex because of his own ageing eyes, or, indeed, whether he might have deployed them in her presence on one or more occasions.[4]

The Piggle continued to engage with the eyebath bottle and did so, once again, in the ninth consultation on Friday, 29th January, 1965. In fact, during this session, she toyed with the bottle several times across the psychoanalytical hour and even put it into her mouth, producing "sucking noises" (Winnicott, 1977, p. 118) in the process, which Winnicott (1977, p. 118) described as "very near to a generalized orgasm".

In his published account of the tenth consultation of Tuesday, 23rd March, 1965, Winnicott (1977, p. 123) took great pains to inform his readers that the toys in his consulting room had remained constant throughout the analysis of the Piggle, but that he had introduced the Optrex eyebath between the first and second consultations. We might well hypothesise that Winnicott's injury occurred during mid-1963, and that he placed the Optrex in his office, on ophthalmological advice, during the early part of 1964.

By Wednesday, 16th June, 1965—the eleventh appointment— Winnicott boasted not one, but two, Optrex eye cups in his consulting room. Unsurprisingly, the Piggle became extremely curious and began to play with these items even more extensively, staring at the world through one of the blue glasses and placing the other one on top of a toy truck. In the twelfth consultation, on Friday, 8th October, 1965, the Piggle used a red crayon to draw a picture of a lamp lady, which she then crowned with an Optrex cup as a hat of sorts.

One imagines that the Piggle might well have engaged with the Optrex on numerous other occasions, although Winnicott may not have written about each and every one of these episodes in his relatively short study of his child patient. But, certainly, the Optrex may well have represented a part of Winnicott's body to the Piggle, which she might have wished to touch and swallow and incorporate. For Winnicott himself, the Optrex bottle and eye cups served as a constant reminder of his potentially great physical pain and suffering—a fact never previously reported in the literature.

Section three: 1966

Throughout the year 1966, the ageing man continued to work with some very disturbed adult psychiatric patients who taxed him considerably

(Winnicott, 1966c). Undeterred, he performed his duties as President of the British Psycho-Analytical Society, and he also persevered with his foreign travels. In early February, 1966, he lectured extensively in Geneva, in Switzerland, and then, in Milan, in Italy; and later that month, he flew to Leiden, in The Netherlands, to deliver several more talks.

On Thursday, 7th April, 1966, Winnicott turned seventy years old. His former trainee, Dr Peter Tizard, who subsequently became a distinguished professor of paediatrics, telephoned Winnicott to offer him happy birthday greetings. As a scientific researcher, Tizard then clarified his well wishes, noting, "I should say the anniversary of your birthday" (quoted in Tizard, 1981, pp. 267–268). Winnicott responded, "You certainly should," said Winnicott, "thank Heavens one doesn't have to undergo *that* experience more than once!" (quoted in Tizard, 1981, p. 268).

Some weeks later, on Saturday night, 30th April, 1966, the British Psycho-Analytical Society hosted a party at its headquarters on New Cavendish Street, in Central London, in honour of this landmark birthday, for approximately 250 guests (Montessori, 1968), including Winnicott's very first psychoanalyst, the scholarly Mr James Strachey—one of Professor Sigmund Freud's analysands and, of course, translators—whom Winnicott had first consulted, decades previously, in 1923 (Kahr, 2010b; cf. Kahr, 1996a).

In 1966, the Piggle attended for her final three sessions with Donald Winnicott. In the fourteenth consultation, on Friday, 18th March, 1966, the child—now four and a half years of age—began to play with a very new toy, namely, a figure of "a little boy pulling a sleigh with a little girl on it" (Winnicott, 1977, p. 180). One might well surmise that this child who, as a two-year-old girl, could not bear the thought of sharing space with a younger sibling, had, by now, succeeded in enjoying her play with a single toy composed of two people working as a pair, rather than as rivals.[5]

Most touchingly, in her penultimate session—the fifteenth—held on Wednesday, 3rd August, 1966, the Piggle reached for the Optrex glass bottles once again. This time, she placed the cups over her own eyes. Winnicott, in truly spontaneous mode, tensed his orbicularis muscles and succeeded in holding the eye baths on his face without the aid of his hands. After some practice, the Piggle managed to follow suit and clutch one of these glass objects with one of *her* eye muscles. Afterwards, she confessed to Winnicott, "I'd like to take them home with me" (quoted in Winnicott, 1977, p. 190). No doubt, at this point, Winnicott may well have felt satisfied that the Piggle could imitate him, identify with him, and even incorporate him. She had begun to consolidate her internalisation of this child psychoanalytical process—an indication that she had achieved success and could begin to manage without his concrete physical presence, so much so that, at the end of her sixteenth and final session on Friday, 28th October, 1966, he pronounced this five-year-old child as "psychiatrically normal" (Winnicott, 1977, p. 198).

Of course, it would be sheer idealisation to presume that Winnicott's work with the Piggle unfolded in a magical fashion, marked by constant improvement along the way. Throughout the course of treatment, Winnicott possessed the ability to disappoint the Piggle and she certainly enjoyed the capacity to express her displeasure. The unpublished letters from the archives of the Piggle's family reveal that, on one occasion, the little girl told her mother that she felt aware of the presence of a "policeman" (quoted in "Mrs Piggle", n.d. [d]) in her mind—perhaps a transferential reference to the ever-monitoring psychoanalyst. Upon hearing this, Mrs Piggle asked her daughter whether she might wish to share this information with Dr Winnicott; but the Piggle replied, "No, he does'nt [*sic*] understand" (quoted in "Mrs Piggle", n.d. [d]).

Also, in my very first interview with the mother, Mrs Piggle, in 1995, she revealed that although she held Winnicott in high esteem, it saddened her that, from time to time, Winnicott's health situation interfered with the treatment and that, on at least one occasion, he upset the Piggle greatly by not being able to meet with her for a period of time, having promised the child that he would be available. Apparently, the Piggle experienced Winnicott's absence as very painful indeed (Kahr, 1995c).

But on the whole, the treatment worked extremely well. And in one of the mother's untitled notes, contained in "'The Piggle' Papers", we learn that, on another occasion, Mrs Piggle asked her daughter directly what she thought of Winnicott. The little girl responded, "he can make me better" (quoted in "Mrs Piggle", n.d. [a]); and when the mother requested further clarification and wondered which part of the Piggle now felt better, the little girl pointed to her head!

In having undertaken this extraordinary piece of clinical work with the Piggle, Donald Winnicott made a vital contribution to child psychotherapy and child psychoanalysis. He allowed his patient considerable time in which to communicate not only through language but, also, through play. In each consultation, he paid extremely close attention to the Piggle's words and gestures, as demonstrated by his careful written notes and by his foregrounding of detail.

Winnicott also devoted much attention to the trauma of sibling rivalry—a very classical notion—and came to appreciate the little girl's struggle with her new baby sister, Susan. Moreover, he granted considerable authority to the Piggle herself by permitting her to request an "on demand" session with him when it most suited her.

With tremendous clinical intelligence, Winnicott also recognised that the roots of the Piggle's symptoms may have stemmed not only from the recent birth of her younger sibling but, also, from earlier, intrafamilial factors within the Piggle household more generally. Indeed, in his write-up of the twelfth session with the Piggle, he included a letter from Mrs Piggle in which she confessed to Winnicott that she, too, had endured a considerable experience of sibling rivalry during her own childhood with a brother whom she disliked. As Mrs Piggle noted, "My anxieties were very intense at the time of Susan's birth—I forget whether I told you that I have a brother, whom I greatly resented, who was born when I was almost exactly the same age as Gabrielle was when Susan was born" ("Mrs Piggle", n.d. [b] [1965], p. 161).

Throughout the text, Winnicott made no reference at all to the fact that Mrs Piggle grew up in a Jewish family. Perhaps he disguised such biographical information for reasons of confidentiality. But, certainly, he would have appreciated from Mrs Piggle's real name and from her vocal accent and, also, from their many conversations, her status as an émigrée from a persecuted background. Moreover, as I indicated earlier, Winnicott had also known Mrs Piggle's mother—the grandmother of the Piggle—and, together, she and Winnicott had once discussed the case of a little boy whose parents died in the Holocaust.[6]

Thus, although Winnicott undertook this treatment long before the explosion of knowledge about what we would now conceptualise as the intergenerational transmission of trauma (e.g. Krugman, 1987), he certainly remained sensitive to the historical antecedents of the Piggle's struggles, some of which might be rooted in her ancestry.

In view of the richness of the case and the successful outcome of his work, it should hardly surprise us that, in due course, Winnicott began to consider sharing this material with his clinical colleagues and with a wider audience.

Section four: Donald Winnicott's final years

Winnicott conceived the idea of writing up his consultations with the Piggle for publication at least as early as 1965. In an unpublished letter addressed to Mrs Piggle, he opined, "Dont [sic] let this idea of the book get in the way of our ordinary inter-communicating" (Winnicott, 1965i). And only weeks thereafter, he penned a letter to the mother encouraging her to record her own observations: "I am very pleased to get notes if you feel like writing any" (Winnicott, 1965j).

Unsurprisingly, as the intimacy between Winnicott and the Piggle developed between 1964 and 1966, so, too, did the closeness of his relationship with the parents themselves. In 1964, he always wrote to them as "Mr Piggle" and "Mrs Piggle",[7] but by 1966 he began to address them by their forenames. Throughout the treatment, the family maintained ongoing contact with Winnicott both by post and also by telephone. Dr Winnicott even paid a number of visits to the family home in Oxfordshire. The Piggle proved sufficiently important to Winnicott that, even after the conclusion of the treatment, he continued to correspond with her from time to time. In a delightful letter of 21st April, 1967, Winnicott (1967d) wrote to his former child patient having received a drawing from the little girl: "Thank you for your letter and for the lovely picture of me. I am afraid I am not really as beautiful as all that, but as I seem to be crying in the picture I expect that means that I am sad because I have not seen you for so long."

The case had obviously captivated Winnicott sufficiently, and even before the end of the treatment in 1966, he embarked upon the process of transforming his notes into a book. Having published his sturdy text on *The Family and Individual Development* (Winnicott, 1965a) during the early months of 1965, followed by his profound collection of essays,

The Maturational Processes and the Facilitating Environment: Studies in the Theory of Emotional Development (Winnicott, 1965b), which appeared by the summer of 1965, Winnicott suddenly found himself with some breathing space, at least in terms of his writing commitments. With his seventieth birthday looming, Winnicott no doubt felt keen to craft his legacy with all due speed. In fact, he completed the "Introduction" to his draft book about the Piggle on 22nd November, 1965, almost exactly one year *prior* to the conclusion of the formal sixteen consultations with the Piggle, at 10.30 a.m., on the morning of 28th October, 1966.

Throughout the mid-1960s, Winnicott continued to refine his typescript, aided by his long-standing and efficient secretary Joyce Coles. Moreover, he collaborated with Mr Piggle and Mrs Piggle, each of whom provided some additional comments (Winnicott, 1977). Gradually, Winnicott produced a complete text, in pretty good shape; and I had the privilege to consult the original typescript, preserved in "'The Piggle' Papers".

It remains unclear precisely why Winnicott did not then insist upon a swifter publication during the late 1960s, especially as he had a virtually perfect typescript to hand. Perhaps he planned to see how the Piggle would develop over the next few years, in order to be certain that his sixteen consultations actually proved efficacious in an ongoing way. No clinician would wish to boast that he or she had cured a patient successfully only to discover soon thereafter that the patient then suffered from a debilitating relapse (as proved to be the case with Dr Josef Breuer's famous patient, Bertha Pappenheim, better known as "Anna O" (Breuer, 1882, 1895; Freud, 1932; cf. Freeman, 1972; Forrester & Cameron, 1999; Skuse, 2006)).

Winnicott may also have delayed publication because he might have intended to elicit feedback from his psychoanalytical colleagues, especially as his unusual "on demand" arrangement with the Piggle challenged the orthodoxy of five-times-weekly treatment. Consequently, on Wednesday, 15th March, 1967, he presented an informal paper, "Discussion Around a Clinical Detail", at a Scientific Meeting of the British Psycho-Analytical Society on New Cavendish Street in London and offered a preview of his work with this captivating child patient. Apparently, Winnicott had not prepared a formal talk on this occasion, as he had kindly and helpfully agreed to step in at the last minute because of the unexpected illness of a colleague already booked to present a paper on that evening. After he delivered his remarks, Winnicott (1967b) wrote to the parents of the Piggle that, having discussed the case with psychoanalytical colleagues, he had come to appreciate the necessity of generating pseudonyms for the patient and her family in order to protect confidentiality.

Some years ago, while researching in the Archives of the British Psycho-Analytical Society, I had the privilege of listening to a very scratchy, uncatalogued tape recording of this talk, which revealed that, in spite of Winnicott's tremendous seniority at the time, several of his colleagues expressed their doubts and hesitations about the nature of his work. The impact of this evening among his more staunchly con-servative colleagues may also have contributed to Winnicott's hesitation about a more immediate publication.

After speaking to his fellow psychoanalytical practitioners about the Piggle in March 1967, Donald Winnicott undertook many further professional commitments during the remainder of that calendar year. Across 1967, he persevered with his treatments of a large handful of patients, as well as with his teaching commitments, not to mention quite a number of organisational contributions. For instance, in addition to his ongoing work at institutions such as the British Psycho-Analytical Society, the London School of Economics and Political Science, and the Institute of Education, he assumed the vice-presidency of the National Association for Mental Health (Appleby, 1967; Winnicott, 1967c). He also embarked upon a lecture trip to New York City and to Boston, Massachusetts. Winnicott toiled so relentlessly that, in spite of having departed for London from Boston's Logan Airport on Sunday, 16th April, 1967, at 8.00 p.m., arriving in England the following morning, on Monday, 17th April, 1967, circa 8.10 a.m., he resumed his clinical sessions almost immediately and even met with a patient that very eve-ning at 8.00 p.m.—no doubt an unbearably tiring timetable for a man of seventy-one years of age.

His workaholism proved so profound that on 2nd May, 1967, not long after his exhausting international trip, Winnicott actually delivered *three* separate talks. At 12.00 p.m., he spoke to students at the London School of Economics and Political Science in the University of London.

Several hours afterwards, at 7.15 p.m., he presented material to a seminar on autism, sponsored by a pharmaceutical company. And then, later that very night, he taught a group of candidates at the Institute of Psycho-Analysis.

I cannot do full justice to the extent of Winnicott's professional commitments in 1967, but I can report that, during this calendar year, the septuagenarian psychoanalyst not only lectured to numerous London-based organisations but, also, he travelled extensively throughout Great Britain, speaking in Winchester in the county of Hampshire; in Standlake in the county of Oxfordshire; in Plymouth in the county of Devon; and in Radlett in the county of Hertfordshire. In addition to his teaching trips to both New York City and Boston, he also delivered presentations about his work to colleagues in Copenhagen in Denmark; in Paris in France; in Wiesbaden in Germany; and, he even returned that year for a second lecture trip to Boston. Due to sheer exhaustion, he cancelled trips in 1967 to both Italy and Spain.

Amid all these commitments, Winnicott continued to prepare his typescript about the treatment of the Piggle. And, shortly after Christmas, 1967, Winnicott (1967e) wrote—somewhat hastily—to Mr Piggle and Mrs Piggle, with glee, boasting, "I've nearly finished the book. Its [sic] terriffic [sic]."

The following calendar year, 1968, proved even more burdensome for the seemingly tireless and always productive Donald Winnicott. Across the months, he continued to toil incessantly as he had done in previous years. And on 7th November, 1968, he flew—economy class—to New York City, once again, to deliver several more professional papers. Winnicott already suffered from a cold while on board the outbound flight, which no doubt placed him in a physically vulnerable position (Kahr, 1996b). And then, quite tragically, while in Manhattan, he succumbed to a virulent strain of Asian influenza—the so-called "Hong Kong Flu"—and, also, experienced another very serious coronary episode with pulmonary oedema, a frequent complication of valvular heart disease, from which he nearly died. Winnicott required immediate hospitalisation and thus had to spend literally many weeks in the Lenox Hill Hospital on the Upper East Side of Manhattan and could not fly home to London until 20th December, 1968 (Kahr, 1996a).

Although this frail psychoanalyst did manage to resume with patients on 6th February, 1969, he could not work at full capacity and became increasingly frail. He did, however, maintain contact with the Piggle and her family and, on 3rd March, 1969, Winnicott (1969a) sent a letter to his former patient, underscoring that, "I'm getting well now and I like to write to you from time to time." Winnicott (1969a) also promised, "One day I shall be coming along again for a cup of tea or coffee + to see you all."

To the best of our knowledge, Winnicott did not meet personally with any members of the family of the Piggle after his serious illness in Manhattan, and, although he maintained correspondence by post, he could not manage another consultation or visit.

At some point in 1969, the ailing psychoanalyst completed a full draft of his typescript about his child patient, entitled *The Piggle: Her Psychoanalytic Treatment*; and in March of that year, he sent a copy to the parents along with a note, which read, in part, "You are invited to write all over these pages" (Winnicott, 1969b). But in spite of having nearly finished the book, his almost fatal illness in November 1968 prevented him from progressing the typescript through the time-consuming complexities of publication. Hence, in spite of his multi-year work, the book did not appear in print during Donald Winnicott's lifetime.

He died at approximately 4.00 a.m. on Monday, 25th January, 1971 (Khan, 1971), at the age of seventy-four years, from left ventricular failure and myocardial infarction (Kahr, 1996a).

PART FOUR: VEERING TOWARDS PUBLICATION

Following Winnicott's death, Clare Winnicott (1971), his grieving widow, wrote to both Mr Piggle and Mrs Piggle to inform them of the sad news. It seems that through their interconnections with the mental health community, the family already knew of Winnicott's decease and had even managed to attend the funeral.

Sometime later, on 4th June, 1973, Clare Winnicott convened with both parents at her home in Chester Square to discuss the publication of the long-percolating book about their daughter. Previously, these three individuals had not met in person—a testament to Donald

Winnicott's protection of the family's privacy and confidentiality. Afterwards Mrs Winnicott (1973a) corresponded further with Mr Piggle and Mrs Piggle, explaining, "I know Donald gained so much from working with you, and it would be good if others could learn from the experience that you all shared."

As discussions about the publication unfolded, Clare Winnicott (1973b) consulted the parents about what name should be used to refer to her late husband's former child patient. The little girl, now twelve years old, agreed that the book should, in fact, bear the supratitle *The Piggle*.

Mrs Winnicott enlisted the services of Dr Ishak Ramzy to assist her with the editing and preparation of the final typescript of her late husband's work. Born in 1911 in the city of Zagazig in the Nile delta of Egypt, Ishak Ramzy studied psychology in Cairo and then moved to England in order to undertake his doctoral studies at the University of London and to train at the Institute of Psycho-Analysis. He then returned to his native Egypt for several years more, after which Ramzy relocated to Topeka, Kansas, in order to work for the distinguished American psychiatrist and psychoanalyst Professor Karl Menninger. Ramzy would remain in the American Midwest until his death in 1992.

Winnicott knew Ramzy reasonably well from their mutual involvement in the British Psycho-Analytical Society, and, in 1965, Winnicott chaired a Simultaneous Session at the International Psycho-Analytical Congress of the International Psycho-Analytical Association, in Amsterdam, in The Netherlands, at which Ramzy delivered a paper on "Factors and Features of Early Compulsive Formation". The two men remained in contact over the years; and when Ramzy discovered that Winnicott had almost died while lecturing in New York City, he sent him a box of "Holiday Feast" chocolates as a present (Ramzy, 1969a), decades before most members of the public had come to realise that such sugary foods might be inadvisable for cardiac patients.

Certainly, Winnicott held Ramzy in sufficiently high regard because, four years later, in 1969, he invited Ramzy to supervise him publicly on his work with the Piggle, at a Pre-Congress gathering of the International Psycho-Analytical Association in London, prior to a larger meeting of this biannual psychoanalytical congress in Rome. Just as Winnicott had challenged the Freudian orthodoxy of five sessions of child analysis per week in his treatment of the Piggle, so, too, did he subvert the traditional model of supervision in which an older clinician will comment upon the work of a more junior clinician. Ramzy (1969b), some fifteen years younger than Winnicott, accepted this unusual offer to supervise the case and he wrote to Winnicott, "much as it fills me with awe and timidity, neither can submerge the excitement over the fantastic idea of role-reversal". Winnicott also invited Ramzy (1971) to assist with editorial work on the book as early as 1969. Thus, after Dr Winnicott's death, Ramzy became the ideal person to support Mrs Winnicott with the completion of the book.

Clare Winnicott, the widow, maintained quite a vigilant watch over the entire proceedings and, in 1976, she even revised Ishak Ramzy's "Editor's Foreword", in spite of her own health struggles, which, at that time, included a case of shingles (Clare Winnicott, 1976),[8] and, more severely, a malignant melanoma of her foot, which resulted in many surgical procedures and even prompted her doctors to consider amputation (Elmhirst, 1996).

Ishak Ramzy also became a confidant to Mrs Piggle, in particular. In a draft letter to Dr Ramzy, written circa 1973, Mrs Piggle revealed that, in her estimation, Dr Winnicott did not always engage with the full extent of her daughter's struggles. As she confessed, "I would have a few criticism [sic] (which I did not keep from Donald)—to do with the dark aspects of the child's feelings, that may sometimes have appeared to have been slurred over" ("Mrs Piggle", n.d. [c] [c. 1973]). However, in spite of this reservation, she still proclaimed Winnicott's treatment of her daughter as "a marked success" ("Mrs Piggle", n.d. [c] [c. 1973]).

Through this collaboration among Clare Winnicott, Ishak Ramzy, Mr Piggle, and Mrs Piggle, all the relevant adults eventually approved the final text of Donald Winnicott's typescript. Although the Piggle did agree to both the supratitle and the plan to publish the book, she did not read the final typescript at that time ("The Piggle", 2020).

The carefully copy-edited version of this now classic text, entitled *The Piggle: An Account of the Psychoanalytic Treatment of a Little Girl* (Winnicott, 1977), finally appeared in print just before Christmas, 1977 (Clare Winnicott, 1977), in an American edition, wrapped in a light blue cloth binding and a simple dust jacket, produced by the long-standing psychoanalytical publishing house International Universities Press, based in New York City. With much satisfaction, Clare Winnicott

(1977) wrote to Mrs Piggle, "Here it is at last. I do hope you will be happy with it, and feel secretly proud of it, as you are really entitled to!" Not long thereafter, a 1978 British edition, published by the Hogarth Press of London, in association with the Institute of Psycho-Analysis, bound in green cloth, became available for purchase at the cost of six pounds and fifty pence per copy (Winnicott, 1978). The British version formed a part of the series, "The International Psycho-Analytical Library", then under the editorship of Winnicott's one-time analysand Masud Khan. A special "Preface", authored by Clare Winnicott and her psychoanalytical colleague Mr Raymond Shepherd (Winnicott and Shepard [sic], 1977;[9] Winnicott and Shepherd, 1978)—both members of the Winnicott Publications Committee—appeared alongside Ishak Ramzy's (1977, 1978) "Editor's Foreword" in each edition, as well as a charming sketch of Donald Winnicott's working space at 87, Chester Square, drawn by Miss Elizabeth Britton, sister-in-law to the deceased psychoanalyst.

PART FIVE: A WINNICOTTIAN MASTERPIECE

Having embarked upon his medical training as an undergraduate at the University of Cambridge in 1914 (during which time he helped to treat soldiers wounded during the Great War), and having worked with patients until his death in 1971, Winnicott had encountered literally tens, if not hundreds, of thousands of patients across the course of his long and rich clinical career. And although he wrote accounts of a great many of his paediatric, child psychiatric, child psychoanalytical, and adult psychoanalytical cases, he produced only two book-length case histories, namely, his study of the Piggle and, also, a far less well known account of an adult psychoanalysis of a male patient, parts of which appeared during his lifetime (Winnicott, 1954), but the more extended versions of which would not be published until after his death, firstly as a 200-plus page chapter on "Fragment of an Analysis" (Winnicott, 1972) and, subsequently, as a full-length book, *Holding and Interpretation: Fragment of an Analysis* (Winnicott, 1986a).

It remains unclear why Winnicott chose to present *The Piggle* as his sole single-case, book-length documentation of his child psychoanalytical endeavours. Certainly, Winnicott could well have written innumerable collections of comprehensive child case histories throughout his long career as he had no shortage of clinical material at his disposal. Although we cannot provide a clear answer to this question, I have often wondered whether Winnicott, who commenced his work with the Piggle at the age of sixty-seven years, strongly identified with his one-time teacher and one-time clinical supervisor, the legendary Melanie Klein (1961), who, in spite of her immense psychoanalytical experience, only published one book-length case study of her own, *Narrative of a Child Analysis: The Conduct of the Psycho-Analysis of Children as Seen in the Treatment of a Ten Year Old Boy*, which appeared in print shortly after her death. Perhaps Winnicott also wished to bequeath a detailed, post-mortem child case history, just as Klein had done one decade earlier.

We must also consider whether Winnicott, approaching death, began to lament the fact that he had never become a biological parent in his own right, even though he "parented" thousands and thousands of infants and children and adolescents across his very lengthy career. Perhaps the Piggle became something of a symbolic daughter or grand-daughter to Winnicott, worthy of the deep investment of his time and of his passion.

Whatever Donald Winnicott's motivation for writing up this particular case of the Piggle, he has, with the facilitation of Clare Winnicott and Ishak Ramzy, and with the blessing of both Mr Piggle and Mrs Piggle, gifted a remarkable text to mental health workers worldwide.

With the possible exception of Josef Breuer's (1895) iconic case of "Anna O" and of Sigmund Freud's legendary patients, known in the English-speaking world as "Dora" (Freud, 1905a, 1905b), "Little Hans" (Freud, 1909a), the "Rat Man" (Freud, 1909b), and the "Wolf Man" (Freud, 1918), as well as the case of the German jurist Daniel Paul Schreber (about whom Freud (1911) wrote in some detail in spite of never having met this man in person), the little girl nicknamed "the Piggle" may well be the most famous patient thereafter in the entire history of psychoanalysis.

Other clinicians or scholars will no doubt extol the many virtues of Winnicott's work with the Piggle, emphasising its pathbreaking nature, its epitomisation of empathy and clinical intelligence, its foregrounding of sensitive play therapy, its compassion, its humility, and so many other fine achievements. One need not look far in order to appreciate the innumerable virtues and lessons contained within this magnificent work of psychological prose. In many respects, the fact that the Piggle has grown into a remarkably sane and sensitive woman—I can attest to this from my personal acquaintance with her over approximately twenty-five years—provides the best evidence that Winnicott undertook something very special and very lasting, supporting and helping and containing not only the Piggle but, also, her very emotionally sensitive and concerned parents.

Of course, we must not underestimate the fact that, subsequent to her psychoanalytical experience with Winnicott, the Piggle embarked upon a rich and full life and will, no doubt, have received positive and life-enhancing support from family and friends and colleagues and, even, perhaps, from further psychoanalysis in adulthood. Certainly, her foundational work with Dr Winnicott may well have provided a unique opportunity for greater solidity and understanding in childhood.

But Winnicott's monograph also posed a very *vital challenge* to classical psychoanalysis, while, paradoxically, maintaining a very *firm allegiance* to traditional psychoanalysis.

During the early years of the twentieth century, most clinical psycho-analysts insisted upon meeting with their analysands six days per week, from Mondays to Saturdays inclusive. Sigmund Freud (1913) pioneered this deeply intensive model of treatment, which proved to be such a contrast to the more conventional psychiatric practice of the nineteenth century when physicians consulted with their patients only on an occa-sional and irregular basis (cf. May, 2006, 2007a, 2007b). By codifying this clinical procedure in such a predictable and intensive manner, Freud created something very containing for his patients, providing a true experience of reliability and safety.

Some of the pioneers of psychoanalysis would, even, from time to time, treat patients on Sundays as well, thus creating a seven-day psychoana-lytical week. For instance, the distinguished Viennese-born practitioner Professor Paul Schilder, who emigrated to the United States of America, worked with one of his patients, Dr Alexander Reid Martin (1975), from Mondays to Sundays *inclusive*. More recently, the British psychoanalyst Dr Leslie Sohn, who specialised in treating highly psychotic patients, believed that those very vulnerable individuals simply could not tolerate the breaks at weekends, and so, he, too, treated some of his extremely ill patients every single day of the week (Minne, 2019).

Child psychoanalysts such as Anna Freud also championed the intensive treatment of young people, establishing five sessions per week as the gold standard. When Winnicott began to work with little boys and girls at the Paddington Green Children's Hospital, often providing only one or two consultations in total, and, subsequently, when he conducted "on demand" psychoanalyses, he succeeded in irritating Anna Freud, in spite of her affection for the man (cf. Freud, 1968; Kahr, 2021). According to Miss Freud's long-standing colleague Dr Martin James (1991), she actually spoke scathingly of Winnicott's technique, especially his espousal of the "on demand" model.

Even though colleagues questioned Winnicott's (1962f, p. 168) embrace of his model of occasional consultations, to which he sometimes referred as "modified analysis", he continued to champion the fact that, as a child psychiatrist as well as a child psychoanalyst, he could certainly appreciate that not everyone requires a full analysis and that not everyone would enjoy such opportunities. As he wrote in his essay on "The Aims of Psycho-Analytical Treatment", presented to colleagues in the British Psycho-Analytical Society on 7th March, 1962, "In analysis one asks: how *much* can one be allowed to do? And, by contrast, in my clinic the motto is: how *little* need be done?" (Winnicott, 1962f, p. 166). Indeed, not long thereafter, Winnicott described his briefer, consultative, "on demand" work as "snack-bar psychotherapy" (Winnicott, 1963b, p. 344)—often practised from his clinic at the Paddington Green Children's Hospital, to which he referred as his very own "Psychiatric Snack Bar" (quoted in Clare Winnicott, 1978, p. 28)—suggesting that not every patient will require a full five-course meal and that some might well satisfy their cravings with just a little snack!

But in spite of Winnicott's capacity to raise some eyebrows and concerns among his psychoanalytical colleagues for not always practising five-times-weekly child or adult treatment, let us recall that he certainly did *not* invent this more flexible model of "on demand" psychotherapy. Apparently, Sigmund Freud himself would, from time to time, meet with patients on an occasional basis. Indeed, according to his disciple Dr Theodor Reik, Freud referred to this arrangement as "Fractured Analysis" (quoted in Freeman, 1971, p. 96). Reik, likewise, employed fractured analysis in his treatment of his patient Lewis Namier, whose political career prevented him from attending psychoanalysis regularly, as he kept bouncing back and forth among Vienna, London, and Geneva (Freeman, 1971).

Other Freudian clinicians followed suit. For instance, during the 1930s, Dr Ruth Mack Brunswick, the American-born psychoanalyst who worked in Vienna, Austria, would permit her analysand, Dr Muriel Gardiner, to attend on an occasional basis towards the end of her regular analysis. As Gardiner (1983, p. 81) revealed in her memoir, she participated in psychoanalytical sessions "only when I asked for an appointment".[10]

Likewise, in New York City, the German émigrée psychoanalyst, Dr Karen Horney, also acknowledged the need for an "on demand" model, especially for those individuals who live outside major cities. In her popular book, *Self-Analysis*, Horney (1942, p. 28) spoke of the possibility of offering "occasional checkups" for certain patients.

Even as late as 1950, Dr Ernest Jones (1950), a devoted follower of Freud, referred to "fractional analysis" when corresponding with Winnicott about a lengthy treatment.

Thus, Winnicott certainly cannot claim credit for the notion of shortened or occasional sessions—"on demand" psychotherapy—although he certainly foregrounded its possibility and, indeed, its desirability in certain instances.

In some ways, Winnicott's treatment of the Piggle, which consisted of sixteen formal London-based consultations, as well as home visits, not to mention frequent correspondence by post, and telephone calls with Mr Piggle and Mrs Piggle, may well seem rather a hefty treatment by comparison to some of his other work. For instance, in the case of "John", the youngster who stole from his parents and from shops, Winnicott (1956) never even met the child in question and worked exclusively with the mother, in part, because the father objected to psychology on religious grounds; consequently, through his discussions with the mother, Winnicott successfully advised her on the unconscious meaning of her son's behaviours.

Donald Winnicott's embrace of the "on demand" model of treatment developed from many sources, including the fact that, as a hospital physician with thousands of patients entering his clinic, he simply could not provide intensive multi-frequency psychoanalysis or psychotherapy for each of them; therefore, he had to develop a model of more occasional therapeutic consultations. Winnicott found this model of use, recognising that young people often benefit quickly from brief interventions.

But in addition to Winnicott's clinical justification for the "on demand" approach to treatment, he also practised this particular method for personal medical reasons, especially towards the end of his life. For instance, in 1970, not long before his death, a patient, whom I shall designate as "Arabella Bagshawe", approached Winnicott for psychoanalytical treatment; but, owing to his fading physical health, he refused to agree to ongoing, open-ended work and offered "on demand" sessions instead, which proved most useful to the patient, who, years later, spoke to me enthusiastically of her experience with the seventy-four-year-old man (Kahr, 1996c; cf. Kahr, 2020).

Not only did Winnicott promulgate "on demand" treatment in his relationship with the Piggle, but he also developed what he came to call "psychoanalysis *partagé*" (quoted in Winnicott and Shepard [*sic*], 1977, p. viii)—a neologistic English-French phrase meaning "shared psychoanalysis", referring to the fact that, in his work with the Piggle, he also shared his psychoanalytical knowledge with the parents and, consequently, the whole family cooperated and collaborated in the treatment in different ways. In other words, Winnicott believed that one should communicate some of the material to the parents, without breaching the child's confidentiality per se. He also insisted that "psychoanalysis *partagé*" should in no way be confused with family therapy. Winnicott did not intend to "treat" the entire system but focused, instead, on the child with the support of the parents.

Once again, just as Winnicott cannot receive full credit for "on demand" work, he also cannot claim to be the progenitor of "psychoanalysis *partagé*". Most obviously, Sigmund Freud (1909a) had created a shared arrangement many years previously in his work with Herbert Graf, the little boy who suffered from a phobia of horses. Freud had met not only with Herbert Graf but also with the child's father, Max Graf. Freud also knew the mother, Olga Hönig Graf, extremely well, as she had undergone her own psychoanalysis with him years previously (Wakefield, 2007). Thus, in many respects, Freud pioneered this particular model of treatment, although Winnicott elaborated upon it with his tremendous compassion and talent.

Although Winnicott barely refers to the famous case of "kleine Hans" (i.e. "Little Hans") in his writings (e.g. Winnicott, 1960), it may well be that Freud's detailed analysis of the child's precise dialogue and language may have propelled Winnicott towards writing a comparable case by quoting the exact words used by the Piggle. Throughout the history of psychiatry, most cases simply summarised what the patient had spoken, but in Winnicott's text, as in Freud's, more than half a century earlier, the precise voice of the little child still shines through.

PART SIX: CONCLUSION

Donald Winnicott's book, *The Piggle: An Account of the Psychoanalytic Treatment of a Little Girl*, published posthumously, remains one of the most important and enjoyable texts in the entire history of psychoanalysis.

This playful book reminds us of the extraordinary healing powers of the talking cure and of the ways in which a clinician of deep experience and profound compassion and creativity can facilitate the growth of an individual in distress.

Winnicott's text provides clear evidence of the importance of tracking the child's words and gestures and play, and the necessity of interpreting their meaning in a helpful manner, thus facilitating emotional growth and stability. The book also confirms the crucial need for collaborating with the wider system when conducting work with vulnerable populations, whether children, the disabled, the mentally ill, and so forth.

When one studies the life of Donald Winnicott in some detail, one soon comes to appreciate that the treatment of the Piggle unfolded amid a time of great physical distress for this extraordinary psychoanalyst. He not only had to navigate his seventieth birthday and all the developmental vicissitudes of the life cycle, but, moreover, he had to work in spite of having already endured a number of coronary crises, with several more to come, as well as significant ocular pain from at least two patient-induced injuries. A man of considerable sturdiness, Donald Winnicott managed to access his professionalism, his playfulness, and his joy for living, in order to transmit these qualities to the Piggle, in spite of his own quite significant medical struggles.

The case of the Piggle remains a source of engagement and interest and provides the leaping-off point for much creative discussion among child and adult mental health practitioners alike. In this day and age, the need for evidence that psychological treatment really does work certainly predominates. Thus, we may all benefit from the fact that in view of the current-day robustness of the Piggle as a full-grown adult, who daily makes her own compassionate contributions to the world, we have important confirmatory evidence that Donald Winnicott's support of this one-time little girl and her parents has made a truly lasting impact.

Acknowledgements

I wish to express my warm appreciation to Dr Corinne Masur for her kind invitation to contribute a chapter to this edited book and for her encouragement during the writing process and, of course, for her intelligent comments about the first draft of this chapter. I also thank Dr Deborah Luepnitz for having kindly introduced me to Dr Masur and, additionally, for her own scholarship on the Piggle. Moreover, I extend my sincere gratitude to my long-standing colleague, Mrs Kate Pearce, the Publisher of Phoenix Publishing House, who epitomises warm-hearted collaboration, as well her cheerful colleagues, Mr Fernando Marques, the Sales Director, and Mr James Darley, the most convivial of copy editors. I owe my most immense thanks to the Piggle, without whom I certainly could not have written this chronicle. The Piggle very kindly read several drafts and offered helpful comments and corrigenda. Through the generosity and trust of the Piggle, I enjoyed the immense privilege of having studied her numerous family documents and photographs. I must also offer my appreciation to Mr Piggle, the father, and to the late Mrs Piggle, the mother, for their kind communications and reminiscences. Additionally, I would like to thank the sister of the Piggle, who generously granted permission for me to study "'The Piggle' Papers"—a most unique archive which will, in future years, prove indispensable to historians of psychoanalysis.

Notes

1. During the course of my research on the life and work of Dr Donald Winnicott, I discovered several unpublished letters between Winnicott and the grandmother of the Piggle, in which these two concerned individuals corresponded about the case of a little boy whose parents had died in the Holocaust. Although

in my historical research I always endeavour to provide detailed scholarly references to all facts, on this occasion, owing to confidentiality, I cannot readily reveal the source of these letters, as this would expose the true identity of the Piggle and her family, which Winnicott had worked so hard to preserve across his career. The letters from which this material derives can be found in a public archive; however, I trust that fellow clinicians (as well as fellow historians) who might also come to discover this stash of correspondence will also honour the pledge of confidentiality.

2. Across the years, I have had the privilege of interviewing over fifty of Dr Donald Winnicott's former analysands. In my publications, I have certainly never revealed their real names; however, as one of my interviewees, Jane Shore Nicholas, the former Jane Khan—sometime wife of the psychoanalyst Masud Khan—had already discussed her story in great detail with the American psychoanalytical biographer, Dr Linda Hopkins (2006), and had granted Hopkins permission to print the story in full in her biography of Masud Khan, I have, on this occasion, referred to Jane Shore by her true name.

3. In the original version of this letter of 12th July, 1965, written solely to "Mrs Piggle", Winnicott (1965g) reported, "When I read your letter I do not feel absolutely in despair about the way things are going."

4. It would not be entirely unreasonable to hypothesise that Donald Winnicott might have had to insert drops into his eyes in the midst of psychoanalytical sessions. Several decades ago, Ms Rosemarie Krausz, then a trainee in the Department of Psychiatry at the Sir Mortimer B. Davis Jewish General Hospital in Montreal, Quebec, in Canada, received a diagnosis of Bell's palsy and had to use eye drops every thirty minutes, over a period of fourteen days, even while facilitating psychotherapy sessions (Brown and Krausz, 1984).

5. One could pontificate at length about the unconscious meanings of the Piggle's engagement with this particular toy. The fact that she enjoyed playing with a figurine of a little boy pulling a little girl on a sleigh might symbolise her capacity to tolerate two young children sharing the same space (i.e. working through the sibling rivalry). Alternatively, one might argue that the Piggle enjoyed the notion of the boy *pulling* the girl as a means of control.

6. Please refer to End Note 1 for more details about this piece of biographical data.

7. Needless to say, for reasons of confidentiality, I have used the designations of "Mr Piggle" and "Mrs Piggle". In the original letters, Winnicott addressed the parents by their titles and by their surnames at the outset of their correspondence.

8. In order to differentiate between publications by Donald Winnicott and those written by his second wife, Clare Winnicott, I have, where necessary, inserted the name "Clare" into certain references, in order to provide greater clarity as to the authorship.

9. In the original American edition of the book, the typesetters misspelled the name of Raymond D. Shepherd, a member of the Winnicott Publications Committee, as "Shepard". Although the book renders his name correctly in the "Contents" page, one finds his surname misspelled as co-author of the "Preface". A member of the Independent Group of the British Psycho-Analytical Society, Shepherd devoted much of his life to the editing of many of Donald Winnicott's posthumously published collections of papers, notably, *Deprivation and Delinquency* (Winnicott, 1984); *Home is Where We Start From: Essays by a Psychoanalyst* (Winnicott, 1986b); *Babies and Their Mothers* (Winnicott, 1987); *Human Nature* (Winnicott, 1988); *Psycho-Analytic Explorations* (Winnicott, 1989); *Talking to Parents* (Winnicott, 1993); and *Thinking About Children* (Winnicott, 1996).

10. In the original German version of Dr Muriel Gardiner's (1978, p. 66) memoir, she described her request for occasional sessions with Dr Ruth Mack Brunswick as "nur auf eigenes Ersuchen".

References

Anonymous [Gershy Hepner] (1961). A Personal View – 10: Donald Winnicott. *St. Mary's Hospital Gazette, 67*, 137–138.

Anonymous (2000). Personal Communication to the Author. 15th February.

Appleby, Mary (1967). Letter to Donald W. Winnicott. 4th April. Box 6. File 6. Donald W. Winnicott Papers. Archives of Psychiatry, The Oskar Diethelm Library, The DeWitt Wallace Institute for the History of Psychiatry, Department of Psychiatry, Joan and Sanford I. Weill Medical College, Cornell University, The New York Presbyterian Hospital, New York, New York, U.S.A.

Birt, Doris (1964). Letter to Donald W. Winnicott. 17th February. Box 4. File 12. Donald W. Winnicott Papers. Archives of Psychiatry, The Oskar Diethelm Library, The DeWitt Wallace Institute for the History of Psychiatry, Department of Psychiatry, Joan and Sanford I. Weill Medical College, Cornell University, The New York Presbyterian Hospital, New York, New York, U.S.A.

Breuer, Josef (1882). Krankengeschichte Bertha Pappenheim. Unpublished Typescript. Box 33A. Freud Museum London, Swiss Cottage, London.

Breuer, Josef (1895). Beobachtung I. Frl. Anna O … In Josef Breuer and Sigmund Freud. *Studien über Hysterie*, pp. 15–37. Vienna: Franz Deuticke.

Brown, Ronald D., and Krausz, Rosemarie (1984). The Patient's Unconscious Perceptions of the Therapist's Disruptions. In James Raney (Ed.). *Listening and Interpreting: The Challenge of the Work of Robert Langs*, pp. 21–35. New York: Jason Aronson.

Elmhirst, Susanna Isaacs (1996). Personal Communication to the Author. 7th March.

Forrester, John, and Cameron, Laura (1999). 'A Cure with a Defect': A Previously Unpublished Letter by Freud Concerning 'Anna O'. *International Journal of Psychoanalysis*, 80, 929–942.

Freeman, Erika (1971). *Insights: Conversations with Theodor Reik*. Englewood Cliffs, New Jersey: Prentice-Hall.

Freeman, Lucy (1972). *The Story of Anna O*. New York: Walker and Company.

Freud, Anna (1968). Letter to Donald W. Winnicott. 30th October. Box 7. File 2. Donald W. Winnicott Papers. Archives of Psychiatry, The Oskar Diethelm Library, The DeWitt Wallace Institute for the History of Psychiatry, Department of Psychiatry, Joan and Sanford I. Weill Medical College, Cornell University, The New York Presbyterian Hospital, New York, New York, U.S.A.

Freud, Sigmund (1905a). Bruchstück einer Hysterie-Analyse. [Part I]. *Monatsschrift für Psychiatrie und Neurologie*, 18, 285–309.

Freud, Sigmund (1905b). Bruchstück einer Hysterie-Analyse. [Part II]. *Monatsschrift für Psychiatrie und Neurologie*, 18, 408–467.

Freud, Sigmund (1909a). Analyse der Phobie eines 5jährigen Knaben. *Jahrbuch für psychoanalytische und psychopathologische Forschungen*, 1, 1–109.

Freud, Sigmund (1909b). Bemerkungen über einen Fall von Zwangsneurose. *Jahrbuch für psychoanalytische und psychopathologische Forschungen*, 1, 357–421.

Freud, Sigmund (1911). Psychoanalytische Bemerkungen über einen autobiographisch beschriebenen Fall von Paranoia (Dementia Paranoides). *Jahrbuch für psychoanalytische und psychopathologische Forschungen*, 3, 9–68.

Freud, Sigmund (1913). Weitere Ratschläge zur Technik der Psychoanalyse: I. Zur Einleitung der Behandlung. *Internationale Zeitschrift für ärztliche Psychoanalyse*, 1, 1–10.

Freud, Sigmund (1918). Aus der Geschichte einer infantilen Neurose. In *Sammlung kleiner Schriften zur Neurosenlehre: Vierte Folge*, pp. 578–717. Vienna: Hugo Heller und Compagnie.

Freud, Sigmund (1932). Letter to Arthur Tansley. 20th November, p. 930. In John Forrester and Laura Cameron (1999). 'A Cure with a Defect': A Previously Unpublished Letter by Freud Concerning 'Anna O'. *International Journal of Psychoanalysis, 80*, 929–942.

Gabriel, Pam (1965a). Letter to Donald W. Winnicott. 5th July. Box 5. File 3. Donald W. Winnicott Papers. Archives of Psychiatry, The Oskar Diethelm Library, The DeWitt Wallace Institute for the History of Psychiatry, Department of Psychiatry, Joan and Sanford I. Weill Medical College, Cornell University, The New York Presbyterian Hospital, New York, New York, U.S.A.

Gabriel, Pam (1965b). Letter to Donald W. Winnicott. 5th October. Box 5. File 3. Donald W. Winnicott Papers. Archives of Psychiatry, The Oskar Diethelm Library, The DeWitt Wallace Institute for the History of Psychiatry, Department of Psychiatry, Joan and Sanford I. Weill Medical College, Cornell University, The New York Presbyterian Hospital, New York, New York, U.S.A.

Gaddini, Renata (1996). Personal Communication to the Author. 2nd May.

Gardiner, Muriel (1978). In Wien vom 12. Februar 1934 bis zum Anschluß. In Muriel Gardiner and Joseph Buttinger. *Damit wir nicht vergessen: Unsere Jahre 1934–1947 in Wien, Paris und New York*, pp. 31–72. Vienna: Verlag der Wiener Volksbuchhandlung.

Gardiner, Muriel (1983). *Code Name "Mary": Memoirs of an American Woman in the Austrian Underground*. New Haven, Connecticut: Yale University Press.

Gitelson, Maxwell (1963). Letter to Donald W. Winnicott. 30th October. PP/DWW/M.2/1. Donald Woods Winnicott Collection. Archives and Manuscripts, Rare Materials Room, Wellcome Library, Wellcome Collection, The Wellcome Building, London.

Grosskurth, Phyllis (1986). *Melanie Klein: Her World and Her Work*. New York: Alfred A. Knopf.

Guntrip, Harry (n.d.). Obituary: Donald Woods Winnicott. Unpublished Typescript. PP/DWW/G/6/2. Donald Woods Winnicott Collection. Archives and Manuscripts, Rare Materials Room, Wellcome Library, Wellcome Collection, The Wellcome Building, London.

Hart, Edward (1963). Letter to Donald W. Winnicott. 2nd May. Box 4. File 1. Donald W. Winnicott Papers. Archives of Psychiatry, The Oskar Diethelm Library, The DeWitt Wallace Institute for the History of Psychiatry, Department of Psychiatry, Joan and Sanford I. Weill Medical College, Cornell University, The New York Presbyterian Hospital, New York, New York, U.S.A.

Hepner, Gershy (1961). Letter to Donald W. Winnicott. 11th November. PP/
      DWW/A/J. Folder 1. Donald Woods Winnicott Collection. Archives and
      Manuscripts, Rare Materials Room, Wellcome Library, Wellcome Collec-
      tion, The Wellcome Building, London.

Hopkins, Linda (2006). *False Self: The Life of Masud Khan*. New York: Other
      Press.

Horney, Karen (1942). *Self-Analysis*. New York: W. W. Norton and Company.

James, Martin (1965). Letter to Donald W. Winnicott. 1st December. Box 5. File 4.
      Donald W. Winnicott Papers. Archives of Psychiatry, The Oskar Diethelm
      Library, The DeWitt Wallace Institute for the History of Psychiatry, Depart-
      ment of Psychiatry, Joan and Sanford I. Weill Medical College, Cornell Uni-
      versity, The New York Presbyterian Hospital, New York, New York, U.S.A.

James, Martin (1991). Lecture on "Has Winnicott Become a Winnicottian?:
      The Importance of Psychiatry". The Squiggle Foundation, Primrose Hill,
      London, at the Primrose Hill Community Centre, Primrose Hill, London.
      16th February.

Jones, Ernest (1950). Letter to Donald W. Winnicott. 3rd October. PP/DWW/
      B/A/16. Donald Woods Winnicott Collection. Archives and Manuscripts,
      Rare Materials Room, Wellcome Library, Wellcome Collection, The
      Wellcome Building, London.

Kahr, Brett (1994a). Telephone Interview with Donald Campbell. 2nd May.

Kahr, Brett (1994b). Interview with Susanna Isaacs Elmhirst. 30th May.

Kahr, Brett (1994c). Interview with Malcolm Pines. 3rd October.

Kahr, Brett (1994d). Interview with Joyce Coles. 18th December.

Kahr, Brett (1995a). Letter to "Mrs Piggle". 7th November. "The Piggle" Papers.
      London.

Kahr, Brett (1995b). Interview with Agnes Wilkinson. 31st January.

Kahr, Brett (1995c). Telephone Interview with "Mrs Piggle". 12th December.

Kahr, Brett (1996a). *D. W. Winnicott: A Biographical Portrait*. London: H. Karnac
      (Books).

Kahr, Brett (1996b). Telephone Interview with Katharine Rees. 3rd January.

Kahr, Brett (1996c). Interview with "Arabella Bagshawe". 12th March.

Kahr, Brett (1996d). Interview with "The Piggle". 2nd April.

Kahr, Brett (1997). Interview with "Edmund Fothergill". 3rd January.

Kahr, Brett (2003). Masud Khan's Analysis with Donald Winnicott: On the Haz-
      ards of Befriending a Patient. *Free Associations*, *10*, 190–222.

Kahr, Brett (2005). Interview with Pearl King. 20th October.

Kahr, Brett (2009a). Telephone Interview with Olive Stevenson. 16th June.

Kahr, Brett (2009b). Telephone Interview with Gershon Hepner. 5th August.

Kahr, Brett (2009c). Interview with Jane Shore Nicholas. 21st August.

Kahr, Brett (2010a). Interview with Peter Bruggen. 10th February.

Kahr, Brett (2010b). Interview with Richard Michael. 26th March.

Kahr, Brett (2015). "Led Astray by Their Half-Baked Pseudo-Scientific Rubbish": John Bowlby and the Paradigm Shift in Child Psychiatry. *Attachment: New Directions in Psychotherapy and Relational Psychoanalysis, 9*, 297–317.

Kahr, Brett (2018). The Public Psychoanalyst: Donald Winnicott as Broadcaster. In Angela Joyce (Ed.). *Donald W. Winnicott and the History of the Present: Understanding the Man and His Work*, pp. 111–121. London: Karnac Books.

Kahr, Brett (2019a). The First Mrs Winnicott and the Second Mrs Winnicott: Does Psychoanalysis Facilitate Healthy Marital Choice? *Couple and Family Psychoanalysis, 9*, 105–131.

Kahr, Brett (2019b). John Bowlby and the Birth of Child Mental Health. *Attachment: New Directions in Psychotherapy and Relational Psychoanalysis, 13*, 164–180.

Kahr, Brett (2020). "I wish your life didn't have to be so difficult": Winnicott's Last Three Patients. Unpublished Typescript.

Kahr, Brett (2021). *Winnicott's Anni Horribiles: The Creation of 'Hate in the Counter-Transference'.* London: Routledge/Taylor and Francis Group, and Abingdon, Oxfordshire: Routledge/Taylor and Francis Group. [In Press].

Karpf, Anne (2014). Constructing and Addressing the 'Ordinary Devoted Mother'. *History Workshop Journal*, Number 78, 82–106.

Khan, M. Masud R. (1971). Letter to Alfred Flarsheim. 2nd February. Box 8. File 11. Donald W. Winnicott Papers. Archives of Psychiatry, The Oskar Diethelm Library, The DeWitt Wallace Institute for the History of Psychiatry, Department of Psychiatry, Joan and Sanford I. Weill Medical College, Cornell University, The New York Presbyterian Hospital, New York, New York, U.S.A.

King, Pearl (1997). Talk on Sept. 5, 1987 on the Twentieth Anniversary of the Founding of the Finnish Psycho-Analytical Society. In Aira Laine, Helena Parland, and Esa Roos (Eds.). *Psykoanalyysin uranuurtajat Suomessa*, pp. 161–168. Kemijärvi: LPT Lapin Painotuote Oy.

King, Pearl (2001). Personal Communication to the Author. 27th August.

Klein, Melanie (1961). *Narrative of a Child Analysis: The Conduct of the Psycho-Analysis of Children as Seen in the Treatment of a Ten Year Old Boy.* London: Hogarth Press and the Institute of Psycho-Analysis.

Krugman, Steven (1987). Trauma in the Family: Perspectives on the Intergenerational Transmission of Violence. In Bessel A. van der Kolk (Ed.). *Psychological Trauma*, pp. 127 –151. Washington, D.C.: American Psychiatric Press.

Law, Frank W. (1963). Letter to Donald W. Winnicott. 2nd July. Box 4. File 4. Donald W. Winnicott Papers. Archives of Psychiatry, The Oskar Diethelm Library, The DeWitt Wallace Institute for the History of Psychiatry, Department of Psychiatry, Joan and Sanford I. Weill Medical College, Cornell University, The New York Presbyterian Hospital, New York, New York, U.S.A.

Martin, Alexander Reid (1975). Untitled Oral History of Karen Horney. American Academy of Psychoanalysis. Cited in Susan Quinn (1987). *A Mind of Her Own: The Life of Karen Horney*, p. 445, n. 13. New York: Summit Books/Simon and Schuster.

May, Ulrike (2006). Freuds Patientenkalender: Siebzehn Analytiker in Analyse bei Freud (1910–1920). *Luzifer-Amor, 19*, Number 37, 43–97.

May, Ulrike (2007a). Neunzehn Patienten in Analyse bei Freud (1910–1920): Teil I: Zur Dauer von Freuds Analysen. *Psyche, 61*, 590–625.

May, Ulrike (2007b). Neunzehn Patienten in Analyse bei Freud (1910–1920): Teil II: Zur Frequenz von Freuds Analysen. *Psyche, 61*, 686–709.

Minne, Carine (2019). Personal Communication to the Author. 14th November.

Montessori, Mario M. (Ed.). (1968). Report of the 25th International Psycho-Analytical Congress, pp. 116–148. *Bulletin of the International Psycho-Analytical Association. International Journal of Psycho-Analysis, 49*, 116–157.

"Mr Piggle" and "Mrs Piggle" (1964a). Letter to Donald W. Winnicott. 4th January. In Donald W. Winnicott (1977). *The Piggle: An Account of the Psychoanalytic Treatment of a Little Girl*. Ishak Ramzy (Ed.), pp. 5–7. New York: International Universities Press.

"Mr Piggle" and "Mrs Piggle" (1964b). Letter to Donald W. Winnicott. n.d. In Donald W. Winnicott (1977). *The Piggle: An Account of the Psychoanalytic Treatment of a Little Girl*. Ishak Ramzy (Ed.), pp. 96–97. New York: International Universities Press.

"Mrs Piggle" (1964). Letter to Donald W. Winnicott. n.d. In Donald W. Winnicott (1977). *The Piggle: An Account of the Psychoanalytic Treatment of a Little Girl*. Ishak Ramzy (Ed.), pp. 63–65. New York: International Universities Press.

"Mrs Piggle" (n.d. [a]). Untitled Note. "The Piggle" Papers. London.

"Mrs Piggle" (n.d. [b] [1965]). Letter to Donald W. Winnicott. n.d. In Donald W. Winnicott (1977). *The Piggle: An Account of the Psychoanalytic Treatment of a Little Girl.* Ishak Ramzy (Ed.), p. 161. New York: International Universities Press.

"Mrs Piggle" (n.d. [c] [c. 1973]). Draft Letter to Ishak Ramzy. n.d. "The Piggle" Papers. London.

"Mrs Piggle" (n.d. [d]). Draft Letter to Donald W. Winnicott. n.d. "The Piggle" Papers. London.

Palmer, Vicki (1967). Letter to Joyce Coles. 20th September. Box 6. File 14. Donald W. Winnicott Papers. Archives of Psychiatry, The Oskar Diethelm Library, The DeWitt Wallace Institute for the History of Psychiatry, Department of Psychiatry, Joan and Sanford I. Weill Medical College, Cornell University, The New York Presbyterian Hospital, New York, New York, U.S.A.

Ramzy, Ishak (1969a). Letter to Louise Carpenter. 14th January. Box 7. File 11. Donald W. Winnicott Papers. Archives of Psychiatry, The Oskar Diethelm Library, The DeWitt Wallace Institute for the History of Psychiatry, Department of Psychiatry, Joan and Sanford I. Weill Medical College, Cornell University, The New York Presbyterian Hospital, New York, New York, U.S.A.

Ramzy, Ishak (1969b). Letter to Donald W. Winnicott. 10th July. Box 7. File 16. Donald W. Winnicott Papers. Archives of Psychiatry, The Oskar Diethelm Library, The DeWitt Wallace Institute for the History of Psychiatry, Department of Psychiatry, Joan and Sanford I. Weill Medical College, Cornell University, The New York Presbyterian Hospital, New York, New York, U.S.A.

Ramzy, Ishak (1971). Letter to Clare Winnicott. 26th March. PP/DWW/G/6/1. Folder 2. Donald Woods Winnicott Collection. Archives and Manuscripts, Rare Materials Room, Wellcome Library, Wellcome Collection, The Wellcome Building, London.

Ramzy, Ishak (1977). Editor's Foreword. In Donald W. Winnicott. *The Piggle: An Account of the Psychoanalytic Treatment of a Little Girl.* Ishak Ramzy (Ed.), pp. xi–xvi. New York: International Universities Press.

Ramzy, Ishak (1978). Editor's Foreword. In Donald W. Winnicott. *The Piggle: An Account of the Psychoanalytic Treatment of a Little Girl.* Ishak Ramzy (Ed.), pp. xi–xvi. London: Hogarth Press and the Institute of Psycho-Analysis.

Robinson, Kenneth (1965). Official Opening of the Conference. In *The Price of Mental Health*, pp. 4–12. London: National Association for Mental Health.

Skuse, Richard A. (2006). *Sigmund Freud and the History of Anna O.: Reopening a Closed Case.* Houndmills, Basingstoke, Hampshire: Palgrave Macmillan.

"The Piggle" (2017). Personal Communication to the Author. 25th January.

"The Piggle" (2020). Personal Communication to the Author. 23rd February.

Tizard, J. Peter M. (1981). Donald Winnicott: The President's View of a Past President. *Journal of the Royal Society of Medicine, 74*, 267–274.

Wakefield, Jerome C. (2007). Max Graf's "Reminiscences of Professor Sigmund Freud" Revisited: New Evidence from the Freud Archives. *Psychoanalytic Quarterly, 76*, 149–192.

Winnicott, Clare (1971). Note to "Mrs Piggle" and "Mr Piggle". n.d. February. "The Piggle" Papers. London.

Winnicott, Clare (1973a). Letter to "Mrs Piggle" and "Mr Piggle". 4th June. "The Piggle" Papers. London.

Winnicott, Clare (1973b). Letter to "Mrs Piggle" and "Mr Piggle". 5th September. "The Piggle" Papers. London.

Winnicott, Clare (1976). Letter to "Mrs Piggle". 18th July. "The Piggle" Papers. London.

Winnicott, Clare (1977). Letter to "Mrs Piggle". n.d. "The Piggle" Papers. London.

Winnicott, Clare (1978). D.W.W.: A Reflection. In Simon A. Grolnick, Leonard Barkin, and Werner Muensterberger (Eds.). *Between Reality and Fantasy: Transitional Objects and Phenomena*, pp. 17–33. New York: Jason Aronson.

Winnicott, Clare (1982). Letter to James W. Anderson. 23rd September. PP/DWW/H/3/1. Folder 2. Donald Woods Winnicott Collection. Archives and Manuscripts, Rare Materials Room, Wellcome Library, Wellcome Collection, The Wellcome Building, London.

Winnicott, Clare, and Shepard, Raymond D. [*sic*] (1977). Preface. In Donald W. Winnicott. *The Piggle: An Account of the Psychoanalytic Treatment of a Little Girl*. Ishak Ramzy (Ed.), pp. vii–ix. New York: International Universities Press.

Winnicott, Clare, and Shepherd, Raymond D. (1978). Preface. In Donald W. Winnicott. *The Piggle: An Account of the Psychoanalytic Treatment of a Little Girl*. Ishak Ramzy (Ed.), pp. vii–ix. London: Hogarth Press and the Institute of Psycho-Analysis.

Winnicott, Donald W. (1931a). *Clinical Notes on Disorders of Childhood*. London: William Heinemann (Medical Books).

Winnicott, Donald W. (1931b). A Clinical Note on Convulsions, p. 257. In Anonymous. British Paediatric Association: Proceedings of the Fourth Annual General Meeting. *Archives of Disease in Childhood, 6*, 255–258.

Winnicott, Donald W. (1932). Growing Pains; the Problem of Their Relation to Acute Rheumatism, p. 227. In Anonymous. British Paediatric Association:

Proceedings of the Fifth Annual General Meeting. *Archives of Disease in Childhood, 7*, 225–229.

Winnicott, Donald W. (1933). Pathological Sleeping. *British Journal of Children's Diseases, 30*, 205–206.

Winnicott, Donald W. (1939). The Psychology of Juvenile Rheumatism. In Ronald G. Gordon (Ed.). *A Survey of Child Psychiatry*, pp. 28–44. London: Humphrey Milford / Oxford University Press.

Winnicott, Donald W. (1940). The Deprived Mother. In John Rickman (Ed.). *Children in War-Time: The Uprooted Child, the Problem of the Young Child, the Deprived Mother, Foster-Parents, Visiting, the Teacher's Problems, Homes for Difficult Children*, pp. 31–43. London: New Education Fellowship.

Winnicott, Donald W. (1942). Child Department Consultations. *International Journal of Psycho-Analysis, 23*, 139–146.

Winnicott, Donald W. (1945). Primitive Emotional Development. *International Journal of Psycho-Analysis, 26*, 137–143.

Winnicott, Donald W. (1948a). Children's Hostels in War and Peace: A Contribution to the Symposium on "Lessons for Child Psychiatry". Given at a Meeting of the Medical Section of the British Psychological Society, 27 February 1946. *British Journal of Medical Psychology, 21*, 175–180.

Winnicott, Donald W. (1948b). Pediatrics and Psychiatry. *British Journal of Medical Psychology, 21*, 229–240.

Winnicott, Donald W. (1953). Psychoses and Child Care. *British Journal of Medical Psychology, 26*, 68–74.

Winnicott, Donald W. (1954). Withdrawal and Regression. In Donald W. Winnicott (1958). *Collected Papers: Through Paediatrics to Psycho-Analysis*, pp. 255–261. New York: Basic Books.

Winnicott, Donald W. (1956). The Antisocial Tendency. In Donald W. Winnicott (1958). *Collected Papers: Through Paediatrics to Psycho-Analysis*, pp. 306–315. London: Tavistock Publications.

Winnicott, Donald W. (1957a). *The Child and the Family: First Relationships*. Janet Hardenberg (Ed.). London: Tavistock Publications.

Winnicott, Donald W. (1957b). *The Child and the Outside World: Studies in Developing Relationships*. Janet Hardenberg (Ed.). London: Tavistock Publications.

Winnicott, Donald W. (1958). *Collected Papers: Through Paediatrics to Psycho-Analysis*. London: Tavistock Publications.

Winnicott, Donald W. (1960). The Theory of the Parent–Infant Relationship. *International Journal of Psycho-Analysis, 41*, 585–595.

Winnicott, Donald W. (1961a). The Effect of Psychotic Parents on the Emotional Development of the Child. *British Journal of Psychiatric Social Work*, 6, 13–20.

Winnicott, Donald W. (1961b). The Paediatric Department of Psychology. *St. Mary's Hospital Gazette*, 67, 188–189.

Winnicott, Donald W. (1961c). La Théorie de la relation parent-nourrisson. Janine Massoubre (Transl.). *Revue Française de Psychanalyse*, 25, 7–26.

Winnicott, Donald W. (1961d). Loving. *New Statesman*. 5th May, pp. 722–723.

Winnicott, Donald W. (1961e). The Paediatric Department of Psychology. Typescript. PP/DWW/A/J. Folder 1. Donald Woods Winnicott Collection. Archives and Manuscripts, Rare Materials Room, Wellcome Library, Wellcome Collection, The Wellcome Building, London.

Winnicott, Donald W. (1961f). Letter to Gordon Levinson. 3rd July. Box 3. File 4. Donald W. Winnicott Papers. Archives of Psychiatry, The Oskar Diethelm Library, The DeWitt Wallace Institute for the History of Psychiatry, Department of Psychiatry, Joan and Sanford I. Weill Medical College, Cornell University, The New York Presbyterian Hospital, New York, New York, U.S.A.

Winnicott, Donald W. (1961g). Letter to Michael H. Harmer. 28th September. Box 3. File 3. Donald W. Winnicott Papers. Archives of Psychiatry, The Oskar Diethelm Library, The DeWitt Wallace Institute for the History of Psychiatry, Department of Psychiatry, Joan and Sanford I. Weill Medical College, Cornell University, The New York Presbyterian Hospital, New York, New York, U.S.A.

Winnicott, Donald W. (1962a). Reply. *International Journal of Psycho-Analysis*, 43, 256–257.

Winnicott, Donald W. (1962b). La Première année de la vie: Conceptions modernes du développement affectif au cours de la première année de la vie (I). Jeannine Kalmanovitch and Janine Massoubre (Transls.). *Revue Française de Psychanalyse*, 26, 477–490.

Winnicott, Donald W. (1962c). Hayatin ilk yili. *Tipta yenilikler*, 7, 4–8.

Winnicott, Donald W. (1962d). Adolescence. *New Era in Home and School*, 43, 145–151.

Winnicott, Donald W. (1962e). Introduction. In Robert W. Shields. *A Cure of Delinquents: The Treatment of Maladjustment*, pp. 9–10. London: Heinemann Educational Books.

Winnicott, Donald W. (1962f). The Aims of Psycho-Analytical Treatment. In Donald W. Winnicott (1965). *The Maturational Processes and the Facilitating*

Environment: Studies in the Theory of Emotional Development, pp. 166–170. London: Hogarth Press and the Institute of Psycho-Analysis.

Winnicott, Donald W. (1963a). The Young Child at Home and at School. In William Roy Niblett (Ed.). *Moral Education in a Changing Society*, pp. 96–111. London: Faber and Faber.

Winnicott, Donald W. (1963b). Dependence in Infant Care, in Child Care, and in the Psycho-Analytic Setting. *International Journal of Psycho-Analysis*, *44*, 339–344.

Winnicott, Donald W. (1963c). Symposium: Training for Child Psychiatry. *Journal of Child Psychology and Psychiatry and Allied Disciplines*, *4*, 85–91.

Winnicott, Donald W. (1963d). Regression as Therapy Illustrated by the Case of a Boy Whose Pathological Dependence was Adequately Met by the Parents. *British Journal of Medical Psychology*, *36*, 1–12.

Winnicott, Donald W. (1963e). The Development of the Capacity for Concern. *Bulletin of the Menninger Clinic*, *27*, 167–176.

Winnicott, Donald W. (1963f). Symposium: Training for Child Psychiatry. *Journal of Child Psychology and Psychiatry and Allied Disciplines*, *4*, 85–91.

Winnicott, Donald W. (1963g). Struggling Through the Doldrums. *New Society*. 25th April, pp. 8–11.

Winnicott, Donald W. (1963h). Psychiatric Disorder in Terms of Infantile Maturational Processes. In Donald W. Winnicott (1965). *The Maturational Processes and the Facilitating Environment: Studies in the Theory of Emotional Development*, pp. 230–241. London: Hogarth Press and the Institute of Psycho-Analysis.

Winnicott, Donald W. (1964a). *The Child, the Family, and the Outside World*. Harmondsworth, Middlesex: Penguin Books.

Winnicott, Donald W. (1964b). The Neonate and His Mother. *Acta Paediatrica Latina*, *17*, Supplement, 747–758.

Winnicott, Donald W. (1964c). The Concept of the False Self. In Donald W. Winnicott (1986). *Home is Where We Start From: Essays by a Psychoanalyst*. Clare Winnicott, Ray Shepherd, and Madeleine Davis (Eds.), pp. 65–70. Harmondsworth, Middlesex: Penguin Books/Pelican Books.

Winnicott, Donald W. (1964d). Letter to "Mrs Piggle". 25th June. "The Piggle" Papers. London.

Winnicott, Donald W. (1964e). Letter to Michael Duane. 2nd November. Box 5. File 6. Donald W. Winnicott Papers. Archives of Psychiatry, The Oskar Diethelm Library, The DeWitt Wallace Institute for the History of Psychiatry, Department of Psychiatry, Joan and Sanford I. Weill Medical College,

Cornell University, The New York Presbyterian Hospital, New York, New York, U.S.A.

Winnicott, Donald W. (1965a). *The Family and Individual Development*. London: Tavistock Publications.

Winnicott, Donald W. (1965b). *The Maturational Processes and the Facilitating Environment: Studies in the Theory of Emotional Development*. London: Hogarth Press and the Institute of Psycho-Analysis.

Winnicott, Donald W. (1965c). A Child Psychiatry Case Illustrating Delayed Reaction to Loss. In Max Schur (Ed.). *Drives, Affects, Behavior: Volume 2. Essays in Memory of Marie Bonaparte*, pp. 212–242. New York: International Universities Press.

Winnicott, Donald W. (1965d). The Price of Disregarding Research Findings. In *The Price of Mental Health*, pp. 34–41. London: National Association for Mental Health.

Winnicott, Donald W. (1965e). Letter to Roger Money-Kyrle. 14th May. Box 5. File 5. Donald W. Winnicott Papers. Archives of Psychiatry, The Oskar Diethelm Library, The DeWitt Wallace Institute for the History of Psychiatry, Department of Psychiatry, Joan and Sanford I. Weill Medical College, Cornell University, The New York Presbyterian Hospital, New York, New York, U.S.A.

Winnicott, Donald W. (1965f). Letter to "Mr Piggle" and "Mrs Piggle". 12th July. In Donald W. Winnicott (1977). *The Piggle: An Account of the Psychoanalytic Treatment of a Little Girl*. Ishak Ramzy (Ed.), p. 145. New York: International Universities Press.

Winnicott, Donald W. (1965g). Letter to "Mrs Piggle". 12th July. "The Piggle" Papers. London.

Winnicott, Donald W. (1965h). Letter to Pam Gabriel. 27th September. Box 5. File 3. Donald W. Winnicott Papers. Archives of Psychiatry, The Oskar Diethelm Library, The DeWitt Wallace Institute for the History of Psychiatry, Department of Psychiatry, Joan and Sanford I. Weill Medical College, Cornell University, The New York Presbyterian Hospital, New York, New York, U.S.A.

Winnicott, Donald W. (1965i). Letter to "Mrs Piggle". 10th November. "The Piggle" Papers. London.

Winnicott, Donald W. (1965j). Letter to "Mrs Piggle". 5th December. "The Piggle" Papers. London.

Winnicott, Donald W. (1966a). A Psychoanalytic View of the Antisocial Tendency. In Ralph Slovenko (Ed.). *Crime, Law and Corrections*, pp. 102–130. Springfield, Illinois: Charles C Thomas, Publisher.

Winnicott, Donald W. (1966b). Comment on Obsessional Neurosis and 'Frankie'. *International Journal of Psycho-Analysis, 47*, 143–144.

Winnicott, Donald W. (1966c). Letter to John Davis. 14th February. Box 5. File 10. Donald W. Winnicott Papers. Archives of Psychiatry, The Oskar Diethelm Library, The DeWitt Wallace Institute for the History of Psychiatry, Department of Psychiatry, Joan and Sanford I. Weill Medical College, Cornell University, The New York Presbyterian Hospital, New York, New York, U.S.A.

Winnicott, Donald W. (1967a). The Aetiology of Infantile Schizophrenia in Terms of Adaptive Failure. In Donald W. Winnicott (1996). *Thinking About Children*. Ray Shepherd, Jennifer Johns, and Helen Taylor Robinson (Eds.), pp. 218–223. London: H. Karnac (Books).

Winnicott, Donald W. (1967b). Letter to "Mrs Piggle" and "Mr Piggle". 17th March. "The Piggle" Papers. London.

Winnicott, Donald W. (1967c). Letter to Mary Appleby. 6th April. Box 6. File 6. Donald W. Winnicott Papers. Archives of Psychiatry, The Oskar Diethelm Library, The DeWitt Wallace Institute for the History of Psychiatry, Department of Psychiatry, Joan and Sanford I. Weill Medical College, Cornell University, The New York Presbyterian Hospital, New York, New York, U.S.A.

Winnicott, Donald W. (1967d). Letter to "The Piggle". 21st April. "The Piggle" Papers. London.

Winnicott, Donald W. (1967e). Letter to "Mrs Piggle" and "Mr Piggle". 27th December. "The Piggle" Papers. London.

Winnicott, Donald W. (1968a). The Non-Pharmacological Treatment of Psychosis in Childhood. In Hermann Stutte and Hubert Harbauer (Eds.). *Concilium Paedopsychiatricum: Verhandlungen des 3. Europäischen Kongresses für Pädopsychiatrie. Wiesbaden, 4. – 9. Mai 1967*, pp. 193–198. Basel: Verlag S. Karger.

Winnicott, Donald W. (1968b). The Squiggle Game. *Voices: The Art and Science of Psychotherapy, 4*, 98–112.

Winnicott, Donald W. (1969a). Letter to "The Piggle". 3rd March. "The Piggle" Papers. London.

Winnicott, Donald W. (1969b). Note to "Mr Piggle" and "Mrs Piggle". n.d. March. "The Piggle" Papers. London.

Winnicott, Donald W. (1971). *Therapeutic Consultations in Child Psychiatry*. London: Hogarth Press and the Institute of Psycho-Analysis.

Winnicott, Donald W. (1972). Fragment of an Analysis. Alfred Flarsheim (Annot.). In Peter L. Giovacchini (Ed.). *Tactics and Techniques in Psychoanalytic Therapy*, pp. 457–693. New York: Science House.

Winnicott, Donald W. (1977). *The Piggle: An Account of the Psychoanalytic Treatment of a Little Girl*. Ishak Ramzy (Ed.). New York: International Universities Press.

Winnicott, Donald W. (1978). *The Piggle: An Account of the Psychoanalytic Treatment of a Little Girl*. Ishak Ramzy (Ed.). London: Hogarth Press and the Institute of Psycho-Analysis.

Winnicott, Donald W. (1984). *Deprivation and Delinquency*. Clare Winnicott, Ray Shepherd, and Madeleine Davis (Eds.). London: Tavistock Publications.

Winnicott, Donald W. (1986a). *Holding and Interpretation: Fragment of an Analysis*. London: Hogarth Press and the Institute of Psycho-Analysis.

Winnicott, Donald W. (1986b). *Home Is Where We Start From: Essays by a Psychoanalyst*. Clare Winnicott, Ray Shepherd, and Madeleine Davis (Eds.). Harmondsworth, Middlesex: Penguin Books/Pelican Books.

Winnicott, Donald W. (1987). *Babies and Their Mothers*. Clare Winnicott, Ray Shepherd, and Madeleine Davis (Eds.). Reading, Massachusetts: Addison-Wesley Publishing Company.

Winnicott, Donald W. (1988). *Human Nature*. Christopher Bollas, Madeleine Davis, and Ray Shepherd (Eds.). London: Free Association Books.

Winnicott, Donald W. (1989). *Psycho-Analytic Explorations*. Clare Winnicott, Ray Shepherd, and Madeleine Davis (Eds.). London: H. Karnac (Books).

Winnicott, Donald W. (1993). *Talking to Parents*. Clare Winnicott, Christopher Bollas, Madeleine Davis, and Ray Shepherd (Eds.). Reading, Massachusetts: Addison-Wesley Publishing Company.

Winnicott, Donald W. (1996). *Thinking About Children*. Ray Shepherd, Jennifer Johns, and Helen Taylor Robinson (Eds.). London: H. Karnac (Books).

Zetzel, Elizabeth (Ed.). (1964). The Finnish Study Group, p. 625. *125th Bulletin of the International Psycho-Analytical Association. International Journal of Psycho-Analysis*, 45, 618–625.

CHAPTER THREE

Reappraising Winnicott's *The Piggle*: a critical commentary*

Christopher Reeves

PART I: INTRODUCTION AND THE TREATMENT

Introduction

"You may find it pretty dreadful as analysis, but it should lead to a useful discussion." With these words Donald Winnicott first introduced an American psychoanalyst friend, Ishak Ramzy, to the analytic case notes of a little girl patient of his. This occurred in the summer of 1969 when Winnicott, on an impulse, invited Ramzy, a former supervisee then in London on a brief visit, to a reversal of their former roles: he would conduct a public supervision of Winnicott as the latter presented a session from this girl's treatment before an international gathering of psychoanalysts. Ramzy agreed and the "supervision" duly took place a few days later. It marked Winnicott's first airing of the case that would eventually

---

* This chapter is made up of two previously published papers: Reeves, C. (2015a). Reappraising Winnicott's *The Piggle*: A critical commentary. Part I. *British Journal of Psychotherapy*, 31(2): 156–190. And: Reeves, C. (2015b). Reappraising Winnicott's *The Piggle*: A critical commentary: Part II. *British Journal of Psychotherapy*, 31(3): 285–297. Copyright © 2015, John Wiley and Sons, reprinted by permission of John Wiley and Sons.

be published after his death as *The Piggle* (Winnicott, 1977), the name by which the patient was known within the family. The treatment of Gabrielle (her actual name) had reached its conclusion three years earlier. For Winnicott it had been a spur to much new thinking about the theory, practice, and aims of analysis in the interim.

"Pretty dreadful as analysis". Of course, Winnicott did not really believe this, otherwise he would scarcely have considered it suitable for public consumption. Yet he may well have anticipated that this would be a fairly widespread verdict on his handling of the case among certain sections of his prospective audience. An eminent figure in the British Psycho-Analytic Society and well respected abroad, Winnicott had acquired a reputation as someone who was indisputably "good with children". The many professionals, psychoanalysts and psychiatrists among them, who attended his "open clinics" at Paddington Green Hospital attest to his immediate rapport with them, whatever their age. Even those among his professional colleagues inclined to baulk at the description of him as a psychoanalytic "genius" (e.g. Isaacs-Elmhirst, 1996) were ready to acknowledge his unrivalled "openness to the mind of the child", that empathic quality which Heimann, in her paper "About Children and Children-no-longer" (1980) described as the one indispensable prerequisite for the child analyst. This attribute called for a certain childlike adaptability, the capacity to get into the skin of the child while remaining in one's own. And it was one that Winnicott patently possessed.

Yet such "openness to the child" came with a rider. The question it raised was this. In analysis, or analytically inspired psychotherapy, how far should such openness, and with it such adaptability, extend? Winnicott's answer seems to have been "as far as the patient's needs required it". And what contributed to the reservations felt by some among his analytic colleagues was his apparent readiness in line with this to subordinate the demands of technique to the needs of the patient, whether child or adult. Certainly, Winnicott was not noted for orthodoxy of method, strictness of technique, detachment, or analytic neutrality as usually understood. Moreover, he disclaimed belief in the universal efficacy of interpretation as the primary means of bringing about psychic change. Compounding these perceived failings, he seemed to take delight in attacking the pretensions of psychoanalytic conventions and the pretentiousness of orthodox practitioners. He won no plaudits, for instance, for claiming in a paper on psychoanalytic technique written shortly before the public event referred to above: "I interpret to the patient so as to show the limits of my understanding" (Winnicott, 1971, p. 86). Such public disparagement of what was generally regarded as the psychoanalyst's principal therapeutic instrument was unlikely to resonate with his audience.

The Piggle is one of only two substantial psychoanalytic case histories to have been published under Winnicott's name. Predictably, in view of the received view among his professional colleagues of him as a somewhat idiosyncratic practitioner, the book was greeted ambivalently on its posthumous appearance in 1977, and has enjoyed a chequered history within the psychoanalytic community ever since. Critics saw it as proof of sentimentality and defective technique—a case of "Winnicott wanting to be loved by his patients"—whilst among those who generally admired his insightfulness there were some who were dismayed by his technical lapses and by his readiness to admit them so candidly. So it is perhaps both surprising and significant that *The Piggle* was the first work of his prepared for posthumous publication under the direction of his widow and literary executor, Clare Winnicott. In doing so, she was fulfilling a cherished project Winnicott had intended to realise himself, had he lived longer. Evidently, so far from being embarrassed by it, he was keen for analysts and others to learn from the case and from his handling of it.

So the importance of *The Piggle* as a testament cannot be doubted. But a testament to what exactly? To the value of analytic treatment "on demand"? The possibilities and limits of interpretation? The therapeutic importance of play with young children? The importance of allowing the child's natural maturational processes to overcome neurotic conflicts and crises? The value of engaging the parents in the therapeutic process? All these topics are commented on in passing, yet without Winnicott supplying a clear pointer as to their relative importance for himself, and, by implication, his prospective readership. Nevertheless, what we take that estimate to be is likely to determine how we understand and appraise the work as a whole.

Winnicott described *The Piggle* as being "partly written by the parents" and as comprising "excerpts from letters about Gabrielle and of my clinical notes attempting to give a detailed description of the psychoanalytic interviews" (Winnicott, 1977, p. 1). The order in which these contributions are put is revealing: parents' first, his own second (although in reality the patient's own words, either verbatim or summarised, occupy by far the largest amount of text). As for Gabrielle herself, she is reported retrospectively by the parents as at the time imagining that Winnicott was actually engaged in writing his autobiography when he was busy note-taking during the sessions: that is to say, she thought he was writing about himself, not about her; or perhaps more precisely, writing about her but in relation to himself (this being a neat, yet apt, mirror inversion of the analyst's conventional transference/countertransference reportage).

If the purpose of writing up *The Piggle* case history was to some extent indeterminate for the participants, what is the reader to make of it? First, there is the question of its genre: is it the story of a therapeutic encounter with an unusually articulate small child designed to be read by a lay readership, or a psychoanalytic case study primarily intended for fellow professionals? The philosopher, Martha Nussbaum (2003), is one of several commentators who view it as a type of intergenerational narrative, calling it "one of the great examples in English literature of an adult entering the wild conflict-ridden world of a young child". The fact that it has remained in print for almost half a century certainly confirms its enduring popularity. Yet was it Winnicott's or his widow's purpose simply to present a dialogue between an elderly doctor and an articulate small child so as to show how enlivening such an encounter could be? Maybe its author, inclined as he was to self-deprecation, would have been content with such a description. But not so his widow. She was in no doubt about the work's import: it was, and should be recognised as a substantive contribution to the theory of psychoanalytic technique. To that end she was anxious that it should published as a volume in the International Psycho-Analytical Library, just as Melanie Klein's *Narrative of a Child Analysis* (1961) had been. The commissioning editor of this prestigious series at the time was Masud Khan. In her covering letter to him she claimed *The Piggle* to be an example of "D.W.W. at his best", and went on: "I hate the idea of exposing this very tender piece of work to the world where it will not be understood, or rather where it runs great risk of being misunderstood" (C. Winnicott to Masud Khan, May 27, 1974). Khan's response is revealing of the reaction that was to become fairly commonplace among the psychoanalytic confraternity— that of damning the work with faint praise:

I have now read this manuscript with great care ... It is not suitable for inclusion in the [Psycho-analytical] Library because, in spite of the extremely interesting clinical dialogue that evolves between the child and Winnicott, it lacks that intensity of transferential rapport which constitutes a psycho-analytic relationship ... Please don't mistake me for saying that it is for these reasons a less interesting case history of Winnicott's. It has a unique flavour to it and is very moving in a happy sort of way. (Masud Khan to C. Winnicott, July 8, 1974)

In short, it confirmed what was already known, namely that Winnicott was "good with children" (in a happy sort of way), but not much more. After this rebuff there followed three years of fraught negotiation before the book appeared, involving Clare Winnicott, the mother of Gabrielle, the agent for the publishers and the same Ishak Ramzy, whom Winnicott had initially persuaded to supervise his case presentation and subsequently invited to edit the manuscript. When it finally appeared in print, the text was much as Winnicott had left it at his death, but Ramzy's planned critical apparatus was omitted in deference to the family's wishes. Masud Khan wrote to Clare Winnicott again at this point:

I have seen *The Piggle* in the I.U.P. edition, and even though we have taken it into the Library, I must confess that all the notations in the margin are utterly idiotic and unhelpful. After all, this is not a primer for "O" level students, and it does injustice to Winnicott. (Masud Khan to Clare Winnicott, January 1978)

This time in her reply she made her feelings plain about what she took to be such gratuitous slighting of her late husband's treasured work. She wrote:

In regard to the marginal notes in *The Piggle*, I want you to know that these are D.W.W.'s own which he made during the sessions to clarify things for himself as he went along, and he included these notes himself in the final typescript which he prepared for publication. Nothing has really been altered on the script as he left it ... Therefore if the marginal notes do an injustice to D.W.—he did it to himself. In my view very few people are anywhere near their "O" levels in the understanding of his work. And he knew this. (C. Winnicott to Masud Khan, January 1978)

Equally revealing of her concern to express Winnicott's intentions without gloss is her plea to Ishak Ramzy as the latter was about to embark on writing his editorial introduction:

> I am going to be very brave and dare to suggest to you that it would not be appropriate to pay a tribute to Donald and his work in the Foreword. I am heartily tired (and so would Donald have been) of *eulogies*. What is far more important and convincing to the reader would be an incisive, insightful comment on his work—even if it were critical in a constructive way. I do hope you understand what I mean. People can so easily sing his praises (and I have to listen to a lot) but very, very few really understand in a deep way, or in any honest way try to understand. But I am not deceived by praises. (C. Winnicott to Ishak Ramzy, January 8, 1974)

Even though Clare was convinced that the book carries an important message for the psychoanalytic community, she would perhaps have admitted that what precisely that message consisted of is not clearly spelt out by Winnicott. *The Piggle* does not have the least appearance of being a didactic tome. Its style is conversational, almost casual. In Winnicott's own preface there is no addressing the reader save in a very general way. He confines himself instead to sketching out the broad particulars of the case, how he came to be involved, and how long the treatment lasted. He concludes the preface with some general remarks aimed principally at a psychoanalytic readership, about how the treatment should best be categorised in clinical terms. Once the account proper of the therapeutic process begins his commentary is sparing on the technical aspects of the case. As for his marginal notes (preserved in the telegraphic form in which they were originally jotted down) along with the summaries at the conclusion of each session, these seem to be directed as much towards himself and the parents as to the reader. So if we are to heed Clare's call to try to understand "in a deep way", we are evidently expected to do so by witnessing and reflecting on an unfolding therapeutic process without too many preconceptions, rather than by being led by Winnicott step by step and taught as we go along. To quote from his preamble: "I have added comments [to my clinical notes], but not enough—it is hoped—to prevent the reader from developing a personal view of the material and its evolution" (1977, p. 1).

One could easily dismiss such an invitation to follow the track of one's own thoughts and reach one's own conclusions as not intended seriously. But that would be a mistake. It is a characteristic of much of Winnicott's writing during the last five years of his life that it is interrogative rather than affirmative. The dictum about his own interpretive activity within analysis—"I interpret mainly to let the patient know the limits of my understanding" (Winnicott, 1971, p. 86)—could be applied equally to his theoretical endeavours, particularly where he felt that he was breaking fresh ground. There is ample evidence that in the process of refining or modifying his formulations he sometimes used his audience, and the reception it accorded him, to ascertain for himself whether his findings were substantive or in need of redrafting. This manner of proceeding is apparent in the case of his well-known 1968 paper "On the Use of an Object" (Reeves, 2007). It is my belief that *The Piggle* falls into this category of self enquiry, and that Winnicott recognised as much, though in this instance (and maybe in the interests of confidentiality) he did not publish the manuscript in time to get a guiding response during his lifetime.

So, we are being invited to form "a personal view" of the material. However, to develop this personal view in an objective manner necessarily entails first taking into account Winnicott's own understanding of the material as it emerges from his commentary, and also the climate of psychoanalytic practice which shaped his view of it. To this end, and, in particular, in order to prepare ourselves for the task almost half a century on from when the treatment took place (as long a gap in time, incidentally, as that between Freud's pioneering involvement with Little Hans and Winnicott's with the Piggle) it may be useful first to recall some of this theoretical background and context.

The case in context

Gabrielle's treatment took place in the middle years of the 1960s. At the beginning of that decade two notable child analytic case histories had appeared, both of which Winnicott was very familiar with. The first of these was Klein's *Narrative of a Child Analysis*, a work that came to be regarded from the moment it was published as a definitive exposition of her way of "doing analysis", even by its non-Kleinian critics (Geleerd, 1963). The second, more modest, account was McDougall and Lebovici's *Dialogue with Sammy*, first published in French in 1960 and reviewed in that form by Winnicott in 1962. These were very different works in style, although the ages of both child patients were similar and the treatment provision the same, namely full-scale child analysis based on the adult model of fifty-minute sessions, five times a week.

Klein's was the account of a four-month treatment period of Richard, a ten-year-old boy that had been conducted in Scotland twenty years before when she (and Richard's family) had left London at the outbreak of war. Despite the incomplete nature of the treatment it was intended to provide for posterity a detailed account of her treatment method and philosophy. Its tone is assured, its conclusions definite. Above all what shines through is Klein's unwavering conviction about the efficacy of interpreting "early and deep" the fantasy content of the child's play material irrespective of his (or her, of course) anxieties and resistances. Her thinking in this regard is perhaps best summed up by Segal and Meltzer in their subsequent review of the book in the *International Journal of Psychoanalysis* (1963). The concept utilised is simply this: that the analytic situation is most securely established by the interpretation of the most pressing anxieties regardless of the developmental level. As a result of this ... the positive transference is fostered, based on the child's desire for understanding and the relief it affords him (p. 511).

I am going to call this technique the use of *commotional interpretations*. The reason for employing the term "commotional" is this. From the starting premise that the strength and impact of anxiety-inducing unconscious fantasies ("phantasies") in Klein's parlance) are the same irrespective of the individual's age and stage of development, there follows a consequent operational injunction: uncover and release these anxieties at the earliest opportunity through verbalising their accompanying fantasy content, so as to foster trust both in the therapeutic process and transferentially in the analyst overseeing it. Such interpretations are commotional because they intentionally promote the release of anxiety related to conflict as a step towards its eventual mitigation, rather than seeking to mitigate anxiety by other means (such as reassurance, or the analysis of the defences), with the aim of allowing for its future emergence in conditions of established trust in the analyst and confidence in the therapeutic process.

Unlike Klein, Joyce McDougall, the co-author of *Dialogue with Sammy* (1960), was a self-confessed novice in the practice of child analysis when she first embarked on the patient's treatment, having previously spent just one year of training under the tutelage of Anna Freud at her Hampstead Clinic. Where Klein proceeded unwaveringly in her methods until the treatment of Richard prematurely ceased owing to her decision to return to London, Sammy's evolved hesitantly over the course of a year through a process of give and take, with analyst and patient endeavouring better to understand each other's perspective and purpose in regard to the treatment, and slowly succeeding in doing so after much intervening strife and challenge, only for this treatment too to be curtailed due to Sammy's sudden return to New York.

Sammy was a floridly psychotic child, whose American parents, like McDougall herself, had found themselves unexpectedly transplanted to Paris. Not only had McDougall never previously conducted a child analysis of any sort; her supervisor and co-author, the French psychoanalyst Serge Lebovici, was himself unfamiliar with the challenges of this type of clinical undertaking, since five-times-a-week analysis was unheard of in France with a patient so young. Thus, where Klein exuded omniscience, McDougall conveyed initial uncertainty and bewilderment in the face of Sammy's insistence that she should write to his dictation, rather than being allowed time and space to formulate interpretations about his defences against anxiety or about the symbolic content of his play or verbal communications, in order to convey these to him in composed and thought-through fashion. Though there was much incidental challenge and commotion within the treatment space when McDougall insisted on maintaining her analytic stance, her aim was not to make commotional interpretations in the sense outlined above. Instead, following the precepts of Anna Freud, she mainly sought to make use of *conjunctive interpretations*, where the manifest content of the child's play material or strategies of defence are first alluded to by the analyst in order to enable the child to make his own connections between thoughts, actions, feelings, and purposes, the more accessible and acknowledgeable ones to start with, later those that were unconscious or unavowed.

> Winnicott's response to both these case histories is reflected in the treatment approach he adopted with the much younger child Gabrielle in *The Piggle*. On the one hand he endorsed Klein's practice of immediately interpreting the dominant anxiety along with its putative underlying fantasy—the use of commotional interpretations; on the other, he lent his approval to McDougall's tentative efforts to build up a treatment alliance in the face of the young child's browbeating and her own uncertainty over whether to comply with Sammy's insistence that she should write down what he said. In his introduction to the English language edition of the book, Winnicott has this to say: "Some patients are lucky when their analysts do not understand too much at the beginning … Gradually they like to be understood, but they may feel cheated if understood so quickly that the analyst seems to be a magician" (Winnicott, 1969).

One may perhaps wonder whether these two viewpoints are in fact compatible. Evidently Winnicott thought they were. One might even suggest that one of his motives for wishing to have *The Piggle* case history published was precisely to show how they could be creatively reconciled. Nevertheless, it was typical of him not to argue the case as such, but instead to leave it to the reader to decide how successfully they were aligned in practice over the course of Gabrielle's treatment.

To return to the earlier pair of published case histories, it is clear from reading them that both young patients seem to have benefited from their analytic encounters and developed an attachment, even lasting affection, for their analysts despite the frequent struggles that took place during their respective sessions. Nevertheless, neither boy was, or felt himself to have been, properly "cured" by the experience of analysis. Indeed, what strikes one most in comparing these two accounts is the relative similarity of outcome (a noticeable but partial improvement), and this despite the considerable disparity in experience of the two psychoanalytic protagonists, as well as their very divergent outlooks and practices in the matter of how, what, and when to interpret, and the degree to which one should, or should not, accommodate to the anxieties and oppositionality of their young patients. Equally striking is the emphasis placed in both accounts on the incompleteness of the treatment. Psychoanalytic treatment is viewed by both as having an implicit time frame dictated by the process of working through of the symbolic material and of the internal defence structures underlying the symptomatology, with no reference to the potentially beneficial effect of ongoing developmental processes in the child.

Winnicott's perspective in *The Piggle* is somewhat different. Though he had previously conducted a number of child analyses according to the conventional parameters of the time, and had Klein as a supervisor and mentor while doing so, he had long since forsaken this type of intensive long-term work with children in favour of more focused interventions—therapeutic consultations, as he called them—based on the principle of doing "as little as was needed" rather than "as much as one was able" (Winnicott, 1962). In *The Piggle* he was combining the expertise gained in both types of treatment approach in order to conduct a psychoanalytic intervention that was intensive without being extensive. It was to be an ongoing and open-ended treatment process, rather than being a time-bound, economic, focused intervention, while being free from the sense of "interminability" that at the time characterised most traditional psychoanalytic treatments, even with children. Insofar as Winnicott wanted to convey a distinctive rationale for his approach to Gabrielle's treatment, it concerned just this aspect, namely his conviction that analytic treatment could and should be continuing without being continuous, allowing space between sessions for the child to process insights at a natural pace. These pauses between sessions, and what happened in them, were in his view as important for growth as what took place in the sessions themselves—hence the detailed account he provides in *The Piggle* of the parents' communications with the child and with himself between times. As for the length of treatment, it should last, he maintained, for as long as the child recognised the need, rather than to the point where the analyst deemed it necessary or desirable to stop. Winnicott put this view succinctly in a sentence quoted by Ramzy in his Introduction: "I do analysis because that is what the patient needs to have done *and to have done with*" (Winnicott, 1962, my italics). There are two further distinctive features of Gabrielle's treatment which serve to set it apart from Klein's treatment of Richard and McDougall's of Sammy. The first concerns the role of play, and the second the direct participation of the parents in the therapy.

> The importance of play, of course, is an intrinsic part of all child analysis and psychotherapy, and was accorded a special status by Klein who, as is well known, viewed it as the equivalent for the child to the verbal free associations of adult analysis. However— and this is very marked in her *Narrative of a Child Analysis*—it is play as content rather than playing as activity on the part of the child that is of paramount importance for her, and for McDougall too. With Winnicott, however, the activity of playing itself is the important thing. He indicates as much in one of his rare asides to the reader: "It is not possible for a child of this age to get the meaning out of a game unless first of all the *game is played and enjoyed*. As a matter of principle, the analyst always allows the enjoyment to become established before the content of the play is used for interpretation" (1977, p. 175).

Winnicott's conception of play as being at once expressive and mutative has a venerable history within psychoanalysis, being traceable back to Freud's early dictum about "the symptom joining in the conversation" (Freud & Breuer, 1895d). Moreover, the child's playing is regarded by him as at times being solitary and at other times interactive. Thus he notes the occasions when Gabrielle plays in a withdrawn way, excluding him (and in one instance reacting with hostility to his untimely attempt to participate). He notes too when she plays in a solitary way (an instance of being alone in the presence of another—a sign of health); and when she plays participatorily, requiring him to join in the game, rather than being just an observer and note-taker. Conventionally the child psychotherapist is taught to assume the role of non-participant observer and interpreter. Such an unbending position was quite foreign to Winnicott's way of working.

As to the parents' role in their little girl's treatment, Winnicott offers surprisingly few words of comment or explanation in his introduction. It is as if he takes it as a matter of course that the parents would be required to play a large part in it, not just supportively as informants and

conveyors of the child to and from sessions, but also as active participants in the therapeutic management of the child between sessions (and
in the case of the father, sometimes during the actual sessions). However,
The Piggle was not a case of "family therapy" in the conventional sense.
Instead, Winnicott treats the parents as therapeutic co-adjutants, providing the necessary holding environment within which was enclosed
and protected the vital one-to-one therapy process involving himself
and the child. It was likewise a condition of such holding provision that
as the child's therapist he should also be available to the parents so as to
support and sustain them in managing the child in the intervals between
sessions. This distinctive model of therapeutic involvement Winnicott
had gradually evolved over the two previous decades, having abandoned
long-term five-times-weekly analytic therapy with children in favour of
engaging the parents where possible as co-therapists of the child. It owed
much to his theoretical formulations about the importance of "primary
maternal preoccupation" and the function of the protective membrane
and paternal "cover" (Reeves, 2012), as well as to the organisational
elaborations of this by his wife Clare (1962) and by his close colleague
Dockar-Drysdale (1960).

Before turning to an examination of the case history proper, a few
further contextual remarks may be in order to explain how the written account of the treatment itself evolved. Unlike Klein's *Narrative*
and McDougall's *Sammy*, Winnicott's *Piggle* only gradually assumed
the dimensions of a full-blown analytic case with a narrative history
attached to it. At the outset Winnicott almost certainly did not anticipate
seeing the two-and-a-half-year-old Gabrielle over a long period and for
several sessions. From a close reading of the text it seems likely that at
first he intended conducting his usual type of brief clinical intervention
in view of the child's age. It is hard to determine for certain at what point
he first became aware that a more extensive involvement was required of
him in this case. The notes at the end of his account of the first session
(which incidentally includes a separate interview with the mother after
the initial encounter with Gabrielle) show signs of having been written a
little after the event. What is more, there is no indication given at the end
of this first meeting that Winnicott necessarily anticipated a further session taking place with her. That the treatment expanded beyond a single
intervention was because the young patient herself became insistent

that it should, not because Winnicott or the parents had pre-planned a follow-up. By the end of the second session, however, there is a definite sense of a process underway, in which both the child and the therapist are fully engaged and which they expect to continue. Even then, however, it is doubtful whether Winnicott anticipated the treatment lasting as long as it did, in spite of Gabrielle's fairly abrupt "descent into illness" following the second session. Thus at the end of the fifth session, six months after the initial contact, Winnicott seems to have conveyed the impression to the father that the treatment could now be regarded as having achieved as much as was necessary and that the rest of her recovery might be better left to the child's natural maturational capacity, especially given the parents' own considerable investment, insight, and abilities (the mother being herself a child psychotherapist). At the same time he rather bizarrely suggested an alternative: that Gabrielle could to be referred for a full analysis to someone else.

Whatever Winnicott's motives for such an ambiguous recommendation to the parents at this juncture (and, in mitigation, one has to bear in mind the severe pressures upon his time and energies, as well as his acute awareness of his already precarious state of health), what is fairly certain is that Winnicott did not then envisage among the outcomes of the treatment the eventual production of a detailed narrative of what he was later happy to refer to as a "child analysis"—a "finished experience". Only when faced with the perplexity and dismay of the parents at his suggestion of either a termination or a transfer, which they understandably felt as rejecting rather than facilitative, did Winnicott acknowledge his mistake, and in doing so recognise for the first time, in a footnote to the main text at this point (p. 73), that whether he intended it or not, analysis proper was already underway with this child. Thereafter, despite further occasional mishaps due to his unavailability, there is no further question of the treatment being terminated on Winnicott's own prompting rather than the child's.

Nevertheless, there are some indications that Winnicott felt that the treatment had perhaps reached a natural conclusion by November 1965 (a full year before it actually did so). At the end of the thirteenth session he makes a point of saying a definite goodbye to daughter and father, because, as he writes, "I felt that Gabrielle had finished what she wanted to tell me" (p. 176). And at the start of his 1966 appointments diary he jotted a note for himself, "No need to see Gabrielle". It may also be significant that in his later introduction to the text he mistakenly wrote that he saw Gabrielle "on demand" fourteen times, whereas the actual number of sessions is sixteen. Equally surprisingly, he appended the date "Nov. 22nd 1965" at the end of this introduction, not 1966, the year of the last three sessions. The likeliest explanation is that these were accidental mistakes by Winnicott that went unnoticed at the time of publication; even so, they are perhaps unconsciously significant ones. For had the treatment in fact ended at that point, missing from the case, and the case history, would have been one of its striking and important features, namely the manner of its finishing.

Klein, as already mentioned, had terminated her treatment due to her own priorities, but the analysis had not in any sense reached a natural conclusion. McDougall's treatment of Sammy was curtailed by circumstances outside her control, a situation regretted equally by herself and her patient. Again, there was no proper termination. What is distinctive and different about *The Piggle* is that not just the child, but Winnicott also, evidently wanted the treatment to be "done with" by the time it reached its final stage. When, according to the narrative, Gabrielle is busy in the fifteenth session showing that "she wanted to get this treatment—Winnicott—finished off while she was still four", he makes this comment to her in response: "*Me*: I'd like to get finished with you, too, so that I could be all the other Winnicotts and not have to be this special treatment Winnicott invented by you" (p. 191). By then Gabrielle had reached five years, and for her the treatment represented the work of a lifetime; as for Winnicott, he may well have wondered in view of his uncertain health whether he would have an equivalent span of years left to live? In the event, he had. One of the other "Winnicotts" we know for a fact that he still aspired to by then was to author an account of *The Piggle* treatment before death overtook him. If such a wish, or intention, was not there at the start, when, one wonders, did the thought and the wish begin to take hold? And linked to this question is another, more important one: did the intention of eventually using the case material in some way perhaps impact on the therapeutic process itself, and if so, how? In this connection it is noteworthy that at the start of the sixth session Winnicott makes a point of addressing her as Gabrielle rather than "the Piggle" (as he had done previously, adopting her parents' practice).

In the next session she calls him "Mr Winnicott", which he interprets as "a recurrent indication of a non-therapist Winnicott". Each of them in their different ways was perhaps showing how they were gradually ceasing to be "subjective objects" for the other, and instead becoming "objects objectively perceived" (1971, p. 38)—each with other lives outside the therapy.

There was a dimension to Winnicott's involvement and fascination with the Piggle which she could not have recognised, though sensing perhaps that it belonged somehow to his "autobiography". This was the realisation, prompted by his experience of her unusual degree of articulacy, of her being an almost ideal child patient for the purposes of teaching, due to her unmediated exposure to states of mind and feeling, her own and others', before it was developmentally possible for these sensations and sentiments of hers to become bounded by words and concepts, and lose some of their intensity in the process. On the basis of his experience with Gabrielle, therefore, he may have concluded (and wished to communicate) that such states of feeling and internal experience did not need, as they might in a somewhat older child, the laborious and repetitive interpretive "unpacking" that constituted a major part of the conventional technique and practice of child analysis. Instead, what they required was room for play, and for spontaneous, creative mending to take place.

Perhaps it was as a result of this dawning realisation that the number and frequency of Winnicott's interpretations dropped as the sessions progressed, while listening, responding, and finally playing together came to dominate the sessions. On the occasions when Winnicott continued to engage in interpreting the underlying fantasy material in what might be called the classical manner (such as in the twelfth session), he referred to it simply as "playing about with interpretations" (p. 155)—the deliberate choice of the word "play" in this context perhaps indicating his growing recognition of its kinship with Gabrielle's symbolic playing, as though the two of them were engaged on a parallel (dis)course.

Winnicott was always generous in acknowledging his indebtedness to his patients for what he learnt from them. Gabrielle was certainly one of those patients who "taught" him. What exactly she taught him Winnicott may have been unable to specify. Yet this indeterminacy—if such is what it is—he perhaps would not have taken amiss. More important in his view was what benefit future readers would derive from the experience of reading the narrative of their encounter, from reflecting upon that experience and, if they were fellow professionals, allowing this to affect or modify their technique. *The Piggle* was, as he put it to Ramzy, "for discussion"; it was meant to change the way one understands the stresses and strains on a child, and particularly on a firstborn, of adjusting to the presence of a sibling. Such events were part of life, and the practice of therapy, in its immediacy, spontaneity, and creativity, needed to reflect this.

The treatment and case history summarised

Gabrielle's treatment spanned two and three-quarter years and consisted of sixteen sessions. Winnicott allows his case history to unfold in narrative fashion, with the account of each session prefaced by number and date and rounded off with a mixture of summary, comment, notes of telephone messages, and passages from intervening letters between the parents and himself. This way of proceeding may be appropriate as a record. However, and especially given the irregular intervals between sessions, it somewhat obscures the trajectory of the treatment. In particular, the changes occurring in Gabrielle over its course, their sequence and timing become blurred. For the purposes of summarising, therefore, I have chosen to treat the case record rather like the script of a play. I see the unfolding of the "plot" extending over five "acts", each act comprising three "scenes", namely the individual sessions, and concluding with an epilogue (the final session). Approaching it in this manner does run the risk of attributing a greater degree of unity, coherence, and development than is perhaps warranted. Still, I believe it helps one to discern some of the predominant themes as Winnicott saw them emerging and evolving. I have also chosen to treat the text as a play involving two principal characters rather than in the form of one person's version—Winnicott's own—since he was evidently at pains to present the material mainly in the form of an ongoing dialogue between the child and himself, with each one's perspective accorded equal importance. Hence the preponderance of direct speech in his account. The parents' reports, comments, and queries, and Winnicott's responses to them, can be regarded, in terms of my overall analogy, as being rather like a Greek chorus, observing rather than directly involved in the action (except where the father in some of the early sessions becomes an active participant). In my summary, therefore, I have for the most part kept to the material as it emerges in the sessions themselves, only alluding to the parental input and Winnicott's responses to, and comments on it, where Gabrielle's own voice can clearly be identified.

However, there remains another methodological issue to be faced in summarising the record in the form of a dialogue, as I have chosen to do. The two "voices" are not equal, despite Winnicott's wish that they should come across as such. He is the adult, doctor, and scribe; Gabrielle is the child, the patient, and can't write. From the very start this imbalance makes for difficulties in the reporting, despite his attempts to redress it. Winnicott listens intently to her, but does not, I believe, always "hear" her; or rather, does not always, as doctor analyst, light on those matters that seem to be uppermost in her mind at a conscious level. "Black" and "babacar" and "baby" are clearly major topics for both of them. Yet "black(-ness)" and "babacar" are only mentioned by her fifteen times across the sixteen sessions, whereas the word "train" occurs in her conversation no less than sixty-four times in one context or another, yet scarcely ever in his. This absence of reference on Winnicott's part is all the more surprising because, when he interviewed her mother, she told him about her daughter's predominant anxieties, instancing in particular "nightmares about a babacar, and also about a train" (p. 14). Nightmares about a babacar interest him, those about trains seemingly do not. He sees reasons for seizing interpretively on her references to the former words and topics, while ignoring the latter. A similar selectivity is evident in the paucity of comment on her frequent reference to the need for "tying up" and "tidying up", both major preoccupations of Gabrielle, both at home and in the sessions.

The above observations are not intended, at least not primarily, as a criticism of Winnicott. It is generally accepted that a degree of selectivity is inherent in all reporting, as well as in the analysing/interpreting process. As if to compensate for this acknowledged bias Winnicott goes to great lengths to set down Gabrielle's words as far as possible verbatim, encouraging the reader to attend to these first and foremost and make sense of their thrust as much as possible, without immediate reliance on his interpretive activity to be a guide as to their meaning. Accordingly, in summarising the sessions I have chosen to present the session material first from what I take to be the child's own perspective (a rash claim perhaps, but I have stuck as closely as possible to the written account); and only then from Winnicott's. However, in order that this procedure should not seem too piecemeal, I shall do this antiphonal summarising of content "act by act" rather than "scene by scene". One further word of explanation for what follows: in my precis of Winnicott's input I shall distinguish between explicit interpretations made to the child from those internally registered by him as informing his subsequent actions and/or responses. I shall use an initial upper case letter "I" to denote the former, and a lower case letter "i" to denote the latter.

Act 1: sessions 1–3 getting to know you getting to know me

For her **first** session Gabrielle comes accompanied by both parents, but not, seemingly, by her younger sister, Susan, who is often referred to in conversation by Gabrielle as Sush, or "the Sush baby". In later sessions Gabrielle is brought by the father alone.

Winnicott begins by making an observation directed towards the reader: despite her initial shyness in the presence of an elderly stranger, he registers that Gabrielle, whom he habitually addresses as "the Piggle", has the air of someone "ready to do work". He acknowledges her initial anxiety and reticence by not addressing her directly, but instead the teddy she had brought with her, inviting it to come and play with the toys in the play area behind the curtain that separated it off from the consultation area where Gabrielle was sitting with her mother. The father meanwhile had moved out of sight to the waiting room area further down the passage. Evidently the teddy required transporting in order to join in the play with the toys. Gabrielle felt able to leave her mother to fulfil this caretaker role.

Very soon, she allows herself to become engaged in systematically laying out the toys, using the words "another" and "another" and "another" as she picks each of them up one by one. Winnicott takes this comment as a cue to refer to the occurrence of a new baby in her life— Susan's arrival on the scene having occurred eight months previously. Prompted by this mention of the baby, Gabrielle declares: "I was a baby. I was in a cot. I just had the bottle" (1977, p. 10). Significantly, Winnicott adds as an aside at this point that, according to the parents, Gabrielle had in fact never taken to the bottle, unlike her sister, Susan, who had. When Winnicott follows her declaration up with the question, "Where did the baby come from?" the reply he gets ("De cot") seems obvious to her, more so perhaps than it was to him.

Meanwhile the medley of toys occupies her attention. She attempts to insert a stick through the window of a toy car. Winnicott takes this to be a displaced reference to parental intercourse in the making of a baby (I refer to this below, in considering Winnicott's perspective). Gabrielle's response to this suggestion is to say, "I've got a cat. Next time I'll bring the pussycat. Another day" (p. 11). She then wants to go and see her mother.

In this exchange and the previous one I believe that one can detect a difference in their respective points of departure over the matter of the new baby. Winnicott, I believe, supposes that Gabrielle views the advent of her baby sister as the coming-into-being of something that did not previously exist. Gabrielle, on the other hand, seems to indicate that the advent of the baby is problematic for a different reason: it leaves herself (hitherto "the baby" in the family) confused as to who or what she now is: who exactly occupies the position of "the baby"? Herself, or this new "bottle-sucking" creature, so like her, yet also different? And if this new creature is the baby, then is she herself still "a baby" too? Or nobody? Or could it be that she is the baby she is actually observing (a possibility perhaps implied when she says that she was feeding from the bottle when the baby arrived)? However, this perplexing thought that she might *be* the baby ("not herself") is reassuringly countered by the fact that she palpably *has* a baby sister, so she can't herself "be" the baby sister. This in turn perhaps gives rise to her subsequent declaration to Winnicott that she has a cat (i.e. the cat is something that is "hers" but isn't "her") and that she will bring it next time to show him. Nevertheless the issue of the baby's arrival remains clouded in anxious incomprehension, whatever the precise nature of the problem it presents her with. This anxiety Winnicott picks up on by then saying to her: "You feel frightened; do you have frightening dreams?" to which Gabrielle replies: "About the babacar" (p. 11). At this point another unspoken difference seems to occur, over who or what exactly the term "babacar" refers to (a word, which, incidentally, never gets defined). In the text at this point Winnicott claims, as an aside, that Gabrielle's mother had earlier explained that "babacar" was the name the child had invented "in connection with the baby, the Sush baby". But in Winnicott's preamble to this first session something different seems to be implied. He refers to the parents' referral letter, where Gabrielle is quoted as demanding from her mother: "Tell me about the babacar, *all* about the babacar." In the letter the mother goes on to explain for Winnicott's benefit: "The black mummy and daddy are often in the babacar together, or some man alone" (p. 7). In other words, the term in Gabrielle's mind seems to refer primarily to either a place, or a state or a container which someone can be inside, but not to a person. However, Winnicott's next question to Gabrielle: "What does the babacar eat?" assumes that the babacar is an imaginary *being*, to which she replies evasively: "I don't know." She then follows this up with an extended process of tidying up as a prelude to ending the session on her own terms. Everything stowed away, Gabrielle leaves her mother to converse with Dr Winnicott, adult to adult.

After this session, Gabrielle displayed marked uncertainty about whether she wanted to have another meeting with him, telling her parents regretfully, "Dr. Winnicott does not know about 'babacar'" (p. 18). At other times the parents reported her as being unable to sleep at night: "The babacar is taking blackness from me to you, and then I am frightened of you. I am frightened of the black Pigga and the black mummy because they make me black" (p. 21).

In the **second** session Winnicott reports that Gabrielle "immediately took possession, making for the consulting room" but had to stay a while with her father in the waiting room. Once able to begin, she resumed her previous questions about the toys, at the same time talking about her long train journey to London for the session. Then she asked: "Do you know about the babacar?" In response Winnicott asked her to explain what it was, but this she seemed at a loss to do. After unsuccessfully suggesting the babacar might be the baby's car, Winnicott "took a risk" and Interpreted: "It's the mother's inside where the baby is born from." Gabrielle looked relieved and said: "Yes, it's the black inside" (p. 24). (Note how Winnicott has now recognised that "babacar" could be an imaginary location, not necessarily an object to see and touch, like a baby.) There then followed some play with a bucket being filled with toys so that it overflowed, which Winnicott associated with the experience of being sick. He then made a further Interpretation which he regarded as the crux of this session: "Winnicott is the Piggle's baby, it's very greedy because it loves the Piggle, its mother, so much, and it's eaten so much that it's sick" (p. 25). Gabrielle replies affirmatively, quite happy to imagine Winnicott in the role of the voracious baby.

It certainly seems as if these two interpretations marked a turning point in their relationship, giving Gabrielle confidence that Winnicott would indeed be able to make sense of her fears, as the parents had doubtless led her to believe he could. And this confidence was to remain largely intact over the sessions that followed, despite some disappointments. In the remainder of this session, Winnicott enthusiastically invests the role of himself as "the greedy baby" issuing from mummy's tummy. When Gabrielle displays some anxiety at Winnicott taking this role, he Interprets, "You are afraid of the greedy Winnicott baby, the baby that was born out of the Piggle, and that loves the Piggle and that wants to eat her" (p. 28). This interpretation seems to me somewhat rash, as it lends itself to being understood by Gabrielle in a different sense from what he intends to convey. Is it herself, as the Piggle (mother), whom the voracious baby (Winnicott) is supposed to be bent on devouring? Or is it the mother who is being devoured, albeit under the guise of the Piggle, with Gabrielle looking on as a "third party", neither the baby nor the mother, but in some manner able to identify with both? What I feel Winnicott insufficiently grasps hereabouts is that she is still needing to retain the identity of "the baby" as belonging to, and defining herself, notwithstanding the advent of Susan. This is simply because she lacks another identity to occupy in the family constellation without usurping the place and role of another; any residual identity, that is, except the decidedly equivocal one of being (called) "the Piggle". The benefit for her of Winnicott's appropriation to himself of the baby role in their play is that it actualises the possibility of the baby role being abrogated in favour of someone else, and introduces the notion of greed—greed expressed both in usurpation by the baby, and by the displaced ex-baby "Piggle" in retaliation, when she aspires to reclaim the position and the prerogatives of babyhood that were once hers by right but of which she now seems dispossessed. It therefore both relieves her that someone like "Mr Winnicott" could actually imagine doing such a greedy thing, even in pretence, and in equal measure alarms her by acquainting her with the idea that he might actually mean what he so surprisingly and vividly enacts; in other words, that he could give expression to an actual self-aggrandising impulse that was so close to her own.

Later in the session (by which time her father's reassuring presence had been called into the room as an antidote to the antics of Winnicott) the following exchange takes place:

> *Winnicott*: I want to be the only baby; I don't want there to be any more babies.
> *Gabrielle*: I'm the baby too (p. 29).

While this exchange was taking place she was busy enacting "being born" by letting herself descend upside down through her father's out-stretched legs. This wish "to be the baby" undoubtedly has a competitive aspect, both with the "baby-being" Winnicott and even more so with the actual baby Susan. But it is also creative as a piece of *wishful thinking*: thanks to Winnicott's cue, Gabrielle can begin to conceive of the possibility of both imagining and pretending an internal scenario that has hitherto persecuted her as a subjective reality in her waking life and her dreaming. This was a crucially important and liberating realisation for her.

In the **third** session Gabrielle is quite explicit about what she has come for: "I want to know why the black mummy and the babacar" (p. 40). Her use of words should be noted. She does not say "*about*" but "*why*" the black mummy and the babacar. Winnicott, however, assumes throughout this session that these two mean the same thing. Consequently he fastens on trying to unmask the fantasy content behind the blackness attributed to them, whereas Gabrielle, I surmise, is after something slightly different, namely, what is it that makes things seem black, when they are actually not so? Seeming to be black is different from being black, just as fantasy is different from reality. It is noteworthy how in this session, whenever Winnicott elaborates a fantasied greedy impulse attributable to the baby, or attributable to herself in respect of the baby in the light of the previous session's material, Gabrielle unpicks the fantasy from the reality, almost prosaically. She accepts, even welcomes, Winnicott's readiness to re-assume the pretend role of the baby, but is very definite that this enactment shouldn't be too realistic (by, for example, his angrily and impetuously overturning all the toys, as he had done previously) because that would frighten her.

She introduces a new notion at this point by referring to "bryyyh": "I be a baby. I want to be bryyyh." Then (for the first time) she also says: "I am the Piggle." "Bryyyh" evidently means faeces. Winnicott then weaves this new association of baby and faeces into his narrative of the baby's disposition—that it is greedy, and it is cross because the greediness goes unsatisfied. But Gabrielle seems to reject this association. It's not what the baby does, but what she is that seems to her (from one perspective at least), to render the baby "bryyyh". Faeces or sick are the two deposits from her inside which she (Gabrielle) is capable of producing (for a child still in nappies "wee" is not experienced as being expelled). So, she is in an acute dilemma over understanding the coming-into-being of her baby sister. If she identifies with her mother (or rather, requires that her mother be identified with her), then the baby has to be excrement, since that is all she herself is capable of producing. But if the baby isn't excrement, and truly a living creature, as truly a baby as she was, then perhaps she herself, now known as "the Piggle", is the negatively charged "bryyyh", displaced and (ready to be) expelled and barely conceivable any longer as the "good" baby her mother once produced. Perhaps this is where the "black mummy" and "the babacar" gains entrance into Gabrielle's narrative? Towards the end of the session, Winnicott asks her twice whether the meaning of the black mummy and the babacar have now been understood by them both, but she declines to confirm that this has happened. She returns home afterwards in what her parents described as "a foul mood".

I now give what I take to be Winnicott's own perspective on these first three sessions. Some repetition is inevitable, but I hope it will enable the reader to clarify what I have identified as parallel narratives, overlapping at some points, diverging at others.

In the **first** session Winnicott lights first on Gabrielle's opening declaration, "I'm too shy." He does not directly comment on this to her, but notes its significance as an expression both of separateness and aloneness. He had already noted the parent's introductory comment about Gabrielle's state: *She seems to be no longer herself.* The meaning of this for him seems to be, not that she is nobody, but that she is inwardly lost to herself, alienated in a depressive way rather than dissociated in a psychotic way. Once she can allow herself to be in his company and at a slight remove from her parents, he links her preliminary itemising of the toys ("another and another and another") to new appearances (arrivals) and Interprets the repeated "anothers" as referring to the advent of her baby sister: "Another baby, the *Sush Baby*." Gabrielle's immediate readiness to talk about this event confirms that they are in accord over its significance, and over the related issue: where did it come from? From here, however, I have suggested that their paths of reflection and comprehension seem to diverge somewhat. Winnicott interprets Gabrielle's subsequent attempt to insert the figure of a man into the driver's seat of the toy car in terms of a fantasy of parental intercourse towards the production of the baby sister: "I said something about man putting something into woman to make baby" (p. 11). She thereupon indicates that she wants to go to mummy. He asks her about frightening dreams, and she mentions about the "babacar". He asks what the babacar eats and she says she doesn't know. She asks him to draw a picture of a man on a light bulb, but she is really intent on tidying up. He asks whether she gets angry with mummy and interprets that she may be angry with her because mummy and Gabrielle love the same man, daddy. He interprets further that her feelings of anger and exclusion turn the figure of the mother into the "black mummy" of her night-time dreams and daytime anxieties. As she busily tidied up in preparation to leave he gave this intercourse fantasy an oral Interpretation: "You are making babies like cooking, collecting everything up." He commented that he felt "quite safe making this interpretation. At one level this must be true" (p. 12).

It is clear that these several Interpretations are only tangentially related to the manifest content of Gabrielle's play, and not at all to her verbal communications. Furthermore, her behaviour in response to them indicates an increase rather than a lessening of anxiety in relation to Winnicott himself. This does not mean that, in his view at least, they were not necessarily correct or timely. The rationale for his manner of early, even premature, interpretation (which I have labelled *commotional*) had been clearly set out by him in a paper written a few years earlier, on the technique of child analysis:

> In my opinion the sooner the analyst interprets the unconscious the better, because this orientates the child towards analytic treatment, and the first relief undoubtedly gives the first indications to the child that there is something to be got out of

> analysis … the earliest possible moment [ ] is the right moment,
> that is to say *the earliest moment at which the material makes it*
> *clear what to interpret*. What matters for the patient is not the
> accuracy of the interpretation so much as the analyst's willingness
> to help, the analyst's capacity to identify with the patient and so to
> believe in what is needed. (Winnicott, 1958)

In the **second** session Winnicott directs his interpretive "scan" towards her "oral greed". Gabrielle again asks him to draw a face on the little electric light bulb among the assortment of toys, adding on this occasion: "Make it sick" (p. 24). This becomes the theme of the session. He Interprets: "Here is the baby me the Winnicott baby come from the Piggle's inside born out of the baby, very greedy, very hungry, very fond of Piggle, eating Piggle's feet and hands" (p. 26). A little later on in the session she fills a bucket with toys so that its contents overflow. Winnicott goes from drawing the sick figure to enacting the sick baby, sick because it was greedy and ate too much. This fascinates yet frightens her and she requires the presence of her father to continue exploring its implications. She sat on father's lap, saying "I'm the baby too" (p. 29), at which Winnicott, as the other baby, insists on wanting to be the only baby. The rivalry prompts her to say, "Put the baby in the dustbin" (p. 29), whereupon Winnicott tries to ascertain whether her preoccupation with darkness stems from, or is associated with, this wish to see off her sister. Gabrielle, however, counters with: "You're not to be the only baby" (p. 30), and she herself enacts a process of being born by insisting on being repeatedly dropped over the father's shoulders onto the floor. She then says, "I am just born. And it wasn't black inside," which Winnicott takes as confirmation of his earlier interpretation linking "blackness" with the mother's insides.

In the **third** session Gabrielle expresses the wish that Winnicott should not be (act) the baby. He notes how she introduces her word for faeces ("bryyyh") at this point, appearing to associate it with a mental picture of being the baby. At the same time she calls herself "the Piggle" (for the only time in the sessions, at least as reported by Winnicott). Gradually, in the presence of her father she tolerates, even encourages, Winnicott to enact the cross baby who overturns all the toys. He Interprets as he does so: "I wanted to be the only baby so I was sick. Mummy got a bryyyh baby" (p. 43). This leads to her telling Winnicott about dreaming of a black mummy and a babacar coming after her in bed at night. When she follows this by putting an axle from one of the toys in her mouth Winnicott Interprets this as referring to the mother's oral greedy experience of the father's penis, but Gabrielle deflects this interpretation by insisting on tidying up the mess of toys left by the angry baby Winnicott.

In these three sessions we observe Winnicott steadily and consistently interpreting Gabrielle's predominant anxiety in relation to the new baby in terms of rivalry with mother, and of oral greed for the father's penis, displacing mother. He further interprets her sentiments towards the baby in terms of fantasies of how the baby was produced and what it is made of, and her recurrent preoccupation with "black" and "babacar" as associated with hate. By the end of the **third** session Gabrielle is more evidently disturbed than at the beginning of treatment. Winnicott encourages the parents to view this as a positive development, a breaking down of manic defences.

Act 2: sessions 4–6 getting to know myself through you

Between the **third** and **fourth** sessions the family went on holiday and the parents, despite Winnicott's assurances, became very perturbed about Gabrielle's emotional state. In a letter they suggested that maybe after all their daughter required a full analysis, so overwhelmed did she seem to be by misery over her tendency to spoil and by fears of retribution from the black mummy. Winnicott, however, again seeks to reassure them that this is just a temporary phase, and conveys his strong conviction about her innate capacity for self-healing.

This reassurance may have also communicated itself to Gabrielle since she comes to the **fourth** session, which took place six weeks after the previous one, in a much more buoyant mood. Very early in the session she again says: "I came about the babacar" (p. 55), thereby indicating both her continuing confusion and her continuing hope for a resolution of her besetting anxiety. To this Winnicott again proposes an Interpretation in terms of envy, that: "Mummy was angry with Gabrielle because Gabrielle was angry with mummy for having a new baby. And then mummy seemed black" (p. 58). Gabrielle's response to this is to say,

"There's a pretty lady waiting for the car, a nice lady. The black mummy is naughty." This seems to suggest that for her the two mummys have to be kept apart, are separate; she cannot see, or allow herself to see, that the good mummy could become transformed into the black mummy and vice versa. After this she begins a fairly determined tidying up of the room in preparation for departure, even though it is still early into the allotted time for the session. With her father she is insistent: "I want to go; please let me go" (p. 59). Father coaxes her to stay longer, and then the game of the previous session resumes, of her easing herself down between father's legs, as though she was being born from him.

While she is repeating this action, Winnicott perseveres with his interpretation of the Piggle's angry feelings rendering the mother black. Towards the end of the session he asks her directly: "Have I become black?" (p. 60) (as a result of saying these things) to which she replies after a pause: "No." When Winnicott goes on insisting that he is now the black mummy, she repeats her denial of this.

Although Gabrielle rejects the suggestion conveyed by Winnicott that feelings can change the actual appearance of a person between being either "pretty" or "black", she does nevertheless appear to have taken from this communication of his the notion that the impression on her of a person can change. What she seems to be not convinced about, however, is that persons remain the same underneath if the "feel" of them for her changes. Her mother subsequently reported that for some days afterwards Gabrielle would not allow her to kiss her, and when asked why, had replied that she was afraid it would make her(self) black. The reason for this difference is that, in respect of herself, Gabrielle can now feel that she remains the same despite appearing to be different, whereas perhaps she still cannot be sure of this continuity of being in relation to her perception of others.

The **fifth** session took place only a fortnight after the previous one, following her insistent requests to see Winnicott again. This time the heat, the noises from outside intruding from the open windows, and Winnicott's sleepiness meant that the course of the session was more confused than usual. However, Gabrielle seems to have derived two things from it. First, that she was growing bigger (she was now nearing three and thinking about when she would get there—and in doing so be able also to remember a time when she wasn't yet that age). Second, eating made you grow. The conclusion she seems to have drawn is that perhaps babies had a way of coming about otherwise than through defecation: they might actually grow inside the mummy. Winnicott, while acknowledging the insight, is as keen as ever to link it with affective ambition, and ascribes to Gabrielle the wish to have a baby of her own, to rival mummy. She however, wants to claim her anchorage to father, as father: "Who loves daddy? The babacar and mummy" (p. 71). And then she leaves the room.

In the **sixth** session Winnicott Interprets her placing two soft toy dogs together as signifying that they are conjoined so as to make babies, once more laying emphasis on her supposed affective ambition. However, Gabrielle contradicts him, saying: "No, they are making friends" (p. 77). There then follows an important passage of playful exchange where she experiments with the idea of people in relationships with one another, relationships which evolve. She recognises that she and Winnicott are separate persons, each with a mind. Winnicott in his notes called this "a kind of establishment of identities". It starts with her talking about the "Sush baby" who can now begin to walk unaided: "Soon she will grow bigger and bigger and do without mummy or daddy, and Gabrielle will be able to do without Winnicott or without anybody at all" (p. 80). It is noteworthy that Winnicott records scarcely any interpretations during this session. His main contribution to it, he reflected in his subsequent notes, is to have greeted her on arrival as Gabrielle, not Piggle.

Viewing these sessions now from Winnicott's perspective I see him at the beginning of the **fourth** session as taking her new sense of purpose, exhibited in her play, to be a sign of her positive feelings towards him and to the therapeutic process. When he voices this, she responds: " 'Cos I like you to blow up the balloon!" (p. 57), indicating an appreciation of his playfulness. Later he again asks her why she likes him and this time she says: "Because you tell me about the babacar." Then comes: "There is the black mummy" (Winnicott incidentally does not say what object she is alluding to). He next attempts to find out whether the primary characteristic of the black mummy was her cross-ness. He suggests that it might have something to do "with mummy being angry with Gabrielle because Gabrielle was angry with mummy for having a new baby" (p. 58), repeating his earlier and now standard interpretation. However, Winnicott's interpretation only seemed to lead once more to heightened anxiety on Gabrielle's part and she went to her father and pleaded with him to take her home. The father demurred, and instead came into the therapy room, where Gabrielle's enactment of being born from him began again. A rather confusing sequence then ensued where Winnicott now Interpreted Gabrielle's wish to be born from father rather than mother. Winnicott thereupon ascribes to himself in the play the role of the jealous mother. Common to both scenarios is the new theme of the excluded third, but it is not the new baby that is, or has to be, excluded, but Winnicott instead. He also notes her increasingly manifest eroticisation and somatic excitement evident in her sucking of the father's thumb, curling up in his lap, and playing at being let down through his legs.

In the **fifth** session Winnicott again fastens on what he sees to be Gabrielle's eroticisation (others might see it as age-appropriate exhibitionism) in relation to himself. When she says: "My hair's curly," while twiddling her "perfectly straight hair", he chooses to Interpret: "You are wanting a baby of your own" (p. 70), to which she replies, "But I've got a girlie-girlie baby." It is at least as plausible to regard her words "My hair's curly" as an acceptance and affirmation by her that while she is still she, others may view her differently at different times. Understood thus the reference she is making would be to the well-known nursery song:

> There was a little girl
> Who had a little curl
> Right in the middle of her forehead. And when she was good
> She was very, very good
> And when she was bad she was horrid!

Winnicott, however, overlooks or ignores this possible association. Instead, his preferred theme, of her wanting a baby of her own, is taken up once more when she conjoins two toy boats. He sees her "eating" outside the door of the consulting room (she had left him alone in the room and made her way to daddy). Again he Interprets: "You were frightened to find you want to make babies by eating the ships" (p. 71). It was in the postlude to this session, while talking with the father, that Winnicott seems to have mooted that, though he found her "normal", there might after all be a reason, or a possibility, of Gabrielle having a full analysis, as the parents had suggested previously.

In the **sixth** session Winnicott begins by greeting her as Gabrielle, rather than as "Piggle", a gesture which he felt was tantamount to an interpretive comment, as if acknowledging thereby her burgeoning self-hood, freed from some of the negative connotations of "Piggle". When she places two soft animals together, and similarly two train carriages, he again Interprets: "They are making babies," to which she counters, "They are making friends." He then attempts a different sort of interpretation: "You could be joining up all the different times that you have seen me," to which she replies, "Yes" (p. 77). This is followed by her saying that she had a small house and a big house. Winnicott uses this image to reflect back to her their separateness yet unity, what he calls "an establishment of identities". When she proceeds from this to talk about herself and Susan both growing up simultaneously, but with herself always the older, she suggests that as part of this process Susan would come to Winnicott, pushing her out of the place she had occupied. In doing so she again took two carriages and rubbed their wheels together. Winnicott asks: "Are they making babies?" She replies that when she lies on her back with her legs in the air she is "not making babies" (p. 80). She tells him she has a sundress and white knickers, and new shoes too. She takes off the shoes to show him, but has difficulty putting them back on. When she returns to the toys, putting them in the bucket he Interprets: "Gabrielle eats up all the world and so she eats too much" (p. 81). She replies, "She doesn't be sick" (and the bucket doesn't overflow). There is a sense of being comfortable in each other's presence, and less wariness on the part of Gabrielle.

Following this session there are signs that both Winnicott and the parents felt that the therapy work had perhaps now been concluded, or at least had reached a stage where Gabrielle's own resources could take over and cope with anxieties and self-doubts in the future. At the end of the session, however, after some seemingly final tidying up, Gabrielle asks: "When shall I come again?" to which Winnicott replies, "In October" (p. 83). It is a very adult-sounding exchange between them and one wonders what this child, not yet three, was able to make of this invitation to return in three months' time. This no doubt conveyed an ambiguous note of partial withdrawal on Winnicott's part, perhaps reflecting his assessment that the "illness phase" was over. But Gabrielle seemed to sense that she hadn't finished the work in hand. Despite the newly evident poise in her—"solidness" was how her mother described it—she continued to be preoccupied with the threatening night-time presence of the "black mummy", although she let her parents know that "she would tell Dr. Winnicott that the black mummy had gone" (p. 87).

Act 3: recognising a difference: "I used to be used to you"

At the start of the **seventh** session Gabrielle marches into the room, somewhat impatient: "Did you hear my bell? I rang three times." She begins setting out the houses in a row, then says: "All the troubles are gone so I've nothing left to tell you. I had a black mummy that troubled me but she has gone away now. I didn't like the mummy and she didn't like me. She talked nonsense to me" (p. 89). In this session Gabrielle seems to do most of the talking, much of it about her holiday in France, of her desire to have been alone there, or friends of her age whom she likes to visit, but now can't visit because of mumps and the fear of contagion. Much of it seems either indefinite or inconsequential. Winnicott confesses to not understanding what she was talking about underneath the chatter. Gabrielle makes no particular effort to let him share her experiences, and when he attempts to play alongside her, or assist in her activity of lining up the carriages of a train, she "almost threw" a tractor at him across the railway line separating them (p. 91). Winnicott isn't clear whether this impulse was prompted by her not wanting the tractor, or not wanting his participation. Much of what Gabrielle expresses reflects differences of understanding, whether it is the fact that in France people speak differently, or the fact that peacocks "don't understand. They just shake their heads like saying no. They never say 'Oh dear'" (p. 93). But more seems to be implied by this perspicacious little girl than simple differences of utterance. She appears to be alluding to a situation of *mis*understanding, where something is said by one person in words which the other is assumed to understand but doesn't; or rather, doesn't understand in the same way, but all the while the mutual incomprehension is never alluded to, so cannot be remedied. There may even be a suggestion here too that her difficulties over the maternal figure, leading to the splitting into mummy and black mummy, had been precipitated by the early experience of hearing her mother switching from talking in a language with which she was familiar, English, to another, German, which Gabrielle did not fully understand, yet in which she recognised her mother to be entirely at home—a "mother tongue" different from her own. Whatever the reason, what is conveyed strongly to Winnicott in this session is that while she remains the same as before, there is nevertheless a barrier between them.

After this session, in which she had clearly demonstrated her separateness from Winnicott, Gabrielle felt an urgent need to see him again. This was in part connected with a recurrent feeling she had that "I haven't paid the black mummy who gave me a lovely wooden cup" (p. 97). Six weeks later, the **eighth** session took place. Evidently, the memory still lingered on of her having almost thrown the tractor at him when she felt "invaded" in the previous session, and she appears to make an effort to involve him, talking about the multitude of "nice" trains he had, and inviting him to find or make an appropriate station for a passing train. At the same time she launches into an extended commentary about her nuisance sister Susan who comes and disturbs her play. Winnicott suggests that her feelings of anger towards Susan makes her sister go black in her eyes, but she initially rejects this suggestion, saying that Susan's troublesome-ness makes Gabrielle cry and shout, which in turn causes her parents to be cross with both of them. Later though she says, "I'm scared of the black Susan; so I play with your toys. Yes, I hate her very much only when she takes my toys away" (p. 103). What seems to have become clarified for her in the course of this session is that love and hate can be felt towards the same person (Susan), and that the person doesn't change as a result; only the feelings change, and these can change again. Perhaps her previous compulsion to "tuck the dark away" (p. 92) because of the fear of irretrievable loss of the "darkened" object has now been diminished, with the result that at the end of this session for the first time she does not assiduously tidy up, but leaves Winnicott to clear up the mess instead.

Between the **eighth** session and the next her mother reported Gabrielle as saying several times: "I have paid the black mummy" (p. 106). There are then a number of exchanges of letter, the sequence of which appears to indicate that Winnicott offered the parents a date for her next session in response to Gabrielle's request, but then had to cancel it, and was unable immediately to confirm an alternative date. The **ninth** session eventually takes place two months after the previous one. Talk about

Susan, her wakefulness, her being "a little monster" is to the fore in her conversation so that Winnicott notes that she is "almost giving me Susan instead of herself". She had a bad cold, asked for a tissue, and then said that "Susan has a bad cold." After talking about this "little monster" of a sister she goes on to speak about the "black mummy", who gets onto her bed, so that she has to insist on her getting off so as to allow her to sleep undisturbed in her own bed. She states that "Daddy says I'm vile" (p. 21). This comes after a mention of "two little Turks"—a reference to her sister and herself as a quarrelsome pair in her parents' eyes. (Or could it be two girls with curls in the middle of their forehead?) It is as if Gabrielle has succeeded in acknowledging her displacement from being the baby following Susan's arrival, but is now having to contend with another sort of displacement, namely that of not being the only "little girl", since Susan is no longer viewable as the baby, but has become another little girl instead, part rival, part playmate. This fresh recognition seems to drive Gabrielle towards a realisation that all relationships evolve, what remains constant is the person underneath. From this recognition she seems to derive a great sense of inner freedom and the session becomes one of almost constant talking on her part, even though Winnicott, on his own admission, begins to feel drowsy. This drowsiness he attributes to her withdrawal into chatter, but the impression that comes across is not that Gabrielle is trying to exclude him (as had happened in the previous session), but that she is now much more secure in herself and therefore less dependent on him. Winnicott implies towards the end of this session that she was still being dominated by the dream of the black mummy, but it could be that Gabrielle now felt emancipated enough to be able to counter the black mummy who had hitherto held sway over her. Yet in order to do so she still has to discover what made things appear black when they weren't actually black. "The black mummy is my bad mummy. I liked my black mummy. Let's play on." Winnicott then writes: "This is when I said it was time to go" (p. 118).

In these three sessions Winnicott's interpretations are markedly less frequent and more "conjunctive" than "commotional", consisting in the main of verbalisations of states of feeling or impulses which were close to Gabrielle's consciousness and had a direct bearing on the content of her speech and play. He lets Gabrielle set the pace, sensing that a process of consolidation of a still precarious (persecution-free) self-identity is taking place. In the **seventh** session he notes her initial touching of him (elbow—in subsequent sessions his leg) and that much of the material she produces is opaque to him though seemingly unproblematic to her. He comments that she appears to be "free at last" (p. 95), reflecting her declaration early in this session: "I had a black mummy that troubled me but she has gone away now" (p. 89). Significantly, Winnicott does not interpret this as post-holiday defensive resistance but allows her separateness and stability to be acknowledged. In the next session, however, her anxieties are in evidence once more, with a focus once again on the invasive presence in her life and feelings of her little sister. Winnicott regularly Interprets her feelings towards the latter as arising from ambivalence: "You hate and love Susan both at the same time" (p. 103). He indicates thereby his perception that her earlier tendency towards splitting into good and bad objects is now being replaced by more depressive forms of anxiety—feelings *in* the self rather than feelings visited *on* the self. Gabrielle does not resist this interpretation, but on the contrary confirms it with extensive associative material. As evidence of this growing freedom from persecutory anxiety he notes her new-found readiness to leave him to clear up the mess of toys at the end.

In the last of these sessions comprising the "Third Act", Winnicott sees Gabrielle's internal struggle between splitting and ambivalence being played out in relation to the black mummy who both assails her and likes her. He links this with the mother's mixture of feelings in relation to giving birth (cf. Winnicott, 1947), but in regard to Gabrielle specifically fastens on the fact that her mother needed her birth (as the first child) in order to discover something new and fulfilling about herself (i.e. that of becoming a mother for the first time). He views this session as one in which a crucial change occurred in Gabrielle, encapsulated in the following dream:

> *Gabrielle:* I was lying all still with my gun. I tried to shoot her [the black mummy]. She just went away. Do you know what people do to me? I was asleep. I could not talk. It was only a dream. (p. 116)

In reporting this dream to the parents afterwards Winnicott said that "Everything led up to the place where the mummy was shot dead. In this setting the black mother is the good mother who has been lost" (p. 118).

In fact, according to his account Gabrielle did *not* say that in her dream she had shot the black mummy. Rather, what she declares is: "I was lying all still with my gun. I tried to shoot her. She just went away" (p. 116). In other words, she claims that she musters resources sufficient to dispose of her, whereupon the black mummy disappears, ceases to be. In Winnicott's version there is a narrative of death, in Gabrielle's one of escape from entrapment. The critical enactment which Winnicott identifies is one that occurs towards the end of the session. Gabrielle takes an Optrex eyebath out from the pile of toys and deliberately puts it in and out of her mouth. This object had been used or taken up by her intermittently during previous sessions, usually accompanied with a question directed to Winnicott about what it was for, as if she saw it as an anomaly among the toys (which in a sense it was). Now was the first occasion, however, on which she seemed to interest herself in it as a significant object, and certainly the first time she had introduced it into her play in this particular way. Winnicott fastens on the erotic nature of her sucking at this point, taking it, as he later told the parents, as representing the point at which she rediscovered "the lost good mother along with her own orgiastic capacity which was lost with the [disappearance of] the good mother" (p. 118). At the moment this enactment occurred in the session, however (as distinct from his thoughts about it after), Winnicott registered something different: "She did something which I am sure had great significance, whatever it symbolized," as if to imply that the unconscious fantasy which he later came to associate with it was not immediately obvious in the context of the other things that she was doing or saying at the time. It could well be that the indeterminacy of her playing at this point was a continuation of the sort of "non-communicative play" that was such a feature of this session. It is very doubtful whether Gabrielle could have related to the actual function of the eyebath. She may well have understood the sound of the word Winnicott used to describe the object as referring to "I" rather than "eye", and seized on it as an expression of "I-ness". What was apparent to Winnicott at the time was "the fact that the whole quality of the session altered". This change of quality does seem to indicate that from that moment onwards her play and communications became more transparent. Could it be that in the process of taking in and extruding the eyebath she was becoming aware of having an inside "I" and an outside "I", that what was inside her was in her own domain, and in that sense belonged to her own "private self", whereas the outside was visible to others, public, and therefore "on show"?

Act 4: recognising separateness: us together, you and I apart

Before proceeding to consider the three following sessions and their verbal exchanges singly, a general change in Gabrielle's behaviour should be noted, one not fully captured in their speech. She is at times much more physically demonstrative than previously towards Winnicott in both an aggressively and a sexual way—"unbuttoned" might best describe it. He mentions her emptying out the insides of the toy animal (session ten) which she herself linked with the evacuation of faeces (p. 131), as well as with the physical discovery of what lies inside and hidden (as in handbags). In the next session the animal's insides have become "perfumed" (p. 139). These now delectable insides have to be evacuated so as to turn into a beautiful baby. Her interest then turns to the penis as either a "snapper" (p. 140) or extractor of some sort (p. 141). Either way the possessor of this item is a "robber"—exciting and wicked. This complex mixture of procreation fantasies is momentarily enacted through physical contact with Winnicott himself by means of a toy tractor on which she was seated and which she pushes towards him (p. 141). Early on in the twelfth session there was a period when she sat on or near Winnicott's shoes and seemed to him to be deriving erotic pleasure from the contact (p. 150). Winnicott appears to have deliberately refrained from commenting on what appeared to be her overt behaviour. However, he did articulate the underlying sexual fantasies he felt were being given expression to by these several successive enactments of hers, fantasies in relation both to parental intercourse, and to himself as a non-father "daddy-man", conveniently older and more vulnerable than her own father, available for play and seemingly single. Winnicott no doubt felt emboldened to make these explicit interpretations to Gabrielle in the knowledge that the parents had reported that at this time Gabrielle (and to a lesser extent her sister) had been expressing new and lively curiosity about babies, intercourse, and the birth process. Winnicott's practice here also accorded with his conviction, one generally accepted among his fellow psychoanalysts, about the actuality and dominance of infantile sexuality and the consequent need for the adult to countenance evidence of it in the feelings and behaviour of the child.

I return now to my session by session account. On the occasion of the **tenth** session there is some internal evidence that, instead of Gabrielle travelling up to London alone with her father, Mother and Susan had also accompanied them. Gabrielle tells Winnicott: "We had great fun in the train all together" (p. 124). Whether or not Susan is somewhere in the vicinity, she is very much a presence in her absence throughout this session, as companion, competitor, and reminder to Gabrielle of a younger, less competent and contained self. Although Winnicott interprets Gabrielle's rivalry with her sister, and her mixture of triumph and guilt at having Winnicott for herself, at least as evident is her sense of having extricated herself from the mess she was formerly in, and that in order to make this transformation irreversible, she would like to invest this messiness in the person of Susan instead. When Winnicott suggests that she would really like to shoot her sister: "Sometimes you shoot her," she replies: "No, sometimes I am at peace with her" (p. 125). While partially acknowledging his follow-up suggestion that she likes coming in order to get away from her, she goes on to say that she will be having lunch soon (presumably "en famille"), so could she come another day instead? There is no further mention here or henceforward of "babacar" or the "black mummy". The company of Susan seems as important to her as the sense of separateness and self-identity that she had so striven for. Insofar as Winnicott represents a former ally in that struggle, he is now, though not exactly redundant, nevertheless a marker of the conflicts from which she feels she is now emerging and wants to put behind her. So his interpretations about the continuing reality of these internal conflicts appear to threaten her, as if inviting her to be retrogressive in order to prolong their association. A solution has to be found which does not involve Susan usurping her place with Winnicott. The figure who is now designated as the one to be "in a mess" is one of the soft toys, a faun, whose insides she has begun to poke out, so that in a little while the sawdust contents of its belly become a deposit in the basket and on the carpet. At the end she leaves Winnicott with the emptied faun and almost accidentally her own toy doll, Frances, that she had brought along with her.

Despite the long interval and the fact that her several requests for another session had not been met, Gabrielle comes to the **eleventh** session in a state of "shy delight". She takes the toy train and immediately joins it to a carriage "because trains don't go without carriages. Susan understands better" (p. 135). She then indicates that she wants to do the talking and Winnicott must do the listening. The train had to be connected together, and connected with the train journey she and her father had made to reach him. Winnicott was required to enlarge the eye of the hook so that two carriages could be joined. While he does this Gabrielle takes the eyebath and uses it in a new way. Treating it as a looking glass, she says: "Dr. Winnicott, you have a blue jacket on and blue hair" (p. 136). This seems to have been the significant moment of the session for Gabrielle, in that she was able to articulate for the first time the recognition that things and people could appear differently *to her* from what they usually were because her perception of them was "coloured", not because they had actually become different. The importance of this realisation is that the blackness which had beset her, and had been linked with darkness (that "turned things black") didn't actually belong to the objects themselves as an actual colour or cover, but pertained to the conditions under which they were seen, and so weren't really the persecutors she felt them to be. Still there are mysterious, unseen, and unseeable aspects to the creatures one knows best, in particular one's parents. Foremost among these mysteries is their joint capacity to produce children, one's sister, and most intriguingly of all, oneself. Parents achieve this by means of processes in which one appears to participate, if only as an end-product, by changing from being nothing into being a baby, and from being a baby into becoming a little sister. Yet all the while, one is completely at a loss over the actual how and the when of the making. This bewilderment Gabrielle tentatively begins to explore with Winnicott during the remainder of the session. He articulates her sense (as he sees it) of intercourse being an illicit "robber" act on the part of the father, acknowledging at this point in a footnote the influence of Klein's formulations on his interpretation. It is uncertain to what extent this actually accorded with Gabrielle's own intercourse fantasies as the session ended at this point. What her comments leading up to this conclusion conveyed, however, was more the imponderability of the whole process and her own inoperancy: being me meant being a child; and being a child meant being excluded, hence ignorant about vital aspects of grown-up experience. As she said, in answer to Winnicott's remark: "What have I listened to to-day?", "One of the neighbours says, 'You tell me and I'll tell you'" (p. 142). Her consolation seems to be that sometimes children are as mysterious to parents as parents are to their children.

Between the eleventh and twelfth session almost four months passed. Gabrielle was desperately keen to see Winnicott in the interval, telling her mother:

> The dream has come again, the cutting up one ... I must go to Mr. Winnicott. *Dr. Winnicott.* Does he make ill people un-ill? I don't think he likes anybody as much as he likes me. He has a lot of delicate things there. I could not take Susan, she would break them. (p. 147)

Yet Winnicott was unable to oblige her. Three weeks later she repeated her request, though in the meantime she had also asked her mother to tell him that she was angry with him and instructed her not to request him to see her again after all.

Unsurprisingly in view of the long intermission the theme of locks and keys looms large in this **twelfth** session. At first Gabrielle is somewhat reserved, fixing her eyes on Winnicott, before going to inspect the toys. She talks at length about the difficulty of the journey on this occasion, when the back of the train caught fire, had to stop for a long time (but luckily no one was hurt), and that this was the reason why they were late in arriving. Winnicott makes no reference to this communication, or to the fact that while saying this she is playing with the toy trains and complaining that some of the carriages have no links, so could not be joined up. It was as if the two of them were in the same room but occupying separate mental spaces, to the point that he began to detect some anxiety in Gabrielle, which manifested itself in her silently observing him sitting on a chair while she played (which, as he mentions, was a departure from his customary position sitting on the floor). Midway through the session, however, there is the beginning of significant exchange. Playing with a black animal that wouldn't stand up properly she says:

> Black is nothing. What is it?
>
> *Winnicott:* Is black what you don't see?
>
> *Gabrielle:* I can't see you because you are black.

Winnicott: Do you mean that when I am away then I am black and you can't see me? And then you ask to come back and see me and you have a good look at me and I am light or something else that isn't black?

Gabrielle: When I go away and look at you you go all black don't you Dr. Winnicott?

She then refers to the handbag she is carrying, and says: "I have got a key in my handbag … It unlocks your door. I lock it for you when you want to go out. You haven't got a key here, have you?" (pp. 152–153). Keys assist in keeping things (and people) inside (and in the dark). Later, after returning from the toilet, she "dived into" the bag she had left behind. She looked for the key which at first she couldn't find, only to discover it lying among the toys she had been playing with. Winnicott took up her earlier suggestion that the key could be used on the lock of the room, at which Gabrielle began to experiment unsuccessfully. Winnicott suggested trying from the other side of the door. She replied that then she would lock herself out, and wanted to be inside: "Then when I tried to go I'd unlock it outside. I wouldn't be able to get in to let myself out. I could only get out if I lock myself in …. Yes, if I lock the outside, I lock you in …' (p. 159). It seems as if towards the end of this session, Gabrielle was beginning to realise that the fact of the change from light to darkness, a transformation which had so beset her previously, wasn't simply or always a result of the loss of light (for example, the lights going out at night), but was, or could be, the result of deliberate choice, of actively locking somebody or something away (in a room, or in a bag), or a person inside locking you out (as when Winnicott did not respond immediately and positively to her requests to see him). Choice, agency, and differentiation now become the focal themes of the concluding sessions. Instead of being frightened, I can frighten; instead of being annihilated, I can annihilate.

From Winnicott's perspective in the **tenth** session and beyond, survival of herself and objects becomes a principal theme. Gabrielle's comments relate mostly to Susan. Winnicott asserts that she wants to shoot her. Gabrielle for her part asserts that she "is [wants to be] at peace with her". But good things (such as "the beautiful stallion") destroy ("trample the wheat"). Later she empties sawdust out of one of the toy animals "leaving you with all the mess". Winnicott introduces a new ingredient into this theme of ambivalence, destruction, and the survival of the object, namely the notion of his own death. He responds to her wish to give him a present for his birthday, the Interpretation that it could well be meant for his death day.

In the **eleventh** session Winnicott relates Gabrielle's anxieties over the fusion of love and hate to her fantasies over her parents' sexual union in the creation of babies. Gabrielle's resistance to this line of Interpretation was evident in her insistence on leaving early. (I shall deal with Winnicott's perspective in this session in greater detail in the final section of this chapter.)

Between this session and the next there stretches a gap of three and a half months, despite Gabrielle's stated wish to see Winnicott sooner. It is no wonder, therefore, that doubts about Winnicott's capacity to "go-on-being" for her become the main focus of the **twelfth** session. There is another change also, in that for the first time, Winnicott sits on a chair rather than on the floor. When she says spontaneously, "Black is what you don't see," he links her sense of "blackness" to the experience of absence in a way that she could readily comprehend. He Interprets her current sense of Winnicott sometimes being absent (i.e. failing her) with experiences of the sometimes absent mother. He goes on to refer to the leather shoulder bag she had brought with her to the session complete with a clasp and key. Its "dark" inside now becomes for Winnicott the dark unknown, linked once again to birth fantasies which he attributes to Gabrielle. As Winnicott says in his notes of this session: "I made quite a lot of interpretations" (p. 157). She had asked about the whereabouts of one of the soft toys whose insides she had evacuated in the previous session, and said "Oh" when shown that it was lying in an envelope, still with its insides outside. Taking his cue from this and from her use of a soldier figure shooting into the church, he Interprets: "You wanted to make a baby out of the mess, but you don't know how to" (which she acknowledges to be the case). He then goes further and, bringing this wish for a baby into the here-and-now transference, interprets: "You are frightened to think that when you love me you tear the stuffing out of my wee-wee." Hereabouts Gabrielle fixes her attention on her handbag (a new acquisition) and its key, but then mislays the key to her handbag, or imagines she does. It is not clear whether at this point she is wanting to preserve herself from the battering of Winnicott's interpretations which do not "fit" her, or whether, on the contrary, her preoccupation with the key is evidence of her acceptance of penetration as a necessary step towards the eventual fulfilment of her desire for a baby—despoliation—as suggested (in Winnicott's eyes) by the very determined way in which she had emptied out the insides of the soft toy in the previous session. At the end of the session she pretends to close Winnicott in the room with her magic key, maybe to "shut him up".

Act 5: recognising separation: I and you going our separate ways

Thirteenth session. Winnicott again notes Gabrielle's shyness on entering the consulting room. It does not have the same quality as the earlier shyness of "not being used" to Winnicott, but is based on a recognition that she was entering, invited, into his space; he was making room for her, but only for a set period: "I haven't seen you for a long time so I was shy when I came to see you, and I shan't see you tomorrow nor tomorrow nor tomorrow" (p. 168). The sense of having to exist separately also leads into the theme of repair: if you can't be mended by an omnipresent mender, you have to become a self-mender. And you can only mend yourself if you are intact enough already. If you are an egg and your shell breaks, then you can't be mended because everything inside has already flowed out: the yolk can't repair the shell. This train of thought ends up with her communication to Winnicott: "Now I don't break any more." And as if to make her meaning crystal clear, namely that she doesn't any longer disintegrate, she then adds: "Now I don't break any more. Now I break things up into pieces" (p. 169). Winnicott recalls his earlier role as that of being her "mender", an observation which prompts Gabrielle to indicate her own new sense of agency in comparison with younger sister Susan, towards whom she is both the generous mender and the ready model of superior competence. In the second half of the session the roles of "mender" and "mended" get interchanged between herself and Winnicott. She acknowledges her indebtedness to him for his mending by making complimentary remarks about the toys in his room and asking him about matters in which she needed instruction (such as how one could light his gas fire), while at the same time recognising that the competence he gave her would enable her to survive and outlive him. This last theme of outliving him found expression in a spontaneously generated game in which she rolled a ruler across the room to hit his knee, whereupon Winnicott made a play of rolling over. She left him to clear up the toys at the end, and at the time he seems to have thought that this would be her last session with him. But more followed. Gabrielle was not yet done.

Three months passed before the next session took place. Again, she recognises the interval that has occurred and that each have had experiences in the meantime, and both had survived. There is reassurance in that and the possibility of pleasurable contact, expressed in her touching Winnicott's knee. She then begins reminiscing, asking about the "dog" (faun) whose innards she had previously disgorged. When shown the envelope with its remains inside, she asks, "Why is he in there? ... You really must have him mended" (p. 181). Here there was latent anxiety about the consequences of past destructiveness, and this became channelled into a prolonged game played about between them and using the full space of the room. It started with a variant of the ruler game from the previous session, except that now each took it in turns to fall over and die. The condition of "being dead" then required the dead person to wake up and on doing so find that the other was not there and had to be found. This was a form of hide-and-seek played out with great zest, but also with an undercurrent of anxiety. Eventually this game evolved into one where she grew inside a house "made of Winnicott", who then pushes her out "in a kind of birth", with the words: "I hate you." This gives expression to the idea of riddance that was to dominate the penultimate session.

Fifteenth session. Four and a half months had elapsed since the previous session. Gabrielle was nearing five, twice the age she was when she first came to see Winnicott. Soon she invited him to continue where her last time's hide-and-seek playing had stopped. When this was exhausted she told of a dream she had had about Winnicott and about diving into a pool in his house, followed by the other members of the family. "It was a good dream" (pp. 187–188). From this she gravitated towards the pile of toys, focusing on a pipe-cleaner figure of a man, which she began to manipulate. As she twisted its legs, Winnicott called: "Ouch." This was the cue to a game of demolishing therapist Winnicott first by means of the toy figure, and then with a piece of paper on which she crayoned, then covered with Seccotine (the name of a popular liquid adhesive of the period), before putting a hole in it so that it could be used as a kite. At the end she said: "All the glue is used up—what shall we do? All the Winnicott, all the pieces, what do we do when all is gone?" (p. 189).

The last session, two months later, was a more self-conscious sort of leave-taking on Gabrielle's part. Winnicott commented: "The session was not like the previous visits. In fact it seemed more like a visit from a friend to a friend" (p. 195). She played briefly with the toys, resumed the hide-and-seek game for a while, then settled down to look at an illustrated book with Winnicott at her side. Looking at the pictures, he reminded her of blackness, but while she was happy to be reminded of the theme, she did not wish to revisit the experiences connected with it. At the end Winnicott says: "I know when you are really shy, and that is when you want to tell me that you love me" (p. 198). Having allowed for the expression of destructive aggression behind the riddance behaviour in the previous session, he now allows the joint recognition of mutual affection to be voiced, which enables them to separate from one another, to preserve a shared memory without the need for the presence and company of each other anymore.

In contrast to his practice in the preceding sessions, Winnicott's commentaries in this last phase of treatment are mostly directed towards verbalising her new-found self-assurance in a non-critical way. He emphasises, however, its source in her confidence in the healing power of Winnicott and the assurance of her having his presence to herself, free from Susan. Referring to her mention of Humpty Dumpty (which had been followed by a "lecture" from her about the difference between hard and soft eggs being a consequence of cooking), he rather obscurely summed up his therapeutic intervention with her as follows: "I put an egg round Gabrielle and she feels alright" (p. 171). At the end—equally obscurely—Gabrielle says, "When the woman comes to mend things, the cook pretends to go to sleep. You have to tell her to wake up, and then she cooks some more" (p. 174)—perhaps a reference to Winnicott's tendency to "absences" both in and between sessions and also to the fact that the help he had provided her with had been intermittent.

The remaining sessions are all concerned with the prospect of termination and her survival. In the **fourteenth** session prominent is a game created between them in which each in turn is "bowled over" and killed by the moving rolling pin. Once dead the surviving player hides, and then has to be looked for by the revived "dead" person who, through being dead, has forgotten where the other one was. This play eventually altered into a game of Gabrielle "being born" out of the curtains, or taking flight, like the wind. In the **fifteenth** session the theme of destroying in order to survive predominates, with Winnicott happily enacting the role of the twisted-up and discarded pipe-cleaner figure. But, he also reciprocated this attitude of dismissal later in the session, confirming that he is quite happy to let her go now "so that I can be all the other Winnicotts and not have to be this special treatment Winnicott invented by you" (p. 191). Very clearly expressed here is the view that a satisfactory ending necessarily involves, along with regret and sorrow sentiments of riddance and relief, sentiments that have to be acknowledged on the part of both patient and analyst.

This foregoing precis of the sessions is inevitably subjective and selective. So before coming to the next part of this essay, to my general review of the material and of Winnicott's handling of it, I recommend the reader now to read the text of *The Piggle* from beginning to end, in order to ensure the proper sense of "clinical dialogue" that Winnicott so desired to engage in with his readers.

PART II: DISCUSSION AND CRITIQUE

If I could think to you without words, you would understand me better
—Samuel Butler, *Life and Habit*, 1877

Discussion

In any critical assessment of *The Piggle*, it is worth stating at the outset that the treatment had an undoubtedly beneficial effect. The second is that as a process it was complete in a way that Klein's (1961) analysis of Richard and McDougall's (1960) of Sammy were not. Of course, these bald statements require some qualification. Gabrielle was only five when the treatment ended. It was therefore impossible to forecast what vicissitudes lay ahead of her in life, and how she would deal with these. Nevertheless, as her parents reported, she had "regained her poise", and her resilience was still evident nine years later at the time her mother wrote the postscript to the published account. These can reasonably be taken for signs of the success of this analysis. As to its completeness, Winnicott declared in his introduction: "It is doubtful … whether a child analysis ought to be thought of as complete when the patient is so young and the developmental processes simply take over as the analysis begins to succeed" (1977, p. 2). Of course, a claim such as the above raises a subsidiary question: might the same positive transformation have occurred naturally anyhow, without Winnicott's intervention? In answer to those who may be inclined to think that this analytic treatment was unnecessary, one can only say that the parents were convinced that without his intervention Gabrielle would have become seriously ill, and Winnicott shared that view. Furthermore, they retained their belief in the necessity of the treatment and of the "on demand" way in which it was carried out, despite being seriously perplexed over what was happening to their daughter at various points along the way, as well as being perturbed by the fact that Winnicott was not always available for Gabrielle when she most needed to see him.

As to the necessity of analytic treatment, Winnicott's view is clear. Analysis is required when "at first illness dominates the scene", but "As the child begins to get free from the pattern of rigid defence organisation that constitutes the illness, it becomes difficult to distinguish between the work done in treatment and the maturational processes' (p. 2). Implicit here is Winnicott's response to those child analysts convinced of the paramount efficacy of full analysis. Among these, Winnicott had counted himself in earlier days:

> In the decade called the thirties I was learning to be a psychoanalyst, and I could feel that, with a little more training, a little more skill, and a little more luck, I could move mountains by making the right interpretation at the right moment … At one time I could have been heard saying that there is no therapy except on the basis of fifty minutes five times a week, going on for as many years as necessary, and done by a trained psychoanalyst. (1970, p. 220)

Klein was foremost among those who continued to believe this. Yet this conviction was widespread in the 1960s and 1970s, not just among her followers, but among those who were trained in child analysis by Anna Freud at her Hampstead Clinic and who joined the ranks of the Association of Child Psychotherapists during its earlier years. The Freudian group might not have shared Klein's belief that there was no essential difference between adult and child analysis, but they did subscribe to the view that five-times-a-week analysis was optimal. With the case of *The Piggle* Winnicott was demonstrating that analytic treatment could be "intensive" without it being an almost daily regimen, and without it having to last for several years.

However, even if one grants that Winnicott makes a persuasive argument for less frequent sessions for children such as Gabrielle, does he make an equally convincing case for a policy of "treatment on demand"? Here, I believe, the evidence is inconclusive. In the first place, one has to consider the term itself: what does "on demand" really mean in practice? Obviously, it is impossible for the analyst to be available with the absolute regularity and predictability that the term implies. For an adult patient the practical limitations implicit in such an "on demand" commitment are likely to be recognised from the outset. But this recognition cannot be taken for granted in the case of a small child, who is inclined to understand the meaning of "on demand" without qualification, and conclude that the analyst is being dishonest if he does not do exactly as he promised. And there is a further consideration to be faced. In the case of a child as young as Gabrielle, is it really possible to distinguish between her own wish to see Winnicott (or her wish not to see him) and the wishes of the parents for her to be seen? Between the expression of the wish and its realisation there is bound to be a gap. The adult patient is able to negotiate with the analyst over how long that gap will be, and therefore to some extent is able to feel in control of events. The small child is not able to do so. However, the most serious argument against describing Gabrielle's treatment as having been "analysis on demand" is that it palpably wasn't always so. There are at least two instances where Gabrielle indicated that she wanted urgently to see Winnicott and yet this did not happen due to his unavailability. On the first occasion, between the fifth and sixth sessions (1977, p. 72), the parents deflected her wish, and on the second (between the eleventh and twelfth sessions), Winnicott told the parents (p. 145) that they would have to wait two months for the next session (in fact it was almost three). As the parents declared, when the child's demand is not met, "there can be very violent repercussions, with inner disaster only very narrowly avoided" (p. 200).

Certainly there may be an argument to be made for adjusting the frequency and timing of sessions to the variable needs of the child patient rather than appearing to prescribe them according to the demand of the doctor, at least in the case of a child with as much natural resources as Gabrielle possessed. But the same positive effect might be achieved by providing a regular session time each month in the knowledge that this could be taken up or passed over at the behest of the child, and also that the child could request an extra session between times. This sort of arrangement might have lessened the sense of the sessions being arranged as though on Winnicott's terms rather than her own or the family's, a sense which Gabrielle gave expression to frequently when she mentioned the length of the journey up to London, and the difficulties she and her father sometimes encountered on the way ("I like you to be near us" p. 68). Above all, it would have given her a sense of entitlement, rather than of being beholden to him. As Winnicott well knew, the dependability of the analyst is always preferable to dependence on the analyst. Yet in the case of *The Piggle* it seems that the latter was fostered more than the former.

I turn now to a consideration of Winnicott's technique within the sessions themselves. After repeated reading of Winnicott's account of the sessions I have come to the conclusion that most of what would usually be called his "deep interpretations", wherein he attributes specific unconscious determinants of an aggressive or sexual sort to speech or actions of the child in the presence of the analyst that seem at variance with their manifest content or conscious intention, these are either not assented to by Gabrielle, or prompt her to diversionary activity. Such resistance takes the form, in the early sessions, of going in search of her father and asking to go home, or else (as in session nine) of withdrawal into solitary play or self-communing in a state of what Winnicott called "quarantine".

Clearly, Winnicott felt that such interpretations, which I have characterised as "commotional", were necessary and effective, and that Gabrielle's aversive reactions, so far from calling them into question, showed their pertinence. However, the view that such interpretations were both correct in themselves and appropriately made can only be sustained on the basis of two further premises: first, that the increased anxiety manifested by the patient after they had been made is indicative of their validity, rather than the opposite; second, that these interventions demonstrably lead to, and are responsible for, observable clinical improvement. The first of these premises was the counter-intuitive view about the validity of symbolic interpretations propounded by Klein, and to some extent endorsed by Winnicott. It was counter-intuitive because the natural conclusion to draw from the child's resistance is, surely, that they were felt by her as being false, or meaningless, or as having no application to her. Given the palpable increase in anxiety and/or avoidance behaviour following them, the position adopted by Winnicott appears to fall foul of the "verifiability principle", inasmuch as, once the relevance of the patient's resistance to an interpretation is discounted as a confirmatory sign, it is hard to find an agreed criterion for determining whether a given interpretation is true or false—unless, that is, one accepts the second premise mentioned above (and overlooks the circularity of the argument in doing so). Then one would be claiming in effect that the only plausible explanation for Gabrielle's improvement over the course of her treatment was that the interpretations Winnicott conveyed to her, of all sorts, but including crucially these "commotional interpretations", were responsible for the positive changes that were brought about, after making due allowance for concomitant maturational processes. Doubtless Winnicott would have preferred a less categorical claim to be made about the effectiveness of his interventions but, heuristically, this alone seems capable of justifying such statements to the reader as the following: "I felt quite safe in making this interpretation. At one level this must be true" (p. 12). Why, in his eyes, must such an interpretation be true? To understand this we must examine his overall standpoint (or at least an essential part of it). The essence of Winnicott's clinical diagnosis of Gabrielle's "descent into illness" (or "no longer being herself" as the parents put it) comprises five principal elements:

1. The birth of her baby sister was a significant shock for her because the effect of Susan's arrival on the scene was to displace her from the position of being "mother's baby" while at the same time feeling herself as exempt from any active part in bringing the baby to birth.

The conjunction of the magnitude of the effect and her total inoperancy in the process was what rendered the event traumatic for her.

2. As a result of this shock, feelings of envy were aroused towards the
   mother for her "baby-making" capacity, while concomitant anger
   threatened further to estrange her from the mother's love.

3. Anger associated with envy and the simultaneous desire not to be
   estranged led to a split in her internal image of her mother, and with
   this split there emerged two separate figures, a "good mummy" and a
   "black mummy" (or "babacar").

4. These feelings also fuelled her wish to have a baby of her own, which
   was to be conceived by ingesting and to be born by excretion. These
   fantasies were configured around the primary areas of sensory excitement at the stage of development she had reached at the time they
   were at their height.

5. As the father was felt to be implicated in the coming to birth of
   her baby sister, but was not the object of the same intense envious
   feelings, her desire for a baby of her own, along with rivalry of the
   mother, fostered in her (or intensified) the wish to have a baby from
   father too.

The interpretive aspect of Winnicott's analytic endeavour focused on
the progressive articulation of these themes, and the slow resolution of
their inherent conflicts, first through insight-giving and then through
Gabrielle's acceptance of her separate identity as a child, no longer a
baby (as desired) or a not-[wanted]-baby (as feared). Her final letting
go in the transference of the subjective Winnicott-as-therapist and her
objective recognition of him as friend and playmate (albeit generation-
ally apart from her and nearer to dying), both mirrored and facilitated
her oedipal, age-appropriate resolution of conflicts vis-à-vis the parents
following the birth of her sister.

I should perhaps declare my own position here. I do not believe that
the above account properly reflects Gabrielle's predicament and its resolution (as will doubtless have become evident in the course of my summary of the sessions). Equally, I feel sure that Winnicott would have
felt that the transference expressions of aggressive and sexual feelings
that found their outlet in the seventh session and especially between the

tenth and twelfth sessions, confirmed the reality of her oedipal feelings and justified his direct and sometimes forceful interpretation of them as regards both content and timing. Since my concern at this stage is to outline and evaluate Winnicott's analysis of the Piggle as it actually occurred, rather than as it might have done, for the present I shall not dwell on a possible alternative way of understanding the material, but confine myself to examining that of Winnicott on his own terms.

Intrinsic to the framework of psychoanalytic theory enclosing Winnicott's clinical diagnosis is a central tenet that harks back to the dawn of psychoanalysis. It is this. Insofar as an infant or small child such as Gabrielle is vested with instinctual impulses, these impulses are to be treated as both *agentive* and *intentional*. That is to say, it is appropriate to say of instinctual behaviour expressive of such impulses: "She wants so and so," or "She is acting like this in order to obtain that." The behaviour is meaningful and aim-directed, not just for the external observer, but also for its source and agency, namely the child. Even if the term "unconscious" is used to qualify the meaningfulness of the behaviour for the doer, this does not detract from the act's intentionality. Unconscious aggression is no less aim-directed than conscious aggression. It can be seen, incidentally, that Gabrielle's parents shared this frame of reference. In their "Afterword" they wrote: "It has been of great value to the parents to be allowed to participate in a process of growth and reparation" (p. 199). "Repair" implies something being done *to* one; "reparation" implies something being done *by* one. Was Gabrielle repaired as a consequence of the treatment, or was she enabled to make reparation for her envious and aggressive attacks (some of which of course were deflected onto herself)? My view is that she was, and felt herself to be, repaired (in part, self-repaired), and that Winnicott came to understand this in the course of treating her (as when he repeatedly refers in the penultimate session to "mending"). The crucial difference between repair and reparation, I believe, is one of the things that Winnicott learnt intuitively from this particular encounter, but conceptually it remained problematic for him.

Let me elaborate this last point. We all comprehend the practical difference between doing and being done to, or in logical terms, between agency and patiency (even if the latter word is not as familiar to us as the former). Much less readily comprehensible is an equivalent disjunction in respect of mental events, events such as having a thought, being struck by an idea, or being overcome with an emotion. Those thoughts or ideas that come to us we typically own as ours: we have them. Those sentiments or emotions that come upon us we do not own in the same way: they overtake us.

In a paper on the technique of child analysis written a couple of years before he began treating Gabrielle, Winnicott wrote: "What matters to the patient is not the accuracy of the interpretation but the analyst's capacity to identify with the patient and so to believe in what is needed and to meet the need as soon as the need is indicated verbally or in non-verbal or preverbal language" (1962, p. 122).

Gabrielle indicated her initial need: she had come about "the baba-car", and Winnicott very clearly represented to her that this was to be his focus too: he wanted them to find out together what it was that was bothering her so much. As I indicated earlier when comparing their initial communications around "the babacar", there was from the outset a noticeable difference in perspective: Winnicott assumed that the babacar was a persecuting object, or person, whereas Gabrielle seemed to imply something more indeterminate, that it was possibly a place, or a state.

However, in the same paper from which I have quoted the passage above, Winnicott went on to refer to a boy patient who said something that felt important enough for him to underline in the text. The boy had said to Winnicott: "But you don't understand, it's not the nightmare I'm frightened of; the trouble is that *I'm having a nightmare while I'm awake*" (ibid., p. 120). The boy in question was ten years old, and able to articulate his predicament in a way that the two-and-a-half-year-old Gabrielle was not yet capable of. But her predicament over the nightmare figure of "the babacar" was, I suspect, of the same order. What is so bad for a ten-year-old about having a nightmare in the daytime rather than at night? It is because in the daytime your thoughts are, or should be, your own, whereas at night thoughts and images just occur to you; you don't "have" them in the same way. Dreams "have" you, whereas you have thoughts or indulge in fantasies, memories, or daydreams. So what the boy was attempting to convey was that he (or his mind) was taken over by the nightmare in the daytime in a way that would be normal only if it happened when he was asleep. So the really frightening thing for him was that this was happening to his waking mind. This power to take over his mind was much more frightening than the actual content of the nightmare, because he was being constrained to react to impressions as veridical which he knew at the same time were counterfactual.

Something similar to this is what Gabrielle needed Winnicott to understand in relation to her "babacar"—that she knew that it was not real, but it felt real. Moreover, its felt presence was compelling and its visitations involuntary. I think that it was only in the ninth session, a year after her first visit, that Winnicott was able to realise and articulate her actual predicament and why it was so persecuting:

> I talked about the black mummy as a dream, trying to make it
> quite clear to Gabrielle that the black mummy belongs to dream-
> ing and that upon waking there are the contrasting ideas of the
> black mummy and real people. The time had come when we
> could talk about dreams instead of an inner reality, delusionally
> "active" inside. (1977, p. 116)

However, there was one important difference between the experience of the ten-year-old boy and Gabrielle. He had reached the stage developmentally of "having a mind of his own", so that the daytime nightmare experience was regressive, causing him to feel as if he were going mad, whereas he had previously felt himself to be ordinarily sane. Gabrielle, however, was just on the way to achieving this stage of "having a mind of her own" when thoughts about the babacar began to assail her following her sister's birth. She was not preoccupied so much with madness as with badness, badness brought about through contamination. The boy knew that what he was experiencing was a dream, and not real. Gabrielle as a two-year-old could not be sure of this, since any thoughts she had were likely to be felt as adventitious, rather than as generated internally: objective and subjective were not yet clearly differentiated. Consequently it was the very invasiveness of the bad thoughts about the bad babacar that made them so overwhelming. She wasn't "having bad thoughts" arising in spite of herself from within, thoughts that made her feel bad and guilty for having them (depressive). Instead she was being attacked by thoughts that seemed alien to her, unwanted, to be disavowed. But she could not locate them as a nightmare, not even as a nightmare occurring to her in the daytime. Kleinian theory postulated that these thoughts were internally instigated, and felt to be external only because of the operation of early schizoid mechanisms, in particular projection. What Gabrielle's experience, as reported by Winnicott, seems to demonstrate rather is that they were introjected as alien and invasive. As such, they occasioned depersonalising anxiety: she no longer felt herself to be the self she was on the way to becoming before their onset.

By the time she had reached the age of three and a half, at the point when in the ninth session Winnicott made the enlightening interpretation mentioned above, Gabrielle was becoming capable of distinguishing inner and outer more securely in spite of the preoccupying "babacar" and "black mummy" ("I have paid the black mummy"). She had come to understand that objects change their appearance, and persons change their "feel", depending on setting, sentiment, or circumstance, but they don't become different objects as a result. Aiding this growing recognition in the face of the persecuting anxieties assailing her was another of Winnicott's "spontaneous gestures"—one person might describe it as a stroke of genius, another as a flash of ingenuity, another as an act of lunacy. It occurred towards the end of the second session, when he began to enact the role of the greedy baby, a sight that both fascinated and frightened her. The vital factor at that moment was that Winnicott was *pretending* to be the baby—pretending in the sense of making-believe. Winnicott intuitively knew that Gabrielle would not mistake himself for the actual Susan whose role he was then assuming; she would know that he was only acting *as if* he was the baby. In the case of the "black mummy" and the "babacar", however, she had been incapable of seeing them as only pretend figures; they were real. She "pre-intended" them. By virtue of his idiosyncratic behaviour Winnicott revealed the possibility of *pretending*. The small child does not begin by having ideas of or about the actual, and then pretending or fantasying about them. Such ideas are (from an adult perspective) delusional before they become illusory. Actual pretending gave Gabrielle the possibility of enabling her to *un*believe her fantasy objects so that she could begin to explore the playful possibilities of "make-believe" based on normal pretence.

What seems to be especially instructive about this episode is that the act of pretending on Winnicott's part was much more "mutative" for Gabrielle than was the content of the pretence itself. Winnicott was set on enacting the greediness of the baby, as if it were paramount to demonstrate this quality of baby-ness as an expression both of her new rival's disposition and of her own. Gabrielle just wanted to follow him in acting the baby, greedy or not. In short, Winnicott fastens on the intending, but Gabrielle on the pretending. This difference of perspective persists throughout, but is ultimately liberating. She spends much of the subsequent sessions pretending in his presence, with Winnicott often not sure what the pretence is really about—as when she puts an axle in her mouth in the third session. In the seventh session Gabrielle says: "I used to be used to you" (p. 93). The conjunction of "I" with repeated "you" in this sentence is perhaps indicative of a passing sense of merger with Winnicott (or rather, a threat of merger) in the way she had previously felt merged, taken over, by the "black mummy". I believe that Winnicott's precipitate verbalisation of "commotional interpretations" in the early sessions may have contributed to this sense of potential merger. However, thanks to his enabling use of pretence in the second session this danger was averted and she was considerably more resilient—and resourceful—in the face of his verbal onslaughts subsequently. Almost paradoxically, as her separate identity became established, so his interpretive narrative woven around the classical analytic themes of childhood desire, rivalry, and envy of the parents took on the semblance of a make-believe system that she could treat as Winnicott's own, antithetic to the belief system that had once been so internally persecuting of her, but which she could now own in memory form as if from the outside, thanks to him.

Concluding critique

I have suggested that the case of *The Piggle* asked questions of Winnicott himself, about his technique, about interpretation, and ultimately about the nature of the therapeutic process itself. To some of these questions he had ready answers and wanted to communicate these to his colleagues through publishing the case. Foremost among these was that on the evidence presented here, an analysis could be intensive without being extensive—at least in respect of children. Indeed, extensive analysis might even be detrimental for a child, interfering with normal maturational processes. Almost as important a lesson to be drawn was about the importance of playing for the process of "working through" internal conflicts, with the important rider that in child analysis play has to be enjoyed for itself, not seen simply as providing matter for the "proper" analytic work of interpretation. Moreover, the child must sense that the therapist not only respects the value of child's play but actually entertains it; and the same applies to the child's conversation.

To some other questions raised by his treatment of Gabrielle, I believe Winnicott had answers at the intuitive level which were not fully worked out conceptually. In particular, he recognised that Gabrielle's anxieties over the "babacar" and the "black mummy" were invasive, that they derived their strength from being what in adult terms would be called delusional, without, however, overrunning her mental capacities to the extent of rendering her psychotic. This recognition led him creatively to seize on the option of "make-believe" play quite early on in the treatment, and this at a critical point when Gabrielle seemingly was beginning to doubt the parents' reassurances that Dr Winnicott was the person who could really help her. Subsequently Winnicott made a series of helpful "conjunctive interpretations" on the subject of the differences between appearance and reality. Later still, and after the treatment was ended, these insights perhaps fed into Winnicott's further reflections on the difference between "subjective objects" and "objects objectively perceived" and about the importance of "the intermediate area of experience" of play and culture. However, I think this whole topic of the balance between play and interpretation remained partially unresolved in *The Piggle*, no doubt being one of those matters intended "for discussion" and a reason for disseminating the case history.

One reason that this technical question remained unresolved, I believe, is that Winnicott had embarked on the treatment of Gabrielle firmly convinced of the efficacy of what I have termed "commotional interpretations" and committed to the traditional psychoanalytic acceptation of unconscious dispositions as being intentional and agentive. He persevered in this belief and frame of reference despite the treatment of Gabrielle appearing to demonstrate the disruptiveness of the one and the inexactitude of the other. Of course, Winnicott might reasonably point to the material surfacing in the course of the tenth, eleventh, and twelfth sessions both as proof of the reality of Gabrielle's oedipal conflicts and as evidence that her behaviour strongly indicated her active desire to have a baby of her own, thereby justifying the bold way that he had interpreted from the outset. Against this, however, it should be noted that the sexually demonstrative behaviour Gabrielle exhibited at this stage of the treatment did not carry over into the last sessions, and that she herself never acknowledged a wish to *have* a baby, at least not while still a child: "We are going to have boy when we are grown up. Me and Susan. We have to find a Daddy man to marry" (1977, p. 117). What she avowed was a wish, or expectation, that there *should be* another baby: "I would like a new baby who doesn't come near me and take my things away" (p. 100). Is there an alternative way of understanding this display of sexualised behaviour and interest without having recourse to Winnicott's "oedipal" interpretation? I believe that there is. The alternative that I propose posits two determining factors. The first of these factors is time specific, the other arises out of the ongoing transference/countertransference relationship between them. I shall deal with each of these aspects in turn.

In a letter from the mother written a few days before the eleventh session she tells Winnicott about Gabrielle: "Of late there has been continuous talk and speculation about babies" (p. 134). This report followed on an earlier communication in which she had detailed some of her daughter's recurrent anatomical questions about fathers and mothers, and noted how these had been followed up with a question about *Dr* Winnicott:

> G: Does he make people better?
> M: Doesn't he make you better?
> G: No, he just talks to me (p. 133).

Setting this preoccupation in a temporal context, it is important to bear in mind that by the time this exchange took place Gabrielle was three years eight months old, and her sister was nearly two years. This means that Susan was now around the same age as Gabrielle had been when her baby sister had arrived on the scene and displaced her from the secure role she had previously occupied, that of being "the baby in the family". Now, in the sessions immediately preceding the eleventh there had been much mention by Gabrielle of Susan's growing up and of her becoming a child in her own right, including "terribly wanting to go to Mr. Winnicott" (p. 126). Meanwhile, as her mother reported (p. 132), she was graduating to "big girl" status through beginning to attend nursery school. The problem for Gabrielle, I suggest, was the following: if she was now the "big" sister and Susan the "small" sister, rather than herself being "the Piggle" and Susan the baby, who or where was the baby now? This may at first sight seem an unlikely question for Gabrielle to entertain in the absence of any evidence that her mother was pregnant or intended to have another baby. However, there was an additional reason, I believe, why it constituted a particular issue for her at this juncture. I have suggested that the earlier transition towards conceiving of herself as a little girl, indeed as still having a place once she had been displaced as a baby by Susan's arrival, had presented her with a special challenge emotionally and conceptually, one that had led her frequently to merge with her sister and submerge her own identity. So, if this had represented such a challenge for herself, should it not also present one for her sister now that she had reached an equivalent age and stage? Yet in order for it to be a comparable challenge for Susan (one that might require her, too, to come to Dr Winnicott for sorting out), there needed to be a newcomer baby. In short, a baby was required in order to occupy a vacant role, but also maybe so as to put her sister on her mettle.

Such a reading of Gabrielle's state of mind at the start of this session is bound to be conjectural. Yet, a degree of credibility is lent to it by the following vignette:

> *Gabrielle*: Susan can't say: "All gone", so she says: "Dad all don." She's silly.
> *Winnicott*: You were two once, and now you are four.
> *Gabrielle*: No, three and three quarters. I'm not quite four.
> *Winnicott*: Do you want to be four?
> *Gabrielle*: Yes. Haha.
> She then sang, while playing with a broken circular object. Pat-a-cake, pat-a-cake, Baker's man, Bake me a cake as fast as you can.
> *Winnicott*: What's the hurry?
> *Gabrielle*: Well it has to be ready before night-time when everyone is in bed. Pull it and pat and make it with p. Put in the oven for Susan and me. (pp. 137–138)

Winnicott, of course, had a different understanding of what Gabrielle was conveying at this juncture. He interpreted the material in terms of Gabrielle's wish to have a baby of her own, in accordance with his overall understanding of her having now reached an oedipal stage. Insofar as Gabrielle does indeed want to have a baby, in the sense of wanting there to be another baby, there is an element in his response that is consistent with what I take to be Gabrielle's primary interest. And she clearly recognises that in Winnicott she has a grown-up who is fully alive to, indeed seems to share, her current interest and preoccupation with the subject of babies and their coming into being. In this respect they are kindred spirits. Nevertheless I also feel that Winnicott's insistence on her supposed wish for becoming a mummy with a baby of her own, when, as I believe, this did not correspond with her actual state of mind, may have been responsible for a distortion of the transference and may have led directly to her displaying more sexualised behaviour in his presence.

My reason for thinking so is this. If what I have outlined above reflects, in part at least, Gabrielle's actual state of mind at this time, then Winnicott's explicit interpretations of sexualised fantasies could well have seemed suggestive to her, not so much of what she *might* be feeling, as of what she *ought* to be feeling. I am simply saying that Winnicott's interpretations may have appeared suggestive to her. I am not saying that they were, or were felt by her to be, seductive. After some initial uncertainty, her trust in *Dr* Winnicott's mending capacity was total. As for *Mr* Winnicott, there is no doubt that the transference bond between them was strong, and that Gabrielle experienced this as something mutual, but also as something tantalising. This seems to be implied by her response to her being told by her mother, between the eleventh and twelfth sessions, that Winnicott would not be able to see her again for two months in spite of being asked to do so: "I don't think he likes anybody as much as me" (p. 147). The pathos behind this remark is palpable, but so is the perplexity: am I loved, or just deluded? For Gabrielle, as for any four year old, it is being loved, not loving, that is all important. The distortion that crept into the transference relationship, I suggest, through Winnicott's over-insistent interpretations, especially when coupled with the occasional delays in seeing her when she had requested a session, is that it was capable of raising the question in her mind, not of whether he liked (loved) her, but why did he? And what was he demanding of her?

As the parents later attested (p. 200), the actual gap of four months in the treatment at this juncture, not of two, could have been, and nearly was, calamitous. In the event, however, it proved to be a providential, if painful, intermission—an instance of the analyst succeeding "by failing, failing the patient's way" (Winnicott, 1962). Gabrielle seems to have concluded that Winnicott could do without her—he might even be dying—so she should learn to do without him too. Consequently, when the sessions resumed Winnicott encountered a much more independent and resilient five-year-old girl. Perhaps the fact that no new baby had arrived, and that there was no Winnicott to see and be seen by, prompted in her a realisation of the difference between the imaginary and the real, subjective apperception and objective perception, a process of necessary disillusionment of a sort which Winnicott was later to discuss in his paper "On the Use of an Object" (1968). She wasn't the Piggle. She was Gabrielle. And while she could not yet quite do without him altogether—there was the last phase of "riddance" to be gone through first—Winnicott was no longer the fantasy "daddy man". Instead he could become the enabling figure of an almost resolved transference, in the poet Peter Levi's memorable phrase, "*the unknown familiar, the never friend*" (Levi, 1973).

To what extent did Winnicott recognise this development, not just in her, but in him? In the paper already referred to, "On the Use of an Object"—incidentally written only two years after he had finished treating Gabrielle—he prefaced his remarks on the subject with the following declaration:

> [I]t is only in recent years that I have become able to wait and wait for the natural evolution of the transference arising out of the patient's growing trust ... and to avoid breaking up this natural process by making interpretations. It will be noticed that I am talking about the making of interpretations and not about interpretations as such ... If only we can wait, the patient arrives at understanding creatively and with immense joy, and I now enjoy this joy more than I used to enjoy the sense of having been clever. (1968)

And in an article of his, written about the same time, we find this:

> Therapy takes place in the overlap of two areas of playing, that
> of the patient and that of the therapist. Psychotherapy has to do
> with two people playing together. The corollary of this is that
> where playing is not possible then the work done by the therapist
> is directed towards bringing the patient from a state of not being
> able to play into a state of being able to play. (1971)

There is a testamentary, almost valedictory quality about these twin
statements. It is perhaps not too fanciful to see them as a belated "realisation" gained through his treatment of Gabrielle, and as incorporating
some of the insights that he had acquired, and wanted to communicate from their encounter, a shared playful experience in which each in
their own way had "made" the other (p. 190). That "making" ultimately
depended on leaving behind not only a relationship, but conceptions
and preconceptions in which each was invested and which each for different reasons needed to shed. Hers beset her as demons; his had been a
system of certainties that once lit his path as a child psychoanalyst like
a beacon, but no longer illuminated in the same way. For Gabrielle this
shedding was a part of growing up; for Winnicott, of "growing down-
wards", a process of "dwindling" that was "painful at first, till you get
used to it" (1970). Communicating this unspoken message that therapy
involved unlearning as much as learning, riddance as much as finding,
was perhaps Winnicott's latent purpose behind the desire to make *The
Piggle* available for "a useful discussion".

References

Butler, S. (1877). *Life and Habit*. London: Fifield.

Dockar-Drysdale, B. (1960). Contact, impact and impingement. In: *The Provision of Primary Experience*. London: Free Association.

Freud, S., & Breuer, J. (1895d). *Studies on Hysteria. S. E., 2*. London: Hogarth.

Geleerd, E. (1963). Evaluation of Melanie Klein's *Narrative of a Child Analysis*.
International Journal of Psychoanalysis, 44: 493–506.

Heimann, P. (1980). About children and children-no-longer. In: M. Tonnesmann
(Ed.), *About Children and Children-no-longer: Collected Papers*. London:
Routledge, 1989.

Isaacs-Elmhirst, S. (1996). Foreword. In: B. Kahr, *D. W. Winnicott: A Biographical Portrait*. London: Karnac.

Klein, M. (1961). *Narrative of a Child Analysis*. London: Hogarth.

Levi, P. (1973). A Good Friday sermon. In: *Collected Poems*. London: Anvil.

McDougall, J., & Lebovici, S. (1960). *Un cas de psychose infantile*. Paris: Presses Universitaires. Translated as *Dialogue with Sammy: Psychoanalytical Contribution to the Understanding of Child Psychosis*. London: Free Association, 1989.

Nussbaum, M. (2003). Dr. True Self: Review of F. Robert Rodman: *Winnicott: Life and Work*. In: *Philosophical Interventions: Reviews 1986–2011*. Oxford: Oxford University Press, 2012.

Reeves, A. C. (2007). The mantle of Freud: Was "The Use of an Object" Winnicott's *Todestrieb? British Journal of Psychotherapy*, 23: 365–382.

Reeves, A. C. (2012). On the margins: The role of the father in Winnicott's writings. In: J. Abram (Ed.), *Winnicott Today*. London: Routledge.

Segal, H., & Meltzer, D. (1963). Evaluation of Melanie Klein's *Narrative of a Child Analysis*. *International Journal of Psychoanalysis*, 44: 507–513.

Winnicott, C. (1962). Casework and agency function. In: *Child Care and Social Work*. Hitchin, UK: Codicote, 1964.

Winnicott, D. W. (1947). Hate in the countertransference. In: *Collected Papers: Through Paediatrics to Psycho-Analysis*. London: Tavistock, 1958.

Winnicott, D. W. (1958). Child analysis in the latency period. In: *The Maturational Processes and the Facilitating Environment*. London: Hogarth, 1965.

Winnicott, D. W. (1962). The aims of psycho-analytic treatment. In: *The Maturational Processes and the Facilitating Environment*. London: Hogarth, 1965.

Winnicott, D. W. (1968). On the use of an object. In: *Playing and Reality*. London: Tavistock, 1971.

Winnicott, D. W. (1969). Preface. In: J. McDougall & S. Leibovici, *Dialogue with Sammy* (English translation of Winnicott [1962] above). London: Hogarth.

Winnicott, D. W. (1970). Residential care as therapy. In: C. Winnicott, R. Shepherd, & M. Davis (Eds), *Deprivation and Delinquency*. London: Routledge, 1984.

Winnicott, D. W. (1971). *Playing and Reality*. London: Tavistock.

Winnicott, D. W. (1977). *The Piggle*. London: Hogarth.

CHAPTER FOUR

The Piggle: rivalrous or bereft?

Corinne Masur

In his book, *The Piggle*, Donald Winnicott revealed his ideas regarding the origin of a little girl's symptoms and fantasies through his interpretations to her and through his margin notes. Largely oedipal in derivation, Winnicott's interpretations eloquently disentangled the Piggle's feelings of terror, anger, anxiety, rivalry, jealousy, and omnipotence. But what of her more conscious affect, sadness? Winnicott largely ignored this powerful feeling.

Donald Winnicott saw Gabrielle, as his young patient was actually named, as a little girl overwhelmed by feelings related to her jealousy of both her mother and her newborn sister. He suggested that Gabrielle resented her mother because her mother was loved more by her father than was Gabrielle herself, she resented her father for loving her mother more, and she resented her little sister for taking possession of their mother's breasts and attentions after her birth when Gabrielle was twenty-one months old.

But, as is often the case with patient material, there are a variety of ways to interpret its meaning. Indeed, it is fascinating to contemplate some of the possibilities which were not prioritised by Dr Winnicott as well as to wonder why he did not consider them more fully. In this chapter the derivation of Winnicott's interpretations of Gabrielle's play material is examined. Specifically, the question is posed as to how it was that Winnicott did not conceptualise the case around another salient aspect of Gabielle's history—one which was not emphasised—in fact, which was not initially mentioned by Winnicott at all.

There was an assumption made from the start of Gabrielle's treatment. Her parents began by writing Winnicott a letter in which they told him that they had been quite anxious about how Gabrielle would react to the birth of their second child and to the subsequent presence of the baby. They said that they felt that Gabrielle was too young to have a sibling at that time. And, after their baby was born, they believed that their worst fears were proven true and that Gabrielle did change. Gabrielle was described by her mother as becoming briefly distressed and jealous after her sister came home and later as listless and "not herself". She experienced sleep difficulties, night-time fears, self-destructive behaviours, and vivid fantasies. Mother also noted that Gabrielle toilet-trained herself within a week at this time.

The parents' description of Gabrielle's history left out an enormous aspect of Gabrielle's experience. Their assumption was that her symptomatology resulted from the birth of their second child and ignored other possible origins for Gabrielle's troubles. What neither they nor Winnicott mentioned was the fact that Gabrielle's mother left her for ten (or possibly more) days to deliver the baby and to recuperate afterwards.

A ten-day stay was common hospital practice for postpartum mothers and infants in the early 1960s in England. Perhaps, as such, this was not seen as significant. And yet, for parents who were as sensitive to their child's feelings as these parents were, it is most striking that this separation was not made more of either by them or by their new consultant, Dr Winnicott.

Even more surprising, at least to a current-day reader and/or practitioner, is the fact that Winnicott seemed to share the assumption that Gabrielle's difficulties originated from the appearance of her sister. He did not make meaning of Gabrielle's sadness and listlessness as recounted by her mother nor did he connect these affects to her experience of actual abandonment. Moreover, the timing of the emergence of Gabrielle's symptoms was left vague—both by the parents and by Winnicott. At what moment did they start? After mother left for the hospital? Immediately upon her return? A week or two later? Or prior to her departure? This is never stated.

In this chapter I intend to explore Gabrielle's material in search of reports from her parents as well as from her play and fantasy material which could indicate feelings of sadness, loss, mourning, and anger related to having been abandoned by her mother. Moreover, I speculate—because that is all it will be—on possible meanings for this omission in Winnicott's understanding of his small patient, because while sadness over departures was mentioned in his sessions notes and in a couple of brief interpretations, it was done only glancingly.

Gabrielle's history and the history of her difficulties

Gabrielle was described by her parents as a person with "great inner resources" (Winnicott, 1977, p. 5). As an infant, she fed well and weaned well having been breastfed for nine months. She was coordinated and rarely fell down. When she did, she rarely cried. She was loved and protected as an infant, as indicated by the following, written by her mother, "We tried hard, I think successfully, to protect her from any impingements which would make her world too complicated" (p. 20). This statement is illustrative of how careful these parents were in regard to their firstborn and how aware they were of their infant's sensitivity and need for a stable, consistent, and loving early environment.

When Gabrielle was eleven and a half months old, her mother became pregnant for the second time. And when Gabrielle was twenty-one months old, her sister, Susan, was born. After the birth, Gabrielle was described by her mother as loving towards her father but "high handed" with her mother (p. 6). Her mother reported that after Susan's birth Gabrielle "ignored" her mother (p. 66). It was implied by the mother that this behaviour and attitude related to the baby's birth.

At some point, when exactly is not made clear, Gabrielle developed distressing symptoms including worries which kept her awake at night. It is notable that it was not mentioned whether Gabrielle suffered these fears, dreams, and fantasies during her mother's absence or only once mother returned. Gabrielle's relationship with her parents changed and she became bored and depressed (as mentioned above). She had "acute jealousy" of her sister after her sister's return from the hospital but, interestingly and importantly, the mother noted that this jealousy did "not last long" (p. 6).

At night Gabrielle called her parents frequently, being bothered by the following fantasies: she had a black mummy and daddy and the mummy would come at night and say, "Where are my yams?" (p. 6). Gabrielle would point to her own chest when saying this. She would also say that the black mummy lived in her tummy, could be talked to on the telephone there, and that the black mummy was ill and was hard to make better. Additionally, she had a fantasy about a "babacar" in which the black mummy and the black daddy and sometimes the black Piggle would be.

Winnicott recommended to the parents that Gabrielle see him "on demand". By this time he had largely given up seeing children in psychoanalysis in favour of seeing children in more limited consultations (Reeves, Chapter Three). However, it must be noted in regard to the on-demand schedule that in fact it was not on *her* demand—Gabrielle was not actually able to see Winnicott when she wanted to due to the family schedule and Dr Winnicott's schedule (Kahr, Chapter Two), and at times she came to see him when she did not want to.

Gabrielle's treatment

The sessions between Gabrielle and Winnicott began when Gabrielle was two years and five months old. With the exception of the very first session when mother was present in the room, and a number of sessions when father joined them at the end, Winnicott was able to see Gabrielle alone in his playroom. Her father sat in the waiting room for most of the sessions.

For the first session, Gabrielle said she was "too shy" (Winnicott, 1977, p. 9) to come in alone, thus her mother sat on the couch in the consulting room for five minutes. Winnicott instructed the mother "not to help at all" and she sat back on the couch with Gabrielle beside her. As a way to engage Gabrielle and without challenging her shy feelings, Winnicott suggested to Gabrielle that she bring the teddy bear which was sitting on the floor by his desk back to where he was sitting so that teddy could see the toys. She did so willingly and then began playing with the toys herself.

Winnicott's very first interpretation to Gabrielle regarded the birth of the "Sush baby" (her name for Susan, her sister). The initial play involved taking trucks and engines out of a toy box and saying "and another one and another one" (p. 10). Winnicott suggested to Gabrielle that this referred to "another baby, the Sush Baby" (p. 10). In his notes he wrote that he received confirmation that this was the correct thing to say as Gabrielle then began to recount the time the Sush baby came. (It is commonplace for psychoanalysts to judge the success of an interpretation by whether or not it is followed by useful material. Generally it is thought that a correct interpretation produces more material.)

A few moments later, Gabrielle began to play with a toy car and tried to put a man in the driver's seat. When she couldn't get him in she tried to push him in with a stick saying, "stick goes in" (p. 11). Winnicott then interpreted, "something about a man putting something inside a woman to make a baby" to which Gabrielle replied, "I've got a cat. Next time I'll bring the pussy cat, another day," and then went to see her mother in the waiting room.

Winnicott understood that at this moment Gabrielle felt frightened and he commented that this anxiety needed to be dealt with. He said, "You feel frightened. Do you have frightening dreams?" (p. 11). And she replied, "About the babacar" and then began to tidy up. Winnicott related this to making babies to which Gabrielle replied, "I must tidy up. Mustn't leave the place untidy." Winnicott asked, "Do you ever feel angry with mummy?" saying that he "linked up the idea of a black mummy with her rivalry with her mother because both of them were in love with the same man, daddy" (p. 12).

The above is a short example of Winnicott's interpretive style in the case of The Piggle. As stated, it can be seen that the interpretive content is Freudian/oedipal, relying heavily on the theory of infantile sexuality. Winnicott interpreted from the point of view of Freudian theory regarding the competitive strivings of the little girl towards her mother for the father's love and the common assumption of sibling rivalry for parental love. His technique (of direct interpretation of primitive material) was much like Melanie Klein's, who was his original inspiration for becoming a child analyst and his supervisor for a number of years. As Reeves (Chapter Three) noted, Klein held an unwavering conviction about the efficacy of interpreting "early and deep" the fantasy content of the child's play material irrespective of his (in this case, her) anxieties and resistances (Chapter Three). And as Reeves noted, Winnicott "endorsed Klein's practice of immediately interpreting the dominant anxiety along with its putative underlying fantasy" (Chapter Three).

We now know Winnicott as one of the psychoanalytic pioneers of understanding both the inner life of the pre-oedipal child and the importance and intricacies of the internal representations of the primary caregiver and the primary dyad (the mother–child relationship). And yet we can see in the above a slant towards the interpretation of triadic material, particularly the oedipal rivalry between mother and daughter for possession of the father and his love.

While sitting with Gabrielle as she played, Winnicott associated immediately to this. He linked Gabrielle's anger to her competition with her mother rather than to her feelings about her mother's abandonment of her during her ten day absence. He also made little of her change of subject from a man putting something in a lady to her cat, and he said nothing about her sudden desire to tidy up.

This is notable. To a current-day practitioner, Gabrielle's change of subject might have indicated an increase in anxiety. The idea that she was anxious would have been corroborated by her impulsive need to tidy things up. The tidying itself might have been interpreted as a desire to escape from primitive impulses, to clean them up, so to speak, to get away from the interpretive material or even to get away from Dr Winnicott and/or from the session itself in so far as cleaning up often precedes leave taking.

Gabrielle might well have felt anxious and scared by her own primitive fantasy material but she might also have been made anxious by Winnicott's interpretation regarding the "man putting something inside a woman". She might already have been experiencing some preoccupation with primitive sexual material related to her mother and father's relationship and the production of an infant and Winnicott may have perceived this and made his interpretation accordingly. However, it is also possible that Gabrielle's anxiety might have been stirred up by a memory of the terror she suffered following her mother's abrupt departure and long stay away. In this very session Gabrielle initially resisted separation from her mother. As a result, Winnicott allowed the mother to come into the playroom. But then when her mother left the room following her five minute stay, Gabrielle was again separated from her mother. Gabrielle might well have felt anxious about this and have been reminded of the longer separation which occurred at the time of her sister's birth. When Gabrielle began to talk about the birth of her sister in the session she might have associated to her mother's long absence just before the baby came home, thus causing her to want to find her mother in the waiting room, which she did go and do. But Winnicott did not see the mother's departure from the consulting room as salient, he did not interpret Gabrielle's need to go see her mother in the waiting room and, evidently, he did not see the mother's departure from the home for ten days as important in the genesis of Gabrielle's symptoms.

How was it that Winnicott did not recognise Gabrielle's many, many references—both direct and indirect—to anxiety and fear of separation in this session and throughout the treatment? And why did he rush immediately, in the very first moments of the first session, to the interpretation of oedipal themes and anxieties? Why not relate Gabrielle's initial anxiety to the fact that this was her first visit with a new person? And furthermore, when she tried to put the man doll into the driver's seat of the car, why not consider this a transference reference, related to Winnicott now being in the dominant position in their play session?

Reeves (Chapter Three) noted Winnicott's "apparent readiness ... to subordinate the demands of technique to the needs of the patient, whether child or adult". However, one must ask whether Winnicott was always able to subordinate the dictates of theory to the needs of his patient, in this case, Gabrielle. I agree with Reeves when he said, "Winnicott listens intently to her, but does not, I believe, always 'hear' her; or rather, does not always, as doctor analyst, light on those matters that seem to be uppermost in her mind at a conscious level (Chapter Three).

Winnicott continued to see Gabrielle for over two years. She must have felt very important—to be meeting with and speaking with and playing with a doctor, to be taking trips with Daddy into London, to be the centre of such intense interest and attention of not one but two men as well as her mother. Moreover, it is of course likely that much of Winnicott's way of understanding Gabrielle's play material and the interpretation of this understanding was of great use to Gabrielle in her recovery. However, it remains of interest to look at Winnicott's particular understanding of Gabrielle's material and to consider that other understandings such as those suggested above might have been as helpful to Gabrielle as those he provided—or at least additionally helpful.

Sadness and mourning in *The Piggle*

References to Gabrielle's sadness and mourning reactions are myriad from the beginning to the end of the case report. For example, in Winnicott's first interview with Gabrielle's mother, the mother reported that recently Gabrielle had started crying when her mother sang her a particular song which she had sung when Gabrielle was a baby. She also reported that at other times Gabrielle would have tears in her eyes while listening to someone hum the song and at still other times Gabrielle would yell for her parents to "STOP" singing the song. The mother also reported that Gabrielle had periods of time during which she "tended to lie in her cot and suck her thumb without playing" (Winnicott, 1977, p. 14).

The fact that Gabrielle cried in reaction to a song from her babyhood obviously indicated that something about the song made her feel upset. It is mentioned in a footnote (p. 13) that the song was about a leave taking and originally sung in German but altered by the parents to English to include the words, "… and the mummy and the daddy will be here". They note that they changed the words—but it is not entirely clear whether this was in reaction to Gabrielle's upset. Upon hearing the words, "and the mummy and the daddy will be here", might Gabrielle's sadness and/or demand that the song be stopped have resulted from the memory which that song provoked of what it was like when her mummy was *not* there during her time in the hospital? This would certainly explain the tears in her eyes and her cries to stop the song. The song delivered a promise which had been grievously broken! And yet no one connected the words of the song and Gabrielle's upset over hearing them to the fact that she had lost her mother for at least ten long days—that her mummy had indeed *not* been there—and then she had lost her mother again, in a different way, when her mother and baby sister arrived home.

Indeed, after the second consultation with Winnicott, Gabrielle woke up one morning in a rage, then retreated to her carrycot, then got inside mother's dressing gown and asked about being born. The mother told her "how she came out" (p. 35) and how she was wrapped in a towel and then Gabrielle said, "And you dropped me" (p. 35). The mother said she had not and Gabrielle said, "Yes you did. The towel was made dirty" (p. 35). So here it is: from almost the beginning of being seen in treatment, Gabrielle let it be known that she felt "dropped" by her mother.

Moreover, once home from the hospital Gabrielle experienced a mother who was different from the mother who left to give birth. Prior to Susan's arrival Gabrielle had been her mother's main focus of attention. Was Gabrielle sad when she heard this song, both remembering the time when she was without her mummy AND realising how much her life had changed since she was that little infant listening to the same song before her mother left for the hospital? Did the song make her sad because she had missed hearing it while her mother was gone? Or could her crying have related to having recently lost her mother's focus? This is all quite speculative. However, the description of Gabrielle lying listlessly in her cot is certainly evocative of sadness and possibly of depression. And her accusation that her mother dropped her speaks to her sense of having been mishandled or having dropped from mother's attention.

To those familiar with the study of depressed toddlers and/or those toddlers who have experienced the loss of the primary object, this reaction is typical (Bowlby, 1960; Furman, 1974; Robertson & Robertson, 1971, 1989). As the Robertsons say in their book, *Separation and the Very Young* (1989), children of two years of age separated from their mothers for ten to twenty-seven days are often anxious, angry, or upset (p. 97). And, as Bowlby (1973) noted, after a toddler has gone without seeing his or her mother for a day or more his/her active protests and anger at the mother's absence often subside into resignation and depression. Gabrielle's feelings of sadness (and possibly of the helplessness and hopelessness which accompany loss) are painfully expressed in the description of her crying and lying in her cot and sucking her thumb without playing following her sister's birth and prior to her treatment with Winnicott.

Furthermore, following the first session, Gabrielle lay in her cot and took "innumerable bottles" (Winnicott, 1977, p. 14), something she had not done before. She declared herself to either be the baby or the mummy but *not* the Piggle as the Piggle was "bad and black" (p. 14). She was also described as lying in bed and crying without knowing why (p. 15). Again, these details provide the picture of a very sad, and possibly depressed little girl who alternately regressed and progressed as ways to escape her current suffering.

Throughout the course of her treatment, Gabrielle and her parents made reference to her very sad feelings and her episodic despondency and lack of energy. But Winnicott's interest seemed to focus more on understanding the origin of Gabrielle's fantasies and unconscious material than on her affects, and particularly her sadness.

Similarly, Gabrielle is described as initially having been a well-coordinated child. But in the mother's report about Gabrielle after the first session, she described Gabrielle as more frequently "falling and crying and feeling hurt" (p. 14). This is another common finding in infants and children after they have been psychically traumatised (Robertson & Robertson, 1989). When children are overwhelmed they may become disorganised on the physical level as well as the psychic. Physiological regulation including the smooth coordination of movement can deteriorate.

Another of the affects Gabrielle associated with herself seemed to be one of hatred—she could not be herself—only the new baby or the mother. Moreover, Gabrielle had scratched her own face at night prior to coming to see Winnicott. It can be speculated that Gabrielle felt anger towards her mother which she then turned towards herself. She saw herself as "bad and black" (Winnicott, 1977, p. 15). This is a well-known defence (primary masochism) in which the infant protects the mother from the infant's hatred of her and turns the hatred towards the self. Winnicott noted (p. 15) that the comment by Gabrielle regarding the Piggle being black and bad referred to the fact that "hate had come in (or disillusionment)". At that moment he did not link the hatred to the mother or the self, merely noting that the hatred was present—although subsequently he did refer to the "hate and love of the mother appearing simultaneously" (p. 16) which he linked to the mother's having become pregnant.

Winnicott understood the material from the first session and the first interview with the mother as indicative of Gabrielle's efforts to work out a new relationship with her mother—a relationship which took into account "her hate of her mother because of her love for her father" (p. 16). From this very early point in the treatment he stated, quite assuredly, that the change in Gabrielle related to the birth of the new child

(p. 16) and her oedipal rivalry with her mother for her father's love. He stated that "the black mummy" was "a relic of her subjective preconceived notion about the mother" (p. 17). He did not link Gabrielle's anger with her mother to the mother's abandonment of her—both postpartum while in hospital and upon her return home when she undoubtedly focused more on the new baby than on Gabrielle. Nor did Winnicott link Gabrielle's calling her mother black and herself black with the possibility of hatred for the mother turned inward.

Following the first session the mother also reported that bedtimes were still difficult, with Gabrielle staying awake until "9 or 10" (p. 17). Bedtime, as we know, is often difficult for toddlers, representing as it does, separation—from the day, from lively activities, and most importantly, from the parents. All this would have been very troubling for Gabrielle but her bedtimes may have been made even harder by her knowledge that her bad dreams came at night and she may have feared experiencing more of these as the time approached to go to bed. In other words, normal separation fears and fears of recurring nightmares may have caused Gabrielle's bedtime difficulties; however, these difficulties might well have also revealed increased fear of separation following her prolonged separation from mother at the time of Susan's birth.

Gabrielle had experienced at least ten days and ten nights without her mother. For a two-year-old child this is a very, very long time. When a mother has to be apart from her infant or toddler, each day that the mother is not available is replete with moments of need for the mother's care, the mother's love, the mother's mirroring of emotion, the mother's limit-setting function (to help control as of yet uncontained impulses), the mother's soothing function (to help regulate affect), etc. And as each day ends and another begins the toddler becomes less and less able to remember the mother (due to the limits of object constancy at this age) including her appearance, her help, her love. At night, the toddler is particularly vulnerable.

During the night, the young child needs to feel safe in order to fall asleep and to maintain sleep. The child who is without her mother, who misses her mother, who needs her mother to help her to feel safe enough to sleep, and the toddler who is anxious about her mother's whereabouts, will likely have terrible difficulties at night and, as was the case with Gabrielle, may develop anxiety dreams, night terrors, and frightening fantasies centring upon the loss of the mother and the fearful reasons for this loss.

Gabrielle's mother noted some days after the first session that Gabrielle seemed listless and sad and she said that Gabrielle admitted to feeling sad (Winnicott, 1977, p. 19). Gabrielle also was overheard calling to her baby (doll?) in the night and talking tenderly to her.

This detail suggests a child who not only resisted sleep but who also felt powerfully lonely and alone in the night. In a defensive manoeuvre, might Gabrielle have displaced her need for company in the night onto her doll (who evidently needed company and kind words) and turned her passive need for soothing into an active attempt to soothe her doll? She thus would have become the soother, or the mummy, rather than being the helpless baby, a position which would have felt intolerable. Might Gabrielle have been re-experiencing what she experienced during her mother's absence and playing out that scene with her doll?

At this point in the narrative Gabrielle's mother revealed her feelings of guilt over "not having arranged to not having a baby again so soon" (Winnicott, 1977, p. 20), perhaps indicating the origin of her assumption that Gabrielle's difficulty came from the birth of the baby. It is well known that mothers often project their own feelings onto their children, especially their very young children, who are unable to report their own opinions about the origin of their distress. Moreover, Gabrielle's mother remembered, later in the treatment, her own feelings of having been replaced by her brother. Again, this experience in the mother's life and her resulting feelings would have provided an opportunity for displacement onto her daughter and a resulting assumption that Gabrielle was suffering due to the birth of her sibling, thus obscuring possible openness to Gabrielle's own subjectivity and other explanations for Gabrielle's suffering.

Further, Gabrielle was described by her mother as spending a lot of time sorting and washing and cleaning (p. 21). This came shortly after having toilet trained herself in a week's time. It seems likely that Gabrielle was acting out of an effort to renounce her earlier dirty ways (soiling in the nappy) in order to become a clean and tidy girl, thus pleasing to her mother. This is supported by the fact that Gabrielle believed that her mother had dropped her just after her birth and that the towel she was wrapped in had become soiled. Through reaction formation she then not only used the toilet, she also cleaned and tidied around the house. She did this in place of playing which the mother reported that she did not do much of at all, instead seeming often to be "at loose ends" (p. 21), yet another sign of preoccupation (and perhaps sadness and/or anxiety) in the young child.

Gabrielle's mother reported at this point that Gabrielle was sometimes naughty and angry but would often give up in the middle of being so in order to become the baby. She also reported that Gabrielle said that she was scared of the black mummy and that the black mummy scratched the mother and pulled off her yams and made her all dirty and killed her with brrrrr (faeces) as well as saying that she herself was bad (p. 21). This behaviour suggests Gabrielle's mixed feelings about her own aggression—her conflict over whether to express these feelings and be naughty/aggressive or to regress instead, becoming a guiltless, passive, and non-aggressive infant.

Might Gabrielle have blamed herself for her mother's departure? Might she have felt that the fact that she was "dirty" (still using the nappy) sent her mother away? During her mother's absence might Gabrielle have worried that she had killed her mother with her brrrrr and with her badness just as she described the black mummy doing?

The above provides abundant evidence of Gabrielle's great sadness, grief, anxiety, and self blame—just in the first several weeks of treatment. There are many more examples throughout the case description but for the purposes of this chapter, these will suffice.

Gabrielle was bereaved. But not just once. She lost the mother which she had had all to herself as an infant and young toddler prior to Susan's birth. She lost the mother who was her mother alone. With the birth of her sister, that mother was gone forever. She also actually lost her mother at the time of her sister's birth—for ten days—a very long time for a toddler. And she lost her mother's focus. As happens to all firstborn children, when a sibling is born, the mother cannot possibly spend as much time and psychic energy on the first child. This is different from having lost the mother she had before her sister's birth. From Gabrielle's subjective point of view, the mother who returned from the hospital, was, quite simply, a different mother. Gabrielle suffered a triple loss: she lost her original mother *and* she lost the focus of her new mother, the woman who was now the mother of two children, *and* she actually lost her real, external mother for ten days.

Winnicott's omission of a formulation revolving around loss

Donald Winnicott is recognised as a psychoanalytic pioneer in understanding the inner life of the pre-oedipal child. He was one of the first to privilege the importance and the intricacies of the child's subjective experience and internal representation of the primary dyad (the mother–child relationship). And yet we can see his slant in the case of the Piggle was towards the interpretation of triadic material, particularly the oedipal rivalry between mother and daughter for possession of the father and his love, and the jealousy of the displaced older child towards a new sibling for the mother's love. It appears that he did not consider Gabrielle's loss of her mother for ten days as a salient dynamic in her symptom formation. When he saw Gabrielle for the first time, Winnicott associated immediately to the theme of oedipal rivalry. He linked Gabrielle's anger to her competition with her mother rather than to her feelings regarding her mother's abandonment of her (during her ten day absence to give birth to Susan and to recover after) and her subjective experience of a different mother.

Why did Winnicott not see Gabrielle's mother's departure from the home as salient and how was it that he did not recognise Gabrielle's many references to sadness, loneliness, grief, and mourning in a more nuanced layering of her feeling-motivation? Why did he rush immediately, in the very first moments of the first session, to the interpretation of oedipal themes and anxieties? Why not, for example, relate her initial anxiety in the first session to the fact that this was her first visit with a new person, and her later anxiety in the session to separation and abandonment feelings?

As stated, after the first session with Dr Winnicott, Gabrielle's parents reported that she allowed herself to be a baby again and to take bottles. She would not allow herself to be called the Piggle—she was either the mother or the baby. She also said that the Piggle was black and bad. She lay in her bed and cried without knowing why. Something was certainly started inside Gabrielle with the beginning of treatment! It appeared that there was a kind of loosening within her—where she could begin to move psychically again, to play with regression and progression, to re-experience her very sad feelings in the context of a now safer environment and to begin to raise the issue of badness, aggression, and blackness.

So, what meaning, if not oedipal rivalry, can be made here? What meaning, different from that given by Winnicott can be elucidated? It seems possible, considering the abandonment she suffered, that one important piece of Gabrielle's work in her treatment was to sort out what had happened when her mother left and why it had happened. It seems quite apparent that after the beginning of her therapy Gabrielle began to be able to re-experience the intense sadness and despondency which she felt during her mother's absence. We know from the work of Spitz, Robertson, Bowlby, Furman, and many others that toddlers who experience the loss of the mother for more than a day or two react in just this way: they experience yearning for mother, sadness at the absence of the usual care given by the mother, and anger at the mother's failure to appear when needed; they protest her absence, they feel sad at the loss of their ability to relate to the mother in the here and now, and they blame themselves for the mother's having disappeared.

The original alliance between mother and infant is perhaps the most significant of all human relationships; it is the wellspring for all subsequent human attachments and it is the formative relationship in the course of which the child will develop a sense of himself (Kennel, Trause, & Klaus,1975, in Masur, 1984). If this relationship is interrupted during the early stages, the effects may be devastating for the young child's future interpersonal relations and personality development (Masur, 1984).

This was known when Winnicott treated Gabrielle. In his introduction to Heinicke and Westheimer's book, entitled, *Brief Separations* (1965), John Bowlby said, "By the early 1950s it was already clear from retrospective research that disruptions of the young child's relationship to his mother could have an adverse effect on his emotional development and mental health" (p. ix). Anna Freud and Dorothy Burlingham had written up their observations of children in the war nurseries in England during WWII (1943, 1944), Bowlby had written on the subject (1953), and James and Joyce Robertson had made several films about the effect of separation on young children and had also written about this (Heinicke & Westheimer). One of the first things Heinicke and Westheimer say in their book on brief separations in young children is this: "All observers agreed that when a 2 year old child is separated from his parents, he frets." They said, moreover, that it had "become clear that forms of fretting ranged from temper-like crying for the parents to quietly watching for their appearance at the window" (1965, p. 1). These behaviours are clearly like those described by Gabrielle's mother of her child as sad, listless, lying in the cot, taking bottle after bottle, etc.

In 1935 Melanie Klein wrote an article entitled, "A Contribution to the Psychogenesis of Manic Depressive States" in which she said that in mourning there is a reactivation of what she called the infantile depressive state. She felt that what was mourned by the infant when confronted with the loss of the mother was the loss of the mother's breast, which represented love, security, and gratification to the infant during what she considered to be the normal infantile depressive phase. According to Klein, what is reactivated following loss later in life is the original loss of the breast accompanied by feelings that the current loss may be due to the individual's own hostile or greedy impulses.

Did not Gabrielle's fantasy/fear/dream of the black mother coming to her asking where her "yams" (breasts) were illustrate Klein's thesis? Would it not have fitted Klein's conceptualisation to see Gabrielle's representation of the loss of her mother for ten days in a fantasy of the loss or destruction of the mother's breast? After all, Gabrielle did indeed lose "the love, security, and gratification" of the mother's presence (and the presence of her breasts) when the mother left to go to the hospital.

Winnicott admitted that he was not a big reader of the analytic literature (Kahr, 2016), preferring to get the sense of an idea and to pursue it himself. But surely he knew of this paper and its basic premise given Melanie Klein's importance to him as his supervisor and her influence within the greater psychoanalytic world at that time.

However, not only had the effect of separation on young children been studied prior to Winnicott's undertaking the treatment of Gabrielle (Arsenian, 1943; Bowlby, 1960, p. 61; Bowlby, Robertson, & Rosenbluth, 1952: Freud & Burlingham, 1942, p. 44; Spitz, 1945: etc., all in Masur, 1984) but Winnicott himself had spoken out against the separation of children from their parents during the Evacuation Scheme in England in the late 1930s and early 1940s. With John Bowlby and Emanuel Miller he "uncompromisingly stated that from a psychological point of view the enforced break up of families and childhood separation from parents entailed in the evacuation scheme had to be regarded as nothing less than a social disaster" (Reeves in Issroff, 2005, p. 192). And Winnicott knew, because the Cambridge Evacuation Survey data had shown it, that children under the age of five were particularly vulnerable to developing difficulties as a result of separation from parents (Reeves in Issroff, 2005), So we must ask, what was it that prevented Winnicott from understanding two-year-old Gabrielle's material through this same lens, the lens of loss?

It seems possible that influences both from within and without were powerful in shaping Winnicott's interpretive understanding of Gabrielle's material. Personal influences always affect the analyst in his or her work as do countertransferential feelings. The analyst's own early experience as an infant and child, family experience, and the influences of education, analytic training, and relationships within the analytic community are pertinent.

The relationship between Winnicott and Bowlby was a fascinating one. John Bowlby is known for having introduced ideas regarding human attachment into the psychoanalytic world. Moreover, in his work, he studied separation, grief, and loss extensively and wrote many papers on these subjects (later to become his three-volume series). And Winnicott and Bowlby were contemporaries, thus ensuring that they would have been at least somewhat familiar with each other's work. However, more than that, they knew each other professionally and played various roles in each other's lives. In fact, Winnicott reviewed Bowlby's 1939 paper for acceptance into the British Psycho-Analytical Society. Winnicott opposed Bowlby's acceptance into the BPAS and was said to have been "ruthless" (Issroff, 2005) in his attack on this and others of Bowlby's papers. And yet when war broke out they joined forces and worked together with Emanuel Miller on behalf of children, opposing the separation of small children from their parents in the effort to evacuate them from London (as mentioned above). Together they wrote to the *British Medical Journal* and separately they testified to governmental commissions including that which resulted in The Curtis Report. In this way we can see Winnicott's clear recognition of the dangers of separating children from parents—even in the face of grave physical danger.

However, Winnicott and others disagreed with Bowlby on many points. Anna Freud wrote to Winnicott that Bowlby "sacrifices most of the gains of the analytic theory, such as the libido theory, the principles of mental functioning, ego psychology, etc. with very little return" (Issroff, 2005, p. 143). She went on to say, "As analysts we do not deal with happenings in the external world but with their representations in the mind" (A. Freud, 1960, in Issroff, 2005). And here may lie one key to how it was that Winnicott formulated the Piggle's mental contents. He and Anna Freud were aligned on these points.

Winnicott may have overlooked Gabrielle's separation from her mother in favour of what he interpreted as her mental representations of oedipal jealousy and fear of retribution as per mainstream psychoanalytic thinking at the time. He may have focused on infantile sexuality at the cost of missing mental representations of loss, grief, and mourning, that is, he may have preferred to look at what Anna Freud had called the representations of the mind rather than what she called the happenings in the external world. And he might have done so at least in part due to his allegiance to the theories of Sigmund and Anna Freud as well as out of opposition to Bowlby's acceptance of happenings in the external world as important in the emotional life of the infant and child.

There is evidence for this: in 1959 Bowlby read his paper, "Grief and Mourning in Infancy" (1960) to the British Psycho-Analytical Society. Winnicott offered a critique. While Winnicott expressed his appreciation for Bowlby's advocacy for the avoidance of unnecessary breaks in the mother–infant relationship, he went on to criticise Bowlby on many other grounds, mostly for his theoretical omissions of Freudian theory (Issroff, 2005). In later years, Winnicott criticised Bowlby for ignoring the role of the subjective object and the difference between losing this object and the external reality object. He also faulted Bowlby on his lack of emphasis on the young child's subjective world, unconscious fantasy, and unconscious conflict.

In the 1960s when Winnicott treated Gabrielle, Bowlby's work was gaining recognition. Is it possible that on either a conscious or an unconscious level, Winnicott stubbornly adhered to certain theoretical constructs out of the aforementioned loyalty to the Freuds and hostility and rivalrous feelings related to Bowlby? Indeed, at one point in a letter to Anna Freud Winnicott said, "I can't quite make out why it is that Bowlby's papers are building up in me a kind of revulsion although he has been scrupulously fair to me in my writings" (Grosskurth, 1986 in Issroff, 2005). Furthermore, Brett Kahr reported to Judith Issroff that he was amused to read the margin notations in Winnicott's copy of Bowlby's 1965 report to the World Health Organization in which Winnicott scribbled "mine" and "taken from me" *many* times (indicating his feelings that Bowlby had stolen ideas from him which he included in his report to the WHO). As Issroff (2005) says, "In light of his litany of criticism of Bowlby's work, there is no need to speculate as to why Winnicott took so little from Bowlby's work" (p. 148).

To continue this theme, Bowlby and Winnicott also disagreed on the young child's capacity to mourn. While Bowlby wrote that the loss of the mother figure gives rise to the processes of mourning in infants and young children even before they have developed a formal capacity to mourn, Winnicott believed that mourning could not occur prior to the achievement of a variety of developmental milestones within the psyche. He said that the ability to mourn "is not to be taken for granted as always being there, as Bowlby implies" (Issroff, 2005, p. 145).

Thus Winnicott may have considered Gabrielle too young to experience grief or to mourn the loss of her mother over the ten days of her absence.

Moving on to other possibilities, Winnicott's own personal history is also relevant here. While Winnicott grew up in a prosperous, middle-class family, it is reported that he saw little of his father due to his father's many business and civic involvements (Kahr, 1996) and there is evidence that Winnicott's mother suffered from episodic depression (Issroff, 2005; Kahr, 1996). It is clear that Winnicott was deeply affected by his mother's state as evidenced by the poem he wrote describing her depression and her weeping (Milner, 2001 quoted in Issroff, 2005). It is also clear that both he and his second wife, Clare, glossed over his mother's depression in each of their (autobiographical and biographical) writings. Why they might have made little of this important aspect of Winnicott's early life is fascinating to consider.

Winnicott spoke of being raised by "many mothers", and he was especially fond of his nanny with whom he stayed in touch over the course of her life. But did these other "mothers" assume greater importance to him due to his actual mother's depressive periods? Did he miss, resent, or feel angry with his mother for her lapses in attention to him and her variations in mood? Might he consequently have felt guilty and needful of making symbolic reparations by caring for her and later, for others, as his chosen career? This is speculative but there is evidence that Winnicott had difficulty with material involving maternal absence or depression.

In her book on Winnicott and Bowlby, Judith Issroff (2005) wrote about a conversation which she had with Marion Milner in which Milner "spoke at passionate length about the way that Winnicott failed her in her analysis with him because he had not adequately dealt with the impact which her mother's depression" had had on her (p. 60). Moreover, it is of interest that Winnicott wrote a paper on the overuse of intellectual ability in the service of manic defence against maternal depression (Winnicott, 1935). Might Winnicott's sensitivity to maternal abandonment have created in him a tendency to use intellectualisation and psychoanalytic theory in order to avoid such material not only within himself but also within his patients? Might he have done this with Gabrielle just as he was reported to have done with Marion Milner? Might this understanding of his inner life have prompted him to write his paper on the overuse of intellectual ability in the service of defence against maternal depression? Was the oedipal level interpretation of patient material in those who had experienced some form of early maternal loss more palatable for Winnicott as a result of the pain which he suffered in considering the loss of a mother—whether his own mother or that of a patient?

Or was Winnicott's interpretation of Gabrielle's material related more closely to the psychoanalytic zeitgeist and to his own training and supervision? Winnicott's training analysis was conducted by James Strachey, six days a week, with interpretations mainly revolving around Winnicott's oedipal desires and his defences against these.

Winnicott later had a second analysis with Joan Riviere who was herself analysed by Sigmund Freud and then Ernest Jones. This is always an interesting element in describing a psychoanalyst who came of professional age in the early or mid twentieth century—how many degrees of separation were there from Sigmund Freud? So, while Winnicott never actually met Freud, he was only separated by one degree in terms of his psychoanalytic lineage. He was, as it were, Freud's psychoanalytic grandchild (Issroff, 2005).

Moreover, Winnicott himself said that he built on Freud and extended Freud's ideas (Winnicott, 1989a, p. 499 quoted in Issroff, 2005). Issroff (2005) writes that late in Winnicott's life it was volumes of Freud that were Winnicott's bedside reading. And as Issroff said playfully, Winnicott may well have seen himself as a footnote to Freud, indicating, of course, his idealisation of Freud and his relative devaluing of his own worth. Given these facts, it is not surprising that as an analyst he might interpret as he was interpreted to in his own analyses in identification with his analysts and as influenced by the father of psychoanalysis.

In the case of *The Piggle*, Winnicott associated the "black mummy" with Gabrielle's anger and rivalry towards her mother. This is in keeping with the above hypothesis that Winnicott was heavily influenced by his own analyses and by Freud's theories. But how is it that Gabrielle's mummy's blackness did not also more immediately connote her absence to Winnicott?

At two years, five months old a child has not established full object constancy. As such Gabrielle's capacity for retaining an image of the mother in her mind for more than a couple of days would have been absent (as discussed previously). In her mother's ten-day absence, is it possible that the mother became black to Gabrielle? After all, black is the colour that can be seen when the eyes are closed—especially at night when asleep or when trying to sleep. Night-time is when Gabrielle had the anxiety/dreams/night terrors about the black mummy and the black yams. Moreover, black is the colour of the darkness.

Black might also be thought of as the colour of something that cannot be seen, that is, which is no longer there. When Gabrielle's mother went away, she could not be seen, and to Gabrielle is it possible that she therefore became black?

This is an interpretation made from what we now would refer to as a pre-oedipal vantage point, that is, relying on what we know of the not yet three-year-old child's capacities and fantasies. How different is this from the way that Gabrielle's experience was understood by Winnicott?

Well, in some ways, Winnicott saw it this way and in some ways he did not.

Gabrielle herself said at the very beginning of treatment that she had come "about the babacar". She asked her mother if Dr W understood about the babacar and she left her first session saying he did not. Clearly what she wanted out of treatment had something to do with the babacar. And in the third session, as Reeves (Chapter Three) notes, "Gabrielle is quite explicit about what she has come for: 'I want to know why the black mummy and the babacar'" (Chapter Three). Her use of words should be noted. She did not say "*about*" but "*why*" the black mummy and the babacar. Winnicott, however, assumed throughout this session that these two meant the same thing. Consequently he fastened on trying to unmask the fantasy content behind the blackness attributed to them, whereas Gabrielle, I surmise, is after something slightly different, namely, what is it that makes things seem black, when they are actually not so? Seeming to be black is different from being black, just as fantasy is different from reality (Chapter Three).

What's more, after the ninth session, Winnicott said in his notes that the session was hard to understand but that he did realise that "In this setting the black mother is the good mother who has become bad" (Winnicott, 1977, p. 228). He also said, "There is now a recollection of an actual mother, orgiastically eaten and also shot in ambivalence, replacing the more primitive split into good mother and black mother related to each other because of the split between the subjective and that which is objectively perceived" (p. 119).

This description is tortured. Why so complex? Yes, we know about the split between the good and the bad mother—and this makes sense. Gabrielle's good mother left her and a bad mother returned with a rival. Gabrielle's internal representation of the good mother may have been sullied by her new experience with a less available mother who now loved the new baby. The good internal representation may indeed have become black under these circumstances. But I find it easier—and less tortured—to understand Gabrielle's image of the black mother as relating to the mother's disappearance, as Winnicott notes, to her absence.

In his notes at this time Winnicott says, "Black mummy is a split off version of the mother, one that does not understand babies, or one who understands them so well that her absence or loss makes everything black" (p. 120). So here he recognised this meaning of Gabrielle's anxious fantasy—but he did not make the interpretation to her or link the idea to her mother's actual and prolonged absence.

The use of "black" in *The Piggle*

Before beginning treatment Gabrielle developed a fantasy involving a black mummy and her black yams. Early in her treatment she talked about herself as black and bad and about the mummy as black. She also began to take pleasure in making "rude noises" with her sister and to talk a great deal about faeces, calling them "brrrrr". The theme of blackness continued to evolve throughout the treatment.

Early in the work Gabrielle gave a reason for her own blackness. She said that rubbing her "wee" is what scared her and made her black (Winnicott, 1977, p. 32). It is well known that when children are anxious, masturbation is one method of self-soothing. Confused as this activity is with powerful bodily sensations and often also with parental prohibitions, it is not uncommon for small children to associate their masturbatory activities with being bad. It is not a stretch of the imagination to consider the possibility that in Gabrielle's mother's absence, Gabrielle was more anxious than usual at night, a time of increased separation fears even in the best of times, and that she may have rubbed herself in order to self-soothe in an attempt to regulate her emotions and to re-establish internal psychic equilibrium.

Mother also reported that at this time Gabrielle said that the black mummy says, "Where are my yams? My yams are in the toilet—water rushing down" (p. 32). There is an indication in the train of association that at that time Gabrielle equated the mother's breasts with faeces. Gabrielle, who was just done with toilet training herself, must have still been close to her own fantasies about the terror of the toilet—the possibility that flushing her own bodily waste meant losing a valuable part of herself. Perhaps she felt angry for having to flush a part of herself away in order to please her mother (by being clean and tidy and toilet trained) and thus wished for retaliation—that is, to flush away a part of her mother, indeed a part of her mother of which she was jealous. Thinking this could have led Gabrielle to fear that her mother would then be very angry with her. The mother reported that after talking about the black mummy, saying that her yams were in the toilet, Gabrielle then said some very nice things about her mother and said she was angry with her father. One possible way of understanding this material might be to see that Gabrielle was trying to appease the angry mother of her fantasy and to reassure her mother that Gabrielle still loved her best.

Gabrielle's mother went on to recount Gabrielle saying that "the black mummy doesn't come". And here we get to what might be considered the crux of the meaning of blackness.

Gabrielle's mother left her. When Gabrielle could not see her mother due to her absence it must have been very difficult for her to bring an image of her mother to mind due to the immature status of her object constancy. At this age object constancy is ephemeral; the ability to bring the image of an absent person to mind, including the absent primary object, lasts at best two to three days. To little Gabrielle, black may have been all she saw when she tried to visualise her mother during most of her mother's absence. She may have equated her mother's absence with her mother being invisible. She may have looked for her mother, especially at night, in the black darkness. She even said that "the black mummy wasn't there and that had something to do with the dark night" (pp. 60–61).

And finally Winnicott and Gabrielle got to this point. Towards the end of treatment, Gabrielle said, "Black is nothing. What is it?" to which Winnicott noted, "I have been very interested in Gabrielle's use of the idea of black, and here was a new version of the theme." He then asked, "Is black what you don't see?" She said, "I can't see you because you are black." (Reversing what is most likely her point, "You are black because I can't see you.") Winnicott said, "Do you mean that when I am away then I am black and you can't see me? And then you ask to see me and have a good look at me and I am light or something else that isn't black?" To this Gabrielle replied, "When I go away and look at you you go all black don't you Dr Winnicott?" (p. 162).

Winnicott then noted that Gabrielle seemed to have dealt with this idea. But had Dr Winnicott fully dealt with the idea?

Here we see the limitations of transference interpretation. It is accepted technique in child work to sometimes leave the child's meaning within the play or within the transference relationship—but in this case one certainly wonders why Winnicott would not have made explicit the connection to Gabrielle's mother's blackness and her absence and the distress that the absence would have caused Gabrielle.

Today, many child analysts are comfortable making such interpretations, which can be considered pre-oedipal level interpretations. We must consider the fact that Winnicott lived within a certain time, when pre-oedipal concerns were being explored by some but perhaps interpreted by few (Klein being a notable exception).

Gabrielle also said, "The black mummy is inside me." What better way to retain the lost object than to put her inside? This might well have been a way that Gabrielle formed a primitive incorporation of her mother in order to keep her present during the mother's actual absence.

Gabrielle's anger and its relation to loss

Mother reported that Gabrielle said that she made the Sush baby black, that she can wear black clothes because she is black and bad, that she broke the black mummy into pieces followed by "My bottom is sore—can I have some white cream?" (p. 37). It seems possible that here Gabrielle was referring to her own angry feelings with her mother, her sister, and herself. She wanted to flush the mother's breasts down the toilet she was so angry—either because she felt that her mother had abandoned her or because she had been eclipsed in her mother's affections by her baby sister—or for both. It may have seemed to Gabrielle that her anger made her mummy, her sister, and herself black and bad. Moreover, her anger was expressed in her fantasy of breaking mummy into pieces. She then punished herself by making her bottom sore—or she may have attempted to soothe herself by rubbing, thus making her bottom sore.

The Robertsons (1989) note in their research, that the children they fostered while the children's mothers were in the hospital having a second child all experienced an increase in hostility towards the mother following their reunion with her. They added that this hostility "carried some potential for disharmony in the mother–child relationship" (p. 99).

Towards the end of the treatment Winnicott and Gabrielle rolled a roller together. When it hit Winnicott's knee, he was "dead" and fell over. This was followed by a forgetting and remembering game which Winnicott linked to his absence (but which might also have been a transference derivative referring to the mother's absence). Interestingly, after this game the Piggle went into the waiting room and asked, "Where's Susan?" indicating, perhaps, that she had had a murderous fantasy regarding her sister and needed to check on the safety and whereabouts of Susan to make sure that she hadn't actually killed her. Winnicott noted that Gabrielle looked happy after this work about life and death and coming and going.

In the next session when playing the roller game Winnicott said, "I forget you and you forget me when we are apart or on holiday but really we know we can find each other" (1977, p. 186). Winnicott interpreted this as preparation for termination. But from the perspective of my argument, I see this work as immensely valuable in helping Gabrielle to work out separations of all kinds, including especially her concerns during her mother's absence that she would never be able to find her mother again. Here Winnicott helped Gabrielle to consolidate an understanding that even when a beloved person is not present, they *can* be found again, even after days and days of waiting to see that person. In this case, Gabrielle had many experiences of waiting to see Winnicott and also had the experience of missing her mother for days and days. Winnicott may also have been right that Gabrielle was anticipating his permanent absence following termination and working on the similarities and differences between this kind of separation and the separation caused by the death of a person. At this point Gabrielle was also older and more able, developmentally, to conceptualise comings and goings and presence and absence in a more mature way.

Throughout the rest of the case write-up, blackness, badness, faeces, and so on are referred to over and over again. But Winnicott did not usually hear this material as related to Gabrielle's struggles with understanding her mother's absence and with why it might have come about. He heard this material differently. While he did refer to blackness possibly being related to absence (p. 160) when he said that black is related to the "denial of absence (looking as denial of not seeing), covering up the memory of the absent object", he did so only two or three times without giving this meaning much emphasis. I have sought here to think about why this might have been.

Countertransference and counter-reaction

One last point can be made about another influence on Winnicott and on Gabrielle. We now know more about the history of Gabrielle's family than was publicly known at the time of the publication of

The Piggle thanks to the work of both Brett Kahr and Deborah Luepnitz (this volume). It turns out that a portion of Gabrielle's mother's family perished in the Holocaust and Gabrielle may have been named for one of these relatives. The Holocaust and the resulting family losses were not discussed in the family—although this does not mean that they were not felt. And, through the process of transgenerational transmission (see Eleftheriadou, Kahr, Kalas Reeves, Luepnitz, and Silber, this volume) could it be that Gabrielle experienced an even greater reaction to the separation in general and the separation from her mother in particular than she might otherwise have?

Moreover, Gabrielle's father also experienced multiple separations from his own father and mother starting in earliest childhood. He grew up in colonial Sudan and at the time of the revolution there, had to leave with his family to go back to Ireland where they had originated. After this, his father travelled a great deal and his mother also travelled. According to Luepnitz (Chapter One) he was cared for by an aunt. Might Winnicott have responded unconsciously—or even consciously—to the family history of separation and loss on both sides, and consequently in his immense sensitivity and empathic attunement have been avoiding the subject in his discussion with them? And might he *not* have interpreted more around this issue to Gabrielle for the same reason? Again, this is speculative—but a provocative possibility.

Conclusion

Winnicott was known for his interest in how "the inner world engages with and is therefore affected by external events" (Issroff, 2005, p. 116). "He was endlessly fascinated by the elaboration and play of conscious fantasy and unconscious inferred fantasy in all areas of his implicit meta-psychological structures" (Issroff, 2001 quoted in Issroff, 2005, p. 116). In the case of *The Piggle*, Winnicott's interest in internal fantasy was primary. In the case of little Gabrielle, his interpretation of her fantasy life was heavily influenced by his theoretical background, the theories of Gabrielle's parents as to the origin of their little girl's troubles, and possibly his own countertransference and counter-reactive feelings rather than by his experience with the separation of children and parents in World War II England.

Overall, Winnicott's ideas were original; they were revolutionary; they were creative, and while they were poorly received in his lifetime (Anna Freud, Melanie Klein, and many members of the BPA and the APA were immensely critical of him) they have become part of the canon for modern-day child psychoanalysis and psychotherapy. However, as I have tried to show here, these ideas and the way he formulated some of his case material were still influenced by the times, by his own personal experience, by his supervision and training, and by his ideological lineage.

References

Arsenian, J. (1943). Young children in an insecure situation. *Journal of Abnormal Social Psychology*, *38*: 225–249.

Bowlby, J. (1953). *Child Care and the Growth of Love*. London: Penguin.

Bowlby, J. (1960). Grief and mourning in infancy. *Psychoanalytic Study of the Child*, *15*: 3–39.

Bowlby, J. (1973). *Attachment and Loss. Vol 2, Separation, Anxiety and Anger*. London: Hogarth.

Bowlby, J., Robertson, J., & Rosenbluth, D. (1952). A Two Year Old Goes to Hospital. *Psychoanalytic Study of the Child*, *7*: 82–94.

Burlingham, D. T., & Freud, A. (1944). *Infants without Families*. London: Allen & Unwin.

Freud, A., & Burlingham, D. T. (1942). *Young Children in War-time*. London: Allen & Unwin.

Freud, A., & Burlingham, D. T. (1943). *War and Children*. New York: Medical War Books.

Furman, E. (1974). *A Child's Parent Dies: Studies in Childhood Bereavement*. New Haven, CT: Yale University Press.

Grosskurth, P. (1986). *Melanie Klein: Her World and Her Work*. London: Hodder & Stoughton.

Heinicke, C. M., & Westheimer, I. J. (1965). *Brief Separations*. New York: International Universities Press.

Issroff, J. (2001). Reflections on *Playing and Reality*. In: M. Bertolini, A. Giannakoulas, & M. Hernandez, with A. Molino (Eds.), *Squiggles and Spaces: Revisiting the Work of D. W. Winnicott, Vol. 1* (pp. 59–70). London: Whurr.

Issroff, J. (Ed.) (2005). *Donald Winnicott and John Bowlby: Personal and Professional Perspectives.* London: Karnac.

Kahr, B. (1996). *D. W. Winnicott: A Biographical Portrait.* London: Karnac.

Kahr, B. (2016). *Tea with Winnicott.* London: Karnac.

Kennel, J. H., Trause, M. A., & Klaus, M. H. (1975). Evidence for a sensitive period in the human mother. *Ciba Foundation Symposiums, 33*: 87–101.

Klein, M. (1935). A contribution to the psychogenesis of manic depressive states. *International Journal of Psychoanalysis, 16*: 145–174.

Masur, C. (1984). Early Childhood Bereavement: Theoretical and Clinical Considerations. Unpublished dissertation, Hahnemann University, Philadelphia, PA.

Robertson, J. (1953). *A Two-Year-Old Goes to Hospital* (Film). University Park, PA: Penn State Audio Visual Services.

Robertson, J., & Robertson, J. (1971). Young children in brief separation: a fresh look. *Psychoanalytic Study of the Child, 26*: 264–315.

Robertson, J., & Robertson, J. (1989). *Separation and the Very Young.* London: Free Association.

Spitz, R. (1945). Hospitalism: An inquiry into the genesis of psychiatric conditions in early childhood. *Psychoanalytic Study of the Child, 2*: 53–74.

Winnicott, D. W. (1935). The manic defence. In: *Collected Papers: Through Paediatrics to Psycho-analysis.* London: Tavistock.

Winnicott, D. W. (1977). *The Piggle: An Account of the Psychoanalytic Treatment of a Little Girl.* London: Penguin.

Winnicott, D. W. (1989). *Psychoanalytic Explorations.* C. Winnicott, R. Shepherd, & M. Davis (Eds.). London: Karnac.

CHAPTER FIVE

Child analysis is *shared*: holding the child's relational context in mind

Laurel Silber

Donald Winnicott referred to his work with his young child patient, Gabrielle, as "shared" or "psychoanalysis *partagé*". He claimed it was "not family therapy—not casework—psychoanalysis shared" (Winnicott, 1977, p. viii) as he incorporated Gabrielle's parents in the work with their child. Winnicott met in individual play consultations with his patient to reflect on her inner life and address her immediate experience and he included exchanges with her parents all as part of the psychoanalytic work. The parents were not referred to another therapist; instead, their parenting role expanded, understanding their child's struggles in new ways through consultations with Dr Winnicott. This relational emphasis placed the child's attachment needs at the forefront, a bold claim within the world of classical psychoanalysis, then a one-person model.

Deborah Luepnitz's (2017) reconsideration of *The Piggle* allows further reflection on the work of a master, with recognition of the multiple ways he played both with the child and within the system in which she was developing. Winnicott's work took place within a particular psychoanalytic context that informed his need to specify that the treatment when "shared" was still psychoanalytic.

My first brush with *The Piggle* occurred while I was in graduate training. My focus at that time was on the way Winnicott operationalised theory into the action of play. I found his interaction with the Piggle fascinating, the play moves, but I also appreciated his way of simultaneously sharing his reflections on the action. His clinical mind was open, juggling theory, developmental perspectives, parental perspectives, and his own reactions to the work. His attention hovered among these vectors while he shifted and engaged in play in the present moment. As a student in training, I found myself intrigued by this type of exposure (the back and forth between action and thought) to a play process. Play struck me as the height of sophistication: abstract thought instantiated in behavioural constructions. An elderly man respected and co-created metaphors with a young child, rich with meaning.

In a different medium, Charles Lutwidge Dodgson, under the pseudonym Lewis Carroll, had the wisdom to recognise the intellect of a young child, Alice Liddell, who he photographed and who served as the muse for the classic story *Alice in Wonderland* (1865). I realise I am mixing art and science, which is risky, but the common thread I want to emphasise across disciplines is the fascination with and respect for a young child's wisdom and the temerity to privilege that. Winnicott brought forward what the Piggle was struggling with from her play gestures in language adults could access. The openness of the text (though identifiers could have been removed!) was consistent with the type of engagement found in the case. Imagining his young child patient's struggles did not eventuate in a collapse into blaming the parents or "becoming the better parent" (problems associated with a one-person model in child work, see Silber, 2015). Rather, he considered parental subjectivity as part of the treatment process. The extent to which he did so will be explored further.

In Winnicott's work with Gabrielle, he entered an attachment context that was undergoing change with the birth of a new sibling. This kind of family expansion involves a shifting of roles and can feel uncertain, even chaotic. However, it seemed that this family system was burdened with escalated fear regarding this change. Winnicott situated himself in the "messiness" of child work; he helped the family sort out the change they were undergoing in their reflections and shared grief. This responsiveness to the system was at odds with established psychoanalysis at the time. Moreover, by generously sharing his original notes on the clinical process alongside the action of the play, the reader was invited to imagine Winnicott's clinical mind as it traversed many developmental miles to ultimately find the mind of his troubled young patient. Gabrielle may have been more available in her interaction with Winnicott due to his being simultaneously connected to her parents in his "sharing". In him they all found a receptive mind, and as a result, what came forward was both riveting and healing.

In Luepnitz's (2017) fortuitous reopening of the case with the adult Piggle, Gabrielle, their sharing co-created more possibilities for examining process then and now. My current focus has shifted from the questions about the play interaction of my training days, to consider the aspect of sharing, and the ways that may have influenced progress in the case. Playing and sharing are related concepts and yet distinct as well. Sharing or working within the attachment context added another layer of complexity.

Additionally, the field has grown up around *The Piggle* case. Attachment research and theoretical advances in relational psychoanalysis have created more ways to think about and elaborate upon Winnicott's notion of sharing. What do we know now that we didn't know then? How can we apply these advances to the process that occurred in the case? This re-examination brings to light new questions and new clinical emphasis connected to the developing field of child relational psychoanalytic work.

Sharing was not family therapy, nor was it casework, but it was a harbinger of the paradigm shifting in child psychoanalysis to child relational psychoanalysis. In the decades following the work detailed in *The Piggle*, keeping parents apart from work with their children was making less and less sense, scientifically and ethically.

So, what did Winnicott mean by sharing in child psychoanalysis? His choice of words was interesting. How were parents a part of the play process in child therapy? What is different about the child therapist's position in the work when the clinical process is shared? How does the child therapist mentalize the multiplicity of subjectivities? In incorporating the child's point of view, the parent's point of view and his or her own point of view, what changes in the work?

To begin unpacking Winnicott's concept of sharing, a link to Philip Bromberg's term, borrowed from adult relational psychoanalysis, "standing in the spaces" (Bromberg, 1998) presents a useful frame.

When moved down the developmental ladder, "standing in the spaces" can expand by referring to *playing in the multiple spaces across multiple minds* in child work. Registering multiple spaces, Winnicott was situated in the relational intersection of subjectivities; he used his mind and was used to scaffold a high wire between the minds of parent and child. The "attachment wires" needed to be untangled, reorganised, reattached through him. While playing in the intersubjective space, the child therapist is in a unique position to wonder who is that child to this parent? Who is that parent? Who is that child? And in further entering the problematic relational crux for the child: in what ways might a parent's dissociated affect, informed by generations, create an obstacle to mind-to-mind sharing? How can child therapists facilitate more collaboration within the intersubjective space so that a child can feel more securely known? Put another way, when a parent holds within him or herself dissociated aspects of affects/experience it serves to obstruct the flow of sharing within as well as across minds. The interference of dissociation to the interaction between parent and child can result in a child's confusion over distortions or affective incoherency, and the felt prohibition to knowing. This problem influences the play, and/or lack of play, in the multiple minds that have entered the therapeutic space. Winnicott's play with the Piggle conveyed this relational difficulty, although he may not have conceptualised it in this way.

Shortly before *The Piggle* was published (1977), three child analysts, Selma Fraiberg, Edna Adelson, and Vivian Shapiro (1975) published a paper: "Ghosts in the Nursery: A Psychoanalytic Approach to the Problems of Impaired Infant–Mother Relationships". This landmark paper was working in a similar clinical area—specifically including the subjectivity of parents in child psychoanalysis. "Ghosts in the Nursery" made the case that it was critical to consider a parent's subjectivity in the work with a young child. The publications were different, and while it is beyond the scope of this chapter to unpack the differences, it is interesting to point out that the shift in attention in child work was moving into the heretofore resisted area of parental subjectivity. The door was opening. Fraiberg and colleagues' (1975) clinical research concluded that ghosts or unformulated feeling state(s) from a parent's past haunt the intergenerational space. To link to the earlier related metaphor, these "ghosts" disrupt the wiring between the generations. The child therapist is in a unique position to detect the interference of ghosts within the attachment context for the child. Sharing—the relational space between the generations—was being scaffolded into the field. Clinical work and attachment research were mutually building to a more complex area within child work, including systems thinking.

The paradigm shift to relational thought in the world of adult psychoanalysis turned on questions of influence (Mitchell, 1997). Like Aron's (1996) concept of mutuality and Benjamin's (1995) feminist critique (along with others)—this shift was connected to the concept of sharing, or, more broadly, appreciating interactive processes within psychoanalysis. In particular, in recognising the ways an adult analyst's subjectivity influences the analysis, not only were the remaining vestiges from the illusion of neutrality being dispelled, but technical advances for working with a two-person model were developing. This changed landscape in adult work informed and perhaps legitimised work on the other side of the binary: work with parents (adults live on both sides of the binary). Opening up the adult analyst's subjectivity created more space: the taboo surrounding work with parents and their influence was being dismantled. In other words, there was growing support to acknowledge the real relationality in work with children (*Relational Child Psychotherapy* co-edited by Altman, Briggs, Frankel, Gensler, and Pantone was published in 2002). Child analysis was indeed shared; no longer was it necessary to downplay that fact to fit in to the one-person model. The rules changed.

Winnicott was less constrained by rules (professional procedural rules of the day) and as such was freer to play than others of his day. He adapted his clinical stance in response to the needs of the system. Might the child's play give him clues to inform clinical direction? At what level should he enter into the interaction? To what extent was fostering parental reflection enough to move a system along? How readily might a parent recover the ability to see/meet the mind of their child? If Winnicott were still alive today, as in really alive, not just playing alive, it would be so interesting to hear him elaborate regarding these assessments. Clinical judgements like the choice of who to engage when within the family system can be complicated. His assessment included a humble respect for the action of development and how treatment interacts with it. Winnicott's knowledge of the nuanced architecture of the

intersubjective space between the generations would have been interesting to probe further. On the child side of the binary in psychoanalysis,
the relational concerns are different in significant ways. Research and
clinical thought in this area has evolved subsequent to Winnicott's work
with the Piggle.

One parameter that conveyed Winnicott's recognition of systems,
and the possibility of navigating shared minds, was that he took pains to
spell out the necessity of *not resolving paradox*, rather, *living with paradox*. By operating at the intersection of subjectivities in the relational
system, it was an imperative to flesh out this concept. Without this concept you can't "stand in the spaces". Holding the tensions of multiple
points of view, and in so doing, the inherent contradictions, without collapse (as in a doer/done-to scenario—either/or, me or you), is informed
by experiential knowledge of wandering in intersubjective spaces. Not
resolving paradox is critical to creating a third position within the intergenerational space. The frame for the therapist's mentalizing matured:
living with the tensions, holding the multiple perspectives, and ponder-
ing connection. Inside the tension, Winnicott described being multiple
"Winnicotts"—he was different in his interaction with each participant,
parent or child, joining them at their different developmental levels;
influencing his process with each by the other. And he was a different
Winnicott with each participant at different moments. This is the therapist's mind moving within the space, playing seriously and expansively.

Disorganised attachment considers the impact of a parent's influence
on the child's development of self. The subject of negative influence
on the part of a parent in child relational work is therefore not a work
around, not dismissed, and not stymied in a blaming or shaming either/
or dynamic, as can happen in a one-person model. The bridge between
attachment research and psychoanalysis was in the process of being con-
structed, expanding possibilities.

In 1965 Mary Ainsworth created the Stranger Situation research
paradigm (see Ainsworth, Blehar, Waters, & Wall, 1978) and in 1969
John Bowlby's first volume on attachment theory, *Attachment and Loss*,
was published. Subsequently, Mary Main and Judith Solomon created
the category of disorganised attachment (1986). And since that time,
Lyons-Ruth (1999) along with others (Fonagy, Gergely, Jurist, & Target,
2002; Hesse & Main, 1999; Lieberman & Van Horn, 2008; Schechter,

2004; Slade, 2005; Solomon & George, 2011; Steele & Steele, 2018; and Tronick, 2007) have elaborated a rich, variegated research base to hold the importance of parent work within the widening scope and shift of child psychoanalysis to parent–child work or relational thought.

In the aftermath of *The Piggle*, attachment research advanced a working understanding of disorganised attachment, which essentially reflected a sharing of pathology between the generations. In connection to this shift, Karlen Lyons-Ruth (2003) stated that the treatment objective in the work with the parent–child relationship was to deepen the "collaboration in the dialogue". Hesse and Main (1999) recognised the frightened parent who in turn frightens the child as a secondary generational effect of trauma. The treatment questions shifted towards the relationship, specifically, helping a parent's mind be open to their child's developing mind.

To briefly summarise the dilemma in disorganised attachment for the purpose of this discussion, the psychic circumstance of a parent's trauma from their childhood culminates in vulnerability (unresolved loss) in the parent–child relationship. Metaphorically speaking, the dissociated experience eventuates in a closed door in a parent's mind. As the child knocks on it, as invariably they will, they become frightened, as does the parent. The door was closed for a reason. The outcome of a parent's reliance on dissociation for past trauma contributes to disorganising attachment for the next generation. The "afterwardness" of trauma (Caruth, 1996) becomes the next generation's trouble (Fraiberg, Adelson, & Shapiro, 1975). The child's experience in the relationship with the parent who is triggered (Coates, 2012), in the midst of a highly evocative "remembering context" (Stern, 2004), results in an affective world that is incoherent. This circumstance frustrates the child's need to organise a representational map of their social world. The intentionality of their caregivers is obfuscated by the parent's internal preoccupations. The child in this context meets a developmental interference and symptoms emerge. This dilemma is an example of the way pathology is shared between generations, as will be explored in the reconsideration of *The Piggle*.

Research has borne out that children's minds are shared in the course of their development (Cozolino, 2010). The minds of parents and their children are wired in relation to each other, primarily through the implicit relational space, the non-verbal behaviour of procedural knowledge. This is also the space that play occupies. Developmental research has identified the primacy of this area of experience for transmission and change (Boston Change Process Study Group, 1998; Seligman, 1999). The child's potential to serve as an evocative trigger to a parent (Coates, 2012) inadvertently provides an opening through the enactment associated with a parent's past trauma. While Winnicott entered this space in the work with the Piggle there was still much to sort out regarding how to use it.

As Deborah Luepnitz (2017) rightfully questions, beyond Winnicott's participation in the therapy process that was shared, did he adequately conceptualise the pathology itself as being shared? It is to this aspect of shared minds, as in the transmission of trauma from parent to child, that I plan to discuss further in concert with Luepnitz's analysis of the case.

Winnicott helped to mark the conceptual space within child psychoanalysis for relational work with children; however, technical advances in recognising and working with the mechanisms of transmission of a parental trauma came later. Historically speaking, when Winnicott spoke of sharing, it came after John Bowlby, another Englishman and prominent child psychoanalyst, was rejected from the British Psycho-Analytical Society (in 1938) for privileging the child's attachment relationship. Bowlby and Winnicott were both white men who received serious professional recriminations for their inclusion of parents. Recognising maternal subjectivity required resistance to the established psychoanalytic order. Like Oedipus' father, Laius, who dismissed the importance of attachment, leaving his son to die on a mountain top, it did not turn out well. However, due to this professional climate, it was a risky business; only the intrepid traveller moved into this space. The psychoanalytic community did not approve of sharing. In Winnicott's use of the term "psychoanalysis shared", he was insisting on expanding the borders of psychoanalysis, not accepting rejection and deportation to another discipline, that is, family therapy, or to downgrade the work with parents to casework. Adopting a two-person model in child psychoanalysis, though more obviously relational, was ironically harder to openly acknowledge.

The toddler (which Gabrielle was when her sister was born), developmentally speaking, generally does not share well. This has to do with the prerequisite cognitive complexity and affective tolerance required for the loss of control in sharing. Similarly speaking, the field also needed a certain degree of maturity to expand theoretical complexity and tolerate the unfamiliarity and unpredictability of process and change happening in a non-linear system (Seligman, 2005). Sharing requires a more complex understanding: the whole being greater than the sum of its parts. At that time it was the individuals that were at the centre of focus, not so much how they were influenced by and integrated within a system.

Now I would like to illustrate these points by discussing the case material presented in *The Piggle*. The shared pathology of Gabrielle and her mother, concretised by Gabrielle in the image of the black babacar, was associated with a witch. Gabrielle had a felt sense of what her mother ultimately communicated with Winnicott: the mother's fear of bringing a sibling into Gabrielle's world. Her mother felt it was too soon. Gabrielle, I believe, felt confused by her mother's guilt and fear regarding this challenge to the relationship. For example, Gabrielle asked her mother if she could suck on her mother's breasts again even though she had not done so for a long while, doing so at a time when her mother was still breastfeeding the younger infant. The boundaries between mother and Gabrielle seemed to collapse at that moment and they seem disoriented. Who was the baby? Gabrielle must have wondered who she was to her mother in light of the fact that there was a *new* baby. She must have wondered where she fitted in. I believe this confusion frightened Gabrielle because it met the mother's confusion and fear (experienced as a "closed door", her mother's absence of a collaborative stance, contributing to confusion about fitting in together). Gabrielle's fear that she could lose her place also became realised, raising the spectre that she could be replaced as opposed to displaced. Gabrielle's mother-as-she-knew-her was lost, simultaneous to her mother becoming the mother to her new sister. Their dyadic structure was regressing from the threat of expansion and change. Another important aspect of the experience of loss at this time, discussed in Corinne Masur's chapter (Chapter Four), was compounded by the mother's ten-day hospital stay. A mutual sharing with Winnicott allowed process around the chaotic affective experience that was evoked. Winnicott reflected on the problem of absence in a play session with the Piggle:

(Absence articulated:)

He said, "I am very interested in Gabrielle's use of the idea of black."

W: Is black what you don't see?

G: I can't see you because you are black. When I go away and look at you you go all black don't you Dr Winnicott?

Margin note: here black is not seeing me when I am absent instead of remembering me in my absence (Winnicott, 1977, p. 153).

During this exploration, the Piggle would leave the consultation room/playroom and say to Winnicott: "I'll not come back." Her father, in the waiting room, coaxed her to return—here she was making her therapist feel the threat of her absence. She was trying to communicate about absence through her actions. In other words, the affective nuance in the parent–child relationship, that felt threatening, was being enacted in the therapeutic relationship. She wanted Winnicott to feel it, therefore the experience could be represented, the trouble brought forward, and potentially understood.

The problem the Piggle faced in experiencing her own disorientation due to a new sibling in the family was that the mother's ability to differentiate herself (her trouble from her past influencing present experience) from the Piggle seemed deeply confused. In this conjecturing, and it is conjecturing, the affective experience between the generations was tangled up. Due to the mother's experience from her childhood (to be elaborated), the marking of the boundaries between herself and her daughter became blurred with a psychic equivalence. In other words, what the mother felt/assumed about the experience was what she imagined her child thought—the psyches lost their markedness and were felt to be equivalent. The ability to imagine, to collaborate across to the other's mind, to register a difference was unavailable due to past trauma. This is the mechanism of transfer—it is in the small exchanges and the absenting of self, or ghosting responsible for distorting and shaping meaning within the connection to self and other. The data is in the rich implicit affective field of knowing and not knowing.

The Piggle's mother explained to Winnicott: "My anxieties were very intense at the time of Susan's birth—I forget whether I told you that I have a brother, whom I greatly resented, who was born when I was almost exactly the same age as Gabrielle was when Susan was born" (Winnicott, 1977, p. 161). Gabrielle's mother reflected that her resentment as a child was expressed in naughtiness and she was brought to child analyst, Anna Freud, to address the troubles she was having. Now that she was a mother she was witness to the next generational moment, and the triggering experience evoked an experience of herself as a perpetrator (a witch) to the Piggle. There was a repetition of the feeling associated with the actions of that time: she brought a version of herself (in the equivalence) to Winnicott. On one level it was her play therapy. Winnicott was working with a past experience of the mother's in the present experience with Gabrielle. The mother was enacting with Winnicott and Gabrielle what had happened in her childhood—a generation removed. One could even conjecture that in that transitional space of a new brother for the mother, feelings from the prior generation's trauma about tragic loss imbued their experience as well. There was much that needed to be metabolised across the generations about loss with and through Winnicott. As Gabrielle played with Winnicott and as Winnicott reflected with the mother about her, the mother was recovering from having confused herself with Gabrielle. She was differentiating from her past, re-representing her past and in so doing rediscovering the boundaries that the intergenerational trauma had compromised. Mother said, "How much writing to you has helped me; somehow to give form to my perplexities and fears, with knowledge that they would be received with great understanding: and feeling of being in relation to you. I am sure all this helped me to work through our anxieties about Gabrielle and again to find our right relationship to her" (p. 161). In the process of sharing minds with Winnicott, the Piggle seemed to have got her mother back. The Piggle's mother could catch her bearings in the heightened emotional landscape and shift to see Gabrielle more clearly. The dyad's normative mourning process, associated with a dyad becoming a triad, could be de-coupled from traumatic loss.

The demand schedule Winnicott tri-created within the treatment was also interesting and may have been part of an active negotiation between Gabrielle and her mother. Gabrielle's request, that she needed to see Winnicott, may have been prompted by an internal state, but perhaps also an external one, as her mother's anxiety may have been escalating. Perhaps a demand for Winnicott emerged at a time when the felt quality of the interaction between them was unsettled. There was a place to go to "make things right between them".

Winnicott operated simultaneously on two levels—he engaged mother's reflective functioning, creating more openness and complexity—helping the mother disengage from a psychic equivalence. The mother could thus shift out of a fear of Gabrielle's resentment (which was projected from her own earlier felt resentment). Meanwhile Winnicott played reflectively with Gabrielle. She was not the cause of mother's fear state. Winnicott uncoupled that idea in Gabrielle, and in so doing, she could feel secure again. Their sharing of affective experience became less confusing and frightening.

Towards the end of the work there was a series of hide and seek games, starting off with Gabrielle killing Winnicott. Imagine the relief she must have felt as she became able to wish to kill and Winnicott could play at being killed, then kill her, then hide. In the end of the play could be a resolution—as Winnicott reflected, that "she forgets me and then I forget her when we are apart or on holiday, but really we know we can find each other" (1977, p. 186).

"Really we can find each other" symbolised the resilience in the attachment. Gabrielle could kill and hate Winnicott but this did not destroy him. It was enormously therapeutic that Winnicott was not afraid of Gabrielle's resentments; he marked them, was curious about the feelings in the play, and imagined with her about them. The Piggle was not omnipotent, she was just angry. Gabrielle's parents gave Winnicott permission to be that "developmental object" while mother caught her emotional bearings and began to be able to tolerate Gabrielle's normal resentments and not signify that she was a bad mother (or "naughty") to have created that feeling in her daughter. In the present moment of the treatment, in the new generation, she arrived at another opportunity to recontextualise her experience.

In a transmitted trauma, or shared pathology, the pair was truly confused; whose fear was whose? If it was the evacuated fear of the parents, what did that mean for the child?

In an illustrative digression, to the crux of the Harry Potter story, there is a quest to find hidden horcruxes (Rowling, 1998). Horcrux symbolised the sealed containers holding a fragmented part of he-who-must-not-be-named, Voldemort's soul. If Voldemort can keep the parts of his soul unintegrated, he achieves immortality (hence the "evil" remained unmitigated, active for generations to come). The past was transmitted, sealed, and hidden, affecting the present. Similar to dissociation, the fragments live on in sealed containers in the mind. In the story, the seventh horcrux was inside Harry Potter (he was a horcrux). He needed to address what became internal to him.

The Piggle began psychotherapy with Winnicott after night terrors in which she feared a "black mummy who lived inside her and made her black". (This happening, at a time when her mother's body had been changing dramatically through a pregnancy/delivery, may have contributed to shaping her fears.) Also, poignant past family history was associated with the Holocaust; history that Gabrielle, as an adult, shared with Dr Luepnitz (Chapter One). The fact that Jews and others were sent on trains to their death day was in the background. The relative for whom Gabrielle was named, Esther, was imprisoned and murdered. One wonders if Gabrielle's fear of poisoning was connected to what was felt and unspoken in her implicit relational space of traumatic fragments. The seal needed to be broken, the contents unpacked. Piggle's mother was not remembering, but possibly reliving through mothering Gabrielle, one generation removed aspects to do with this intergenerational painful experience. In this way she could potentially remember, and the current developmental moment in the generational dialogue would be just that.

Mother began to represent her experience better. This may have eased Gabrielle's sense of having to co-regulate an inchoate fear within herself and between her and her mother. Their shared process was transformed by the inclusion of Winnicott. And with the Piggle, Winnicott could put play back into the space that had been seized by a fearful blackness. Ideas and feelings began to dance with reversals and were imagined without fear of real consequences. An unresolved paradoxical feeling, "Let me be alive when I die," which was said by Winnicott, and often quoted by the Piggle's mother, was played with in the work. He brought life into a space that had been compromised, freighted with transmitted trauma. The ability to play at things, his reframing a birthday as a death day, for example, created implicit space, freeing the Piggle up to think, to not fear her thoughts. Play being reflective thought, Winnicott and she converged multiple parts of her experience into a scenario that made more felt sense to her.

Conclusion

Psychoanalysis is, in reality, always a shared event. Individualised treatment may contribute to an illusion of detachment from the lived relational context. The radical paradigm shift to relational psychoanalysis becomes more radical when working with the child within their relational system. To incorporate the developmental reality, there are more parts of the system to actively consider and work with in the treatment context. Sharing was a bid to expand the scope of what can be known and considered within child psychoanalysis, a bid to hold more complexity of process (both theoretically and procedurally) within the domain of child analytic work.

Winnicott emphasised the importance of creating the space to play for movement and change to happen. When there is play in the system emergence and sharing are inevitable in the therapeutic consultation. That is how change happens. The potential for expanding the collaborative dialogue between the generations rests on this process occurring in the mind of the therapist who holds the subjectivities of the child and parents. The Piggle's mother began to wonder anew about connections between herself and Gabrielle, and in so doing saw herself as different from her daughter, Gabrielle, and different from what she feared, like waking up from a bad dream. Gabrielle's mother became a more relaxed mother in the interaction with Winnicott who was changing the quality of relatedness between them. Winnicott made use of pretend play and pretend thinking and they found what was real, together and apart.

References

Ainsworth, M. D. S., Blehar, M. C., Waters, E., & Wall, S. (1978). *Patterns of Attachment: A Psychological Study of the Strange Situation*. Hillsdale, NJ: Erlbaum.

Altman, N., Briggs, R., Frankel, J., Gensler, D., & Pantone, P. (2002). *Relational Child Psychotherapy*. New York: Other Press.

Aron, L. (1996). *A Meeting of Minds: Mutuality in Psychoanalysis*. New York: Analytic Press.

Benjamin, J. (1995). *Like Subjects, Love Objects: Essays on Recognition and Sexual Difference*. New Haven, CT: Yale University Press.

Boston Change Process Study Group—Stern, D., Sander, L., Nahum, J., Harrison, A., Lyons-Ruth, K., Morgan, A., Brushweilerstun, N., & Tronick, E. (1998). The non-interpretative mechanisms in psychoanalytic therapy: The 'something more' than interpretation. *International Journal of Psychoanalysis, 79*: 903–921.

Bowlby, J. (1969). *Attachment and Loss, Volume 1*. New York: Basic Books.

Bromberg, P. (1998). *Standing in the Spaces: Essays on Clinical Process, Trauma and Dissociation*. New York: Routledge.

Carroll, L. (1865). *Alice's Adventures in Wonderland*. London: Macmillan.

Caruth, C. (1996). *Unclaimed Experience: Trauma, Narrative, and History*. Baltimore, MD: Johns Hopkins University Press.

Coates, S. (2012). The child as traumatic trigger: Commentary on paper by Laurel Moldawsky Silber. *Psychoanalytic Dialogues, 22*(1): 123–128.

Cozolino, L. (2010). *The Neuroscience of Psychotherapy: Healing the Social Brain*. New York: W. W. Norton.

Fonagy, P., Gergely, G., Jurist, E. J., & Target, M. (2002). *Affect Regulation, Mentalization and the Development of the Self*. New York: Other Press.

Fraiberg, S., Adelson, E., & Shapiro, V. (1975). Ghosts in the nursery: A psychoanalytic approach to the problems of impaired infant-mother relationships. *Journal of the American Academy of Child & Adolescent Psychiatry, 14*: 387–421.

Hesse, E., & Main, M. (1999). Second-generation effects of unresolved trauma in nonmaltreating parents: Dissociated, frightened, and threatening parental behavior. *Psychoanalytic Inquiry, 19*: 481–540.

Lieberman, A., & Van Horn, P. (2008). *Psychotherapy with Infants and Young Children: Repairing the Effects of Stress and Trauma on Early Attachment*. New York: Guilford.

Luepnitz, D. A. (2017). The name of the Piggle: Reconsidering Winnicott's classic case in light of some conversations with the adult 'Gabrielle'. *International Journal of Psychoanalysis, 98*(2): 343–370.

Lyons-Ruth, K. (1999). The two-person unconscious: Intersubjective dialogue, enactive relational representation and the emergence of new forms of relational organization. *Psychoanalytic Inquiry, 19*(4): 576–617.

Lyons-Ruth, K. (2003). Dissociation and the parent–infant dialogue: A longitudinal perspective from attachment research. *Journal of the American Psychoanalytic Association, 51*(3): 883–911.

Main, M., & Solomon, J. (1986). Discovery of a new, insecure-disorganized/ disoriented attachment pattern. In: M. Yogman & T. Brazelton (Eds.), *Affective Development in Infancy* (pp. 95–124). Norwood, NJ: Ablex.

Mitchell, S. (1997). *Influence and Autonomy in Psychoanalysis.* New York: Analytic Press.

Rowling, J. K. (1998). *Harry Potter and the Chamber of Secrets.* New York: Scholastic.

Schechter, D. (2004). Intergenerational communication of violent trauma experience within and by the dyad: the case of a mother and her toddler. *Journal of Infant, Child, and Adolescent Psychotherapy, 3*(2): 203–234.

Seligman, S. (1999). Integrating Kleinian theory and intersubjective infant research: Observing projective identification. *Psychoanalytic Dialogues, 9*: 120–159.

Seligman, S. (2005). Dynamic systems theories as a framework for psychoanalysis. *Psychoanalytic Dialogues, 15*: 285–319.

Silber, L. M. (2015). A view from the margins: Children in relational psychoanalysis. *Journal of Infant, Child, and Adolescent Psychotherapy, 14*: 345–362.

Slade, A. (2005). Parental reflective functioning: An introduction. *Attachment & Human Development, 7*: 269–281.

Solomon, J., & George, C. (2011). *Disorganized Attachment and Caregiving.* New York: Guilford.

Steele, H., & Steele, M. (2018). *Handbook of Attachment-Based Interventions.* New York: Guilford.

Stern, D. (2004). *The Present Moment in Psychotherapy and Everyday Life.* New York: W. W. Norton.

Tronick, E. (2007). *The Neurobehavioral and Social-Emotional Development of Infants and Children.* New York: W. W. Norton.

Winnicott, D. W. (1977). *The Piggle: An Account of the Psychoanalytic Treatment of a Little Girl.* London: Penguin.

CHAPTER SIX

A child analyst looks at *The Piggle* in 2020

Justine Kalas Reeves

Introduction: Winnicott's positive effect on the parents and Gabrielle

Commentators and reviewers have agreed that Winnicott's (henceforth, DWW) treatment greatly helped Gabrielle, also called the Piggle, back to her former equanimity (see Bürgin, 2016; Furman, 1979; Reeves, 2015a, 2015b; Teurnell, 1993). She herself said, "Dr Winnicott is a very good maker-better of babies" (*The Piggle*, Winnicott, 1977, p. 107). At this time in the United States, child psychoanalytic trainings are not thriving despite continued community and family need for the contributions of child psychoanalysis. For this reason, it behoves us to take a closer look at Winnicott's flexibility in working with this family to see what we can learn about how psychoanalysis can help families in more realistic ways. Two terms Winnicott uses, "psychoanalysis *partagé*" and "psychoanalysis on demand" warrant elaboration to this end.

With the exception of Furman (1979), the effect of DWW's work with the parents has been little explored. He intended to write more about "psychoanalysis *partagé*"—his term for work with the parents, or shared psychoanalysis—although sadly he did not before he died. DWW served as a *developmental object* (more on this later) for the whole family, haunted as they were with transgenerational Holocaust trauma (Luepnitz, 2017, p. 347) as well as by "ghosts in the nursery" (Fraiberg, Adelson, & Shapiro, 1975). Fortunately, they were also endowed with generous helpings of transgenerational joy. The tender attachment between Gabrielle and her mother with its fledgling separation–individuation process in train (Mahler, 1972) rendered Sush baby's arrival difficult for both. Mother's guilt and anxiety may likely have been heightened by her Tavistock child psychotherapy training as her letters suggest a focus on her daughter's vulnerabilities more than her strengths. Further, she was mothering at a time before the ideal mother of psychoanalysis had been called out for its essentialist misogyny (see Raphael-Leff, 1995 and Balsam, 2017). For women who pursued child psychotherapy trainings and childrearing at close range, exposure to the many kinds of mother–child difficulties could raise anxiety. The mother's letters and involvement in the publication of The Piggle show how she toggled between anxious mum and valued yet preoccupied colleague to DWW, particularly since she was the patient's mother.

Gabrielle and her parents were all gifted with language, and the text of Winnicott's case write-up can nearly be heard for its musicality. Winnicott's and the parents' efforts to preserve Gabrielle's words, play, and a record of the treatment has left us with a rare rendering of parent–toddler and analyst–toddler interaction. And while Gabrielle's reaction to a sibling birth may seem extreme I consider it fairly typical. Her verbal acuity made her reaction appear as more unusual than it actually was, as so often a toddler's despair at being displaced by a sibling is repressed and lost in the clatter of family life. Gabrielle's parents were deeply concerned and interested in Gabrielle's experiences and as such took careful note of them. In her paper on her discovery of the adult Piggle, Deborah Luepnitz reveals that Gabrielle's mother had a deathbed wish to see DWW, revealing his presence in her psyche (Luepnitz, 2017). Indeed, DWW provided a "motherhood constellation" (Stern, 1995), loving guidance, to both parents in their acknowledged helplessness. He also conveyed quiet confidence that all would turn out well while validating their concern that Gabrielle was in major distress.

The context

The Piggle movingly conveys a mother's and toddler's anguish upon the arrival of a new baby girl. The parents worry as they see their robust little Gabrielle, or "Piga", as she calls herself, falter as she scratches her face, resists sleep, has nightmares about a terrifying babacar with a black mummy and daddy and piga who aren't clean. "It's the mother's inside where the baby is born from" (Winnicott, 1977, p. 24) interprets DWW of the meaning of the babacar to which Gabrielle replies, "Yes, the black inside" (p. 24). Gabrielle had toilet trained herself in one week after baby Susan's arrival, and compulsively tidied her toys as she feared losing her mother's love for her dirty, aggressive, black, betrayed feelings towards her (Furman, 1992). Self-soothing failed her. Other times she lost her capacity to play, interact, and be herself. She felt broken, and said, "Mummy loves Susan best" (Winnicott, 1977, p. 104). Sadness, loss, hate, and love permeate the text as the adults help her find relief "lest she should settle down and harden herself against her distress as the only way of coping with it" (p. 7). In the Piggle's words: "The Piga gone away, gone to the babacar. The Piga is black. Both Pigas are bad. Mummy, cry about the babacar!" (p. 7).

That her mother is seemingly not experiencing the same grief adds to Gabrielle's suffering, so she commands her mother to cry as she does. The level of detail in the mother's letters to DWW about Piggle, while in themselves a rich record, also express *her* feelings, since parents initially see their children as extensions of themselves, particularly for mothers in the earliest years when the bodily and psychical boundary is more permeable (Furman, 1996). The new baby and the marriage troubles forced a premature psychical separation for Gabrielle that influenced the sleeping troubles (Daws, 1989), made her shy with others in nursery despite wanting to play, and contributed to mother's insecurities about her importance to her daughter. The mother's yielding to Gabrielle's urgent request to nurse long after weaning shows us mother's guilt at letting go as well. While common enough for a two- to four-year-old child to want to breastfeed upon seeing their mother feeding a new baby (and it is generous that mother allowed her), the several instances described, and the fact of mother gratifying this wish, reflect the real anxiety mother felt to frustrate her daughter. DWW was aware of the extent of mother's guilt and sought to help her, as when he mentioned how families do not always give time for ordinary madness to sort itself out.

In the sequence in which it is established that it is hard for the Piggle to keep a stable image of DWW between sessions, he links "black Winnicott" to a denial of absence, linking this to the black mummy.

As Zaphiriou Woods writes, "Toddlerhood begins when an infant takes his first faltering, but independent steps [which] ushers in intrapsychic separateness, individuation, identity and autonomy, culminating in the toddler achieving inner images of his mother and of himself in her absence such that he can manage himself (body, thoughts, feelings)" (Zaphiriou Woods & Pretorius, 2011, p. 20). The mother's similar interval of a sibling birth in her own childhood made it difficult for her to reassure her daughter that the hating/feeling hated feelings were not the whole story (abiding love remained) since she, too, had felt overwhelmed by her experiences as a toddler, and guilty in the present. As an adult she turned passive into active, being the commissioner of the leave-taking in arranging another pregnancy and baby around the time that Gabrielle would have been testing her own leave-takings with the "excursions and returns that are significant in that if they fail, they alter the child's whole life" (Winnicott, 1966, p. 136).

Working with the parents in *The Piggle*

Gabrielle came to DWW's attention when her mother sent him a letter in January of 1964 when Gabrielle was two years, four months. One wonders if the fact that mother had trained at the Tavistock as a child psychotherapist and had supervision with Melanie Klein (Luepnitz, 2017, p. 350) compelled DWW to take the case despite his scant availability and illness. I say this because his term "psychoanalysis *partagé*" goes against the grain of Klein's conviction that children deserve a space away from parents in child analysis (Klein, 1955), and yet both DWW and Gabrielle's parents make clear how valuable both found the involvement of the parents. In the Afterword written by the parents, they write: "It has been of great value to the parents to be allowed to participate in a process of growth and reparation" (Winnicott, 1977, p. 199). Recent scholarship by Aguayo dates Winnicott's weaning from the Klein group to 1964 (Aguayo, 2018, p. 11), after Klein's death in 1960, and this was a time Winnicott felt freer to boldly assert his differences from Klein. Of Melanie Klein, who supervised Winnicott's early child cases and who analysed his wife Clare, Winnicott wrote: "[Klein] claimed to have paid full attention to the environmental factor, but it is my opinion that she was temperamentally incapable of this" (1962, p. 177).

Winnicott's relationship with the family

Mother's efforts were central to pulling the manuscript of *The Piggle* together, though DWW points out twice (p. 1 and p. 3) that her contributions were done with "*no* view towards publication" (emphasis mine) as if to make it appear there had been no plan during the treatment to collaborate. Yet, DWW made sure to include (p. 161) mother's gratitude that he included her in the treatment: "I have wanted to thank you very much for sending me the typescript of your last session with Gabrielle. It is most generous of you, and I am pleased that you knew how very much I would enjoy reading it."

It is difficult to imagine he did this with other parents, so it seems likely he did this because she was in the same field. He clearly felt enriched by the exchange with this enchanting family, particularly the mother. Similarly, on another occasion in a footnote, DWW includes mother's observation in reference to how "the black inside had to do with hate of the new baby" (p. 30). Again, her remark reads as a colleague's comment, not a mother's: "How strikingly the use of the transference emerges in the knife edge between participation and interpretation" (p. 30).

As it was incomplete, we do not know if DWW intended "psychoanalysis *partagé*" to mean parents' ideas were elicited (so they shared in the problem-solving of therapy), or that parents shared in receiving therapy. Or both. Clare Winnicott reported he did not complete his thoughts on this prior to his death, though he left a note on the manuscript about what he meant by psychoanalysis *partagé*: "Share material with the parents— not family therapy—not casework—psychoanalysis *partagé* (shared). No breach of confidence on their part, and they didn't interfere" (p. viii).

It seems "they didn't interfere" meant the parents maintained boundaries, not telling Gabrielle details of their conversations with DWW, and trusting the therapeutic relationship. Further, this note addressed how child analysts and parents could work together in a manner so as not to interfere with the child–analyst partnership as well as the parent–child one. Winnicott also believed one of the benefits of his "psychoanalysis on demand", which in this case meant sixteen meetings over a little under three years, was that it provided time and space for the relationship between children and parents to strengthen. He wrote, regarding a drawback of child therapy, "Once a child has started treatment what is lost sight of is the rich symptomatology of all children who are being cared for in their own satisfactory homes" (p. 2).

Klein, Winnicott, and Anna Freud

First-generation child analysts felt pressure to endow the field with the same gravitas as adult analysis. To do so, Klein equated play with free association, and provided deep interpretations to dispel anxiety. She avoided work with parents, doctors, or teachers to protect the child's space but also for fear reality elements could dilute the unconscious pith of psychoanalysis. It turns out that these were realistic fears if one knows the history of child analysis in the IPA (Kalas Reeves, 2017). Anna Freud's distinction between play and free association has frequently been misunderstood. Recall that Freud (1914d) abandoned hypnosis for free association because symptoms were thought to re-emerge once the influence of the doctor waned. Anna Freud believed the unconscious fantasies that emerge during play bypassed the child's immature ego since the observing part of the ego is still developing. The young child still requires adults to serve as auxiliary egos and superegos and therefore to equate play with free association implies a very different view of psychic development. Anna Freud very much agreed that young children's play is closer to primary process, so some of their differences could be seen as semantic but the bigger difference is in having different models of the mind and of development. Klein put most pathology as coming from the oral phase whereas Anna Freud felt different vulnerabilities arose from different developmental phases, and that there was a lot more that we did not know as to the aetiology of symptoms than we do know (A. Freud, 1970).

Opinion regarding whether to include the parents in child analysis has varied widely since the beginning, with some analysts promoting it and others not. There was a long period in the 1980s when it was considered best practice to almost never see an adolescent's parents, though that has been reconsidered in the Novicks' (2005) work. It was Masterson and Rinsley (Rinsley, 1981) and others who sought to create a healthier second individuation for adolescents via alternative adults such as the analyst, with the idea amounting to: get the adolescents away from the unhealthy parents who caused the troubles. That attitude is still somewhat prevalent in work with adolescents though now many of us feel far more comfortable if parents of adolescents are seen either by the same therapist/analyst as the adolescent or by another therapist/analyst.

For Winnicott, then, to announce that the parents did not interfere was directed towards Klein's conviction that child analysis was not proper analysis if real parents were included (beyond arrangements and fee), or if the frequency of meetings with the child were fewer than five times per week. DWW and Anna Freud were very interested to determine *the least* intervention necessary to help a child and family since analysis was a big undertaking, whereas Klein argued any child could benefit from analysis.

Anna Freud recommended working with parents though she underestimated the importance of the mother of earliest childhood (preoedipal). Anna Freud's followers, Erna Furman as well as Jack Novick and Kerry Kelly Novick, are most credited with creating a more systematic set of theories and techniques about work with parents in child and adolescent analysis. *Working With Parents Makes Therapy Work* by Jack and Kerry Kelly Novick describes the historic reasons why parent work has traditionally been fraught. In considering the psychodynamic reasons for this resistance, the Novicks suggest child analysts may be:

> driven by rescue fantasies … that use a hostile omnipotent fantasy as a defense against helplessness. The unconscious hostility to parents contained in the therapist's fantasy for rescuing the child may be the element of response to parents' defensive hostility that contributes to the difficulty of the work. In order to feel with parents, especially the mother, the child analyst must become aware of his or her own unconscious primitive wishes, fears, and defensive and reactive rage to the "pregendered" mother, the first object for identification for both boys and girls. (2005, p. 11)

As a child analyst, one regularly hears from adult analysts how much they would have enjoyed staying with child work if not for the parents! When a child analyst can engage the parents as the experts on their child and family, and feel with them, it is under those conditions that the work often proceeds most smoothly. Even adolescents are frequently relieved that parents are seen, understanding that their sessions are utterly confidential as the parents are seen for help *as parents*.

Winnicott felt "that analysis can get in the way of allowing satisfactory homes to tolerate symptoms" (1977, p. 2), an attitude which showed his overall confidence in Gabrielle's sturdiness and that the parents were well beyond "good enough". Indications that this mother felt vulnerable come through in her sincere letters acknowledging her helplessness, guilt, and anxiety. This mother's self-analysing functioning imbued Gabrielle with similar capacities in this family with psychologically minded, musical, eloquent, and playful parents. When the adult Gabrielle was asked about her parents sending her to DWW when the marriage was in difficulties (Luepnitz, 2017, p. 350), I was reminded of the lifelong wish among children of divorce for their parents to reunite. While her mother remained certain for all her days that the treatment was crucial to Gabrielle's development, the adult Gabrielle wished the marital troubles had been treated. An adult would surely realise a divorce in childhood to be more influential than a sibling birth. Was there a relationship between Winnicott's intervention and the end of the marriage? Was mum's devotion to DWW a threat to father? It seems no small accident that in the Afterword, supposedly written by both parents (though I suspect it was alone written by the mother), there is no mention that the parents had separated after the treatment ended.

Hints about the marital troubles?

In a letter from the parents written by father after the first consultation, he wrote:

> I think you were right that we had been too "clever" about our understanding her distress. We felt very involved and guilty about not having arranged to not have a baby again so soon and somehow, her nightly desperate pleading—"Tell me about the babacar"—made us feel under pressure to say something meaningful ... When Susan was born, Gabrielle seemed somehow thrown out of her mould, and cut off from her sources of nourishment.

We found it hurtful to see her so diminished and reduced, and she may well have sensed this. There was also a period of tension between us two [the parents]. (Winnicott, 1977, p. 20)

One can see the guilt in the being too clever (I take this to mean overcomplicated in their interpretations of Gabrielle's behaviour) and the double negatives surrounding sex. The parents felt guilty and responsible for her strong reaction, which led to blaming difficulties between them as a couple. DWW was a great comfort to both parents, particularly mother, as when he reassured them of how she was managing well despite their repeated letters replete with anxiety similar to the one above. The admiration and affection he showed for Gabrielle's struggles as well as her creative ingenuity in playful problem-solving also lessened their helpless guilt as parents and helped them take pride in their daughter. Additionally, he confirmed all the lovely aspects of the parents' childrearing. After the twelfth consultation, mother wrote to DWW:

I would like to tell you—though you may know this—how much writing to you has helped me; somehow to give form to my perplexities and fears, with the knowledge that they would be received with great understanding; and the feeling of being in relation to you. I am sure all this helped me to work through our anxieties about Gabrielle and again to find our right relationship with her. My anxieties were very intense at the time of Susan's birth—I forget whether I told you that I have a brother, who I greatly resented, who was born when I was almost exactly the same age as Gabrielle was when Susan was born. (p. 161)

Here mum expressed how significant his being on the other end of her anxious letters with a thoughtful, loving openness meant to her. She alluded to her own loss of being an only to a mother (she also having been the eldest), another thread in the intergenerational transmission of loss. Interestingly, when mum reported Gabrielle's requests to see DWW, one often has the impression that mother herself wished to see him, or that in sending Gabrielle to DWW she offered her daughter something she considered more valuable than what she herself could offer. Although the letters from mother show that it was Gabrielle requesting these visits, given how closely linked mother–toddler psyches are, these were also mother's wishes. When DWW wrote back that it may have to wait as he was busy or ill, that was another way DWW strengthened this dyad with the implied confidence that they would be fine even if they must wait.

It is irresistible to ask whether Winnicott's idealisation of this family blinded him to the marriage problems. I tried to go back to see if I found that Gabrielle's symptoms can be read as anxiety about her parents' marriage falling apart. The black mummy and babacar are understood by most as relating to Gabrielle being afraid of her aggressive feelings towards her mother for her faithlessness in having another baby. On occasion, there is a black mummy and a black daddy together in her night terrors. Furthermore, she cries when the old parting song "Muss Ich Denn" is sung as a lullaby with the new words her family gave it, "and the mummy and the daddy will be here". Is this sensitive toddler the only member of the family who was onto the marital breakdown? How often do we child analysts suggest that a child's distress is in fact due to this very thing? Quite often. Is the father's guilt, conveyed in the double negatives of the letter above, due to the fact that the new baby was prematurely conceived in the hopes that a new baby could rescue or resuscitate the marriage? All three adults were focused on Gabrielle—was it a *folie* or *ménage à trois*? Mother sent the child analyst observations of her children but rarely much about the marriage or "period of tension". *The Piggle* commemorates a time when the family was intact with both parents actively invested in their children and to one another. Yet somehow they were not able to make conscious, even with the great Winnicott on the case, that the most powerful source of Gabrielle's nightmares may have been the fraying of the marriage. Luepnitz's article shares that both families had loss and trauma, which makes the leaving song "Muss Ich Denn" all the more poignant. Intended as a song about a young man who leaves his sweetheart to go to work faraway, he promises to be faithful and asks her to wait for him. The themes of leave-taking, transformation of relationships throughout the various stages of the life cycle, and trust resonate in Gabrielle and the narrator of "Muss Ich Denn".

The developmental object and trauma

Another way to conceptualise Winnicott's role to the family is to think of him as a developmental object. Tähkä (1993) introduced the term developmental object, which has been elaborated by followers of Anna Freud, Anne Hurry (1998), Jill Miller (2013), and Carla Neely (2020). In addition to the analyst being used as a contemporary object or past (transference) object, the new (developmental) object is created by the patient for the analyst to act differently from the original developmental object being sought in the transference. In Tähkä's words, this new developmental object is based on the analyst's "empathic and/or complementary recognition of the patient's frustrated and arrested developmental needs and potentials" (1993, p. 231). DWW becomes a greedy baby in the first meeting to show Gabrielle he understands what she has just lost and that by playing with those feelings, the fear of one's own aggression is mitigated. When Gabrielle "kills" him and he is still there, it helps her realise there is a big difference between a feeling and reality. The analyst as developmental object can be especially therapeutic when there is transgenerational trauma, as Luepnitz (2017) disinters through sleuthing the suppression of the name "Esther". Not only is the unspeakable part of Gabrielle's name a reference to the trauma of the murdered relatives of the Holocaust but it also connects siblings' births through the generations. Regarding these, Carla Neely writes:

> So often patients come to us having experienced the cumulative trauma of not having been seen, not having been recognized. Analysis then involves an effort to help the patient mourn, to face loss, and to face not only separation but the state of aloneness. In order to recognize and tolerate those affective states in the patient, the analyst will need to be comfortable with those states in herself. It is in this way that she can become a developmental object who provides an opportunity for the patient to create new internal models of self and other. The patient then is aided in taking a new developmental step. When in the throes of transference, the analyst stands in for someone else or a part of the patient's self; in those moments the patient does not realize that the analyst sees him. When the analyst is functioning as a developmental object, the patient has the potential to realize that he is being seen and heard. (2020)

Tracing how the notion of the developmental object links with Anna Freud's work on developmental help, so relevant to child analytic work,

Jill Miller writes: "The analyst is then a developmental object who meets developmental needs not by interpretation, but through the interaction, with the aim of creating new internal models of self and other" (2013, p. 313).

In being able to kill off DWW (Winnicott, 1977, p. 151) and dream of the three-generational family (p. 167) in the pool, Gabrielle demonstrates integration of the hurt parts with the sturdy parts of her self.

Witnessing and the developmental object

If the Piggle's parents contacted me today, after hearing their concerns in a fifteen to twenty minute initial phone call, I would recommend meeting without the child for multiple sessions to see how far we could get. This would signal to the parents that they are the experts on their child, that their commitment to and participation in the work is crucial and that it is neither advisable nor possible for me to do the work without them. In this first phone call I would also mention the dual goals of child analysis, 1) for their relationship with their child to be a lifelong loving and supportive relationship, and 2) to help the child back to the path of progressive development (Novick & Novick, 2005).

One definition the Novicks (2005) have ascribed to parent work is "psychotherapy of the parenting function". By this they mean that developmental interferences to parenting are amenable to therapeutic work using all the techniques we use in psychotherapy and analysis. It is clear from the mother's letters that she suffered guilt about having another baby, identified with the Piggle upon Sush baby's birth, and frequently denied how important she was to her daughter.

Deborah Luepnitz's work showed there was a traumatic history in both parents. For the mother the trauma involved the death of several family members who perished in the Holocaust. The father was an only child whose mother had multiple miscarriages. As such, it would also be important to address mother's survival guilt, which would include thinking with her about the feelings she carried related to the fact that beloved family members perished in concentration camps. We could work on the unspeakable grief Luepnitz's paper highlights regarding the name "Esther". Ilany Kogan and Hillel Klein, psychoanalysts who have written about Holocaust survivors, describe duelling experiences in the creation of a new family:

> The creation of a new family was seen by the survivors as con-firmation of life and denial of the loss of their families … Many survivor mothers were obsessed by their anxieties and fears that their children are or could be injured and destroyed. In the analysis of such cases we discover that the children have been used as symbolic representations of their damaged self. (Klein & Kogan, 1986, p. 46)

The Piggle's nightmares of the black mummy and the babacar are remi-niscent of Primo Levi's description of the SS "men with black patches" (*The Drowned and the Saved*, 1986, p. 78). The text of *The Piggle* does not mention the horrors of the Shoah perhaps due to the fact that this global trauma was so fresh at the time she was treated that it took several more decades before people could speak at any length about the unspeakable horrors of World War II. At the time, Winnicott did not have the work of Ilany Kogan and Hillel Klein (1986), Ira Brenner and Judith Kestenberg (1996), Warren Poland (2000), and others to aid him in thinking about these issues. Witnessing is an analytic attitude that is consonant with the notion of the analyst as developmental object, as listening and witness-ing provide psychic scaffolding for experiences that have not been felt, represented, or talked about as the person feels to do so will risk feeling overpowering shame or harm.

It would be interesting for future research to consider whether the parents' divorce had to do with survivor's guilt, as in an unconscious fantasy along the lines of "I get to live but not thrive"—a theme in the survivor literature. The unconscious compromise formations of survi-vors expose them to what Wurmser (1981) called "the severe neuroses", which can include sadomasochistic patterns of relating. Though specu-lative, it is possible that the parents getting Gabrielle help straight away with one of the finest child analysts felt the best immunity for future health. Obtaining help for themselves and their marriage might have been beyond their capacities at that time. In *The Piggle* itself there is not enough information to speculate on these matters. In an earlier draft,

I described what I thought was a transient beating fantasy in Gabrielle as her attempts to self-soothe did not calm her, and she often engaged in conflictual masturbation after feeling lonely, aggressive, and sad. These ideas warrant further exploration. What we do know is that the adult Gabrielle regrets that her parents did not go for marriage therapy. Divorce is the death of a hope to be together for a lifetime and its sad effects on children are well known.

Conclusion

Winnicott did not get to elaborate "psychoanalysis *partagé*" due to his untimely death. One way of reading *The Piggle* is that it is a requiem, Winnicott's goodbye to the world he wanted to nourish. Each time I read through *The Piggle* I found a new strand to focus on, and at times I felt frustrated with him as if he left a heap of dangling signifiers in need of interpretation. Psychoanalysis *partagé* would have been a significant contribution since up until the mid-1990s the psychoanalytic literature on work with parents was limited to keeping them involved enough to ensure payment and attendance. Finally, this stunning text is hailed for being unique in human literature for showing a toddler's and a mother's subjectivity through the sensitive eyes and observations of parents and DWW who put it all down in words. It is Winnicott's and Piggle's mum's great contribution that they were able to vividly portray Gabrielle's experiences such that readers can comprehend the profound devastation and disruption she felt. When sensitively handled, a new sibling is the best thing that ever happens to a child. Part of getting there for Gabrielle and her parents, which they indubitably do, involved mourning this poignant time that is no more, such that buoyant expectancy of the ongoing transformations of development can prevail. What is dizzyingly brilliant about Piggle's capacity to verbalise and dramatise, and of all the adults with the prescience to register and preserve the evidence of these raw feelings of loss, murder, collapse, and reconstitution is that it is accomplished *despite the powerful human tendency to repress and get rid of these experiences.* I think Winnicott was powerfully aware of how rare and unique this was, as evidenced in a letter to the parents well after their work: "She gave so much of herself to me in those treatment sessions! It was a very rich experience for me …" (Luepnitz, 2017, p. 360).

In order for child psychoanalysis to continue to thrive, DWW's ideas regarding "psychoanalysis on demand" and "psychoanalysis *partagé*" warrant our focused attention. The first idea begs us to re-examine our concrete requirement in psychoanalytic trainings that three to five sessions per week define a treatment as psychoanalytic. The second idea is about the centrality of engaging parents in the child/adolescent work to intervene with greater precision. How can psychoanalysts, who so privilege metaphor, dreaming, and symbols be the hobgoblins of something as concrete as times per week met? The number of people training in child analysis has decreased in the US. This is not the case in Latin America or the UK, though for spurious political reasons the UK-trained professionals, called child psychotherapists, cannot be called "child psychoanalysts" until they qualify as adult psychoanalysts, and therefore operate outside the IPA. Will child analytic trainings wither because we are unwilling to reconsider the frequency issue? As Winnicott said, psychoanalysis is determined by whether the clinician has had an analysis. I do not know the answer to these quandaries but I invite organised psychoanalysis to soberly engage with the loss to our body of knowledge if we cannot attract families to a frequency that *we* need, or to candidates who forego training in child analysis because they doubt they can convince a family to bring a child three to five times per week for at least a year. To be clear, many children, adolescents, and parents would benefit from multiple weekly sessions. The reality, however, is that it has become harder given the menu of mental health offerings that purport to be cheaper in time and money. We can also do a better job of promoting how cost-effective psychoanalytic treatments are in comparison to inpatient programmes, or to long-term sole psychopharmacologic interventions.

References

Aguayo, J. (2018). D. W. Winnicott, Melanie Klein, and W. R. Bion: The controversy over the nature of the external object—holding and container/contained (1941–1967). *Psychoanalytic Quarterly, 87*: 767–807.

Balsam, R. H. (2017). Freud, the birthing body, and modern life. *Journal of the American Psychoanalytic Association, 65*(1): 61–90.

Bürgin, D. (2016). Treatment on demand. *British Journal of Psychotherapy, 32*(3): 347–358.

Daws, D. (1989). *Through the Night: Helping Parents and Sleepless Infants.* London: Free Association.

Fraiberg, S., Adelson, E., & Shapiro, V. (1975). Ghosts in the nursery: A psychoanalytic approach to the problems of impaired infant-mother relationships. *Journal of the American Academy of Child & Adolescent Psychiatry, 14*: 387–421.

Freud, A. (1970). The symptomatology of childhood—a preliminary attempt at classification. *Psychoanalytic Study of the Child, 25*: 19–41.

Freud, S. (1914d). On the history of the psychoanalytic movement. S. E., 14. London: Hogarth.

Furman, E. (1979). The Piggle: An account of the psychoanalytic treatment of a little girl. *Psychoanalytic Quarterly, 48*: 324–326.

Furman, E. (1992). *Toddlers and Their Mothers.* New York: International Universities Press.

Furman, E. (1996). On motherhood. *Journal of the American Psychoanalytic Association, 44*: 429–447.

Hurry, A. (Ed.) (1998). *Psychoanalysis and Developmental Therapy.* London: Karnac.

Kalas Reeves, J. (2017). On losing and being lost without Anna Freud's "revolutionary overhaul". *Journal of the American Psychoanalytic Association, 65*(6): 1077–1101.

Kestenberg, J., & Brenner, I. (1996). *The Last Witness: The Child Survivor of the Holocaust.* Washington, DC: American Psychiatric Press.

Klein, H., & Kogan, I. (1986). Identification processes and denial in the shadow of Nazism. *International Journal of Psychoanalysis, 67*(1): 45–52.

Klein, M. (1955). The psychoanalytic play technique: Its history and significance. In: *Envy and Gratitude and Other Works 1946–1963.* International Psycho-Analytic Library. London: Hogarth.

Levi, P. (1986). *The Drowned and the Saved.* Turin, Italy: Giulio Einaudi.

Luepnitz, D. A. (2017). The name of the Piggle: Reconsidering Winnicott's classic case in light of some conversations with the adult 'Gabrielle'. *International Journal of Psychoanalysis, 98*(2): 343–370.

Mahler, M. S. (1972). On the first three subphases of the separation–individuation process. *International Journal of Psychoanalysis, 53*: 333–338.

Miller, J. M. (2013). Developmental psychoanalysis and developmental objects. *Psychoanalytic Inquiry, 33*(4): 312–322.

Neely, C. (2020). The developmental object and therapeutic action. *Psychoanalytic Study of the Child*. Taylor & Francis Online.

Novick, J., & Novick, K. K. (2005). *Working with Parents Makes Therapy Work*. Lanham, MD: Rowman & Littlefield.

Poland, W. S. (2000). The analyst's witnessing and otherness. *Journal of the American Psychoanalytic Association, 48*(1): 17–34.

Raphael-Leff, J. (1995). Psychoanalysis and feminism. *British Journal of Psychotherapy, 12*(1): 84–88.

Reeves, C. (2015a). Reappraising Winnicott's *The Piggle*: A critical commentary. Part I: Introduction and the treatment. *British Journal of Psychotherapy, 31*(2): 156–190.

Reeves, C. (2015b). Reappraising Winnicott's *The Piggle*: A critical commentary. Part II: Discussion and critique. *British Journal of Psychotherapy, 31*(3): 285–297.

Rinsley, D. B. (1981). Borderline psychopathology: The concepts of Masterson and Rinsley and beyond. *Adolescent Psychiatry: Developmental and Clinical Studies, 9*: 259–274.

Stern, D. (1995). *The Motherhood Constellation: A Unified View of Parent–Infant Psychotherapy*. New York: Basic Books.

Tähkä, V. (1993). *Mind and Its Treatment: A Psychoanalytic Approach*. Madison, CT: International Universities Press.

Teurnell, L. (1993). An alternative reading of Winnicott: The Piggle—a sexually abused girl? *International Forum of Psychoanalysis, 2*(3): 139–144.

Winnicott, D. W. (1962). A personal view of the Kleinian contribution. In: *The Maturational Processes and the Facilitating Environment* (pp. 171–178). New York: International Universities Press.

Winnicott, D. W. (1966). The child in the family group. In C. Winnicott, R. Shepherd, & M. Davis (Eds.), *Home Is Where We Start From* (pp. 128–141). London: Penguin, 1990.

Winnicott, D. W. (1977). *The Piggle: An Account of the Psychoanalytic Treatment of a Little Girl*. New York: International Universities Press.

Wurmser, L. (1981). *The Mask of Shame*. Baltimore, MD: Johns Hopkins University Press.

Zaphiriou Woods, M., & Pretorius, I. (2011). *Parents and Toddlers in Groups: A Psychoanalytic Developmental Approach*. London: Routledge.

CHAPTER SEVEN

Inviting the Piggle into therapy: a contemporary perspective

Zack Eleftheriadou

Introduction

The aim of this chapter is to present a contemporary psychoanalytic therapeutic overview of Donald Winnicott's case of *The Piggle* from an interpersonal framework. The reader will be invited into the consulting room and asked to imagine this family reaching out for help. An outline of the therapeutic process and how we engage with the different family members will be discussed, with the young child being at the forefront of the therapeutic stage at all times. Theoretically, I will draw from Brafman's (2016) supposition that it is more effective therapeutically if we engage with the parents and the child as a system. I will also refer to Stern and colleagues' (1998) and Beebe's (2005) writings regarding the importance of the implicit arena of communication demonstrating why meeting the whole family in person is essential. Finally, I will refer to Fraiberg, Adelson, and Shapiro's (1975) seminal work on intergenerational trauma as a critical part of the assessment process and therapeutic exploration. Many poignant questions raised by the case study will be considered, such as the treatment style, the role of play, and developmental issues. Specific psychoanalytic technique, such as transferential processes are beyond the scope of this chapter (please refer to Reeves, Chapter Three).

Identifying who is the client: therapeutic beginnings

Donald Winnicott's case of Gabrielle or the Piggle (as she was called by her parents) is about a girl of two years and four months, consumed by anxiety and fear which emerged both in her narrative and in her play. In brief, the sequence of events progressed as follows: Gabrielle's mother communicated in writing to Winnicott requesting his therapeutic input. She had already mentioned Winnicott to Gabrielle and Gabrielle in turn had asked to see Winnicott (Winnicott, 1977 p. 7). It is intriguing to think about what it means for a mother of a two-year-old child to seek therapeutic input and whether an admission of this kind by the mother (that she can not help her child but an outsider can) might intensify feelings of not being psychologically held in the child. At the same time, it was probably reassuring to Gabrielle that someone was identified in the parents' minds that could offer help. Of course, it is worth bearing in mind that when Winnicott was treating Gabrielle, adult psychoanalysis had not generally been adapted for work with children. There were challenges for Winnicott on how to treat such a young child, although his vast paediatric experience with infants and young children gave him an advantage.

The main channels of communication between the parents and Winnicott took place via letters. The mother had an initial consultation with Winnicott but it was mainly the father who accompanied Gabrielle to her sessions. Nowadays, it is likely that communication would take place via internet-based means, perhaps with the occasional phone call. Although parents may still provide a great deal of information remotely, what has not changed in psychotherapy is the importance of the face-to-face encounter between parents and clinician. The predominant reason for this is that remote contact is not conducive to cultivating a trusting therapeutic relationship and it can leave key family dynamics unexplored. This might be best understood by turning to Winnicott's famous statement that "There is no such thing as a baby ... if you set out to describe a baby, you will find you are describing a baby and someone. A baby cannot exist alone, but is essentially part of a relationship"

(1964, p. 88). This quote sets the scene for what is now described by contemporary schools of psychoanalysis as an interpersonal or inter-subjective model; in other words, the sense of self and the emotions one experiences are learned and expressed via a relationship. This is a broad psychoanalytic perspective which suggests that although from the beginning we start to develop unconscious intrapsychic lives, there is always an influence from our primary relationships. Following on from this premise, psychological derailment may occur intrapsychically but it may also be fuelled by parental projections. Therefore, a child cannot be understood in isolation without the family, since it is an interrelated system. Brafman (2016) states that from the outset the professional "faces a complex picture, where child and parents are involved in a mutually reinforcing vicious circle and it is virtually impossible to decide what is cause and what is effect" (p. xiv).

He goes on to say:

> Because I believe the persistence of the symptom is probably linked to the child's interaction with one or both his parents, I also try to investigate how they had interpreted their child's symptoms and, consequently, have been dealing with their child's problem prior to seeing me. When the parents realise what has, in fact, been tormenting their child and manage to change their approach to him or her, it is almost certain that the child's symptoms will disappear. (2016, p. 162)

Furthermore, contemporary psychoanalytic theorists favour face-to-face contact because they believe that the most essential aspects in under-standing the quality of relationships are implicit. These include spatial aspects, gestures, voice tone, and rhythm of the interaction. Detailed micro-analysis research examining these elements by Beatrice Beebe (2005) clearly illustrates the mutuality of the mother and baby relation-ship: "It is a 'co-constructed' process in which each partner makes moment-by-moment adjustments in response to the other's shifts in behaviour such as gaze, facial expression, orientation, touch, vocal quality, and body and vocal rhythms" (p. 6).

The narrative between infant and mother can appear coherent, but when watched as tiny segments of micro-moments it can be seen that there are sometimes exchanges which are less than synchronised. These micro-moments occur very quickly and therefore in real time can be easily missed. They are extremely important as they are informative in providing a clearer picture about who is initiating or avoiding interaction at any given time. Another problematic issue with remote contact is that it is difficult for the child to know that the parents have direct access to the therapist, but they do not. This is especially difficult for a young child who cannot hold in mind temporal aspects and for whom waiting to see the therapist can feel unbearable.

Taking all these factors into consideration, in contemporary therapy the parents would be invited on their own for a few sessions. For families like Gabrielle's who don't live in close proximity to the therapist, a clinician might offer extended session meetings (the therapeutic fifty-minute session not being long enough to get a sense of the problem and to take a full developmental history). During the first meeting, the clinician would enquire if the parents had mentioned anything about the therapy to the child. If not, the clinician would carefully work out an acceptable script with them for telling the child about the impending therapy. Parents always add their own psychological slant, but preparation for talking to their child can help them to begin to process their own feelings and to make an explanation to their child which will set the stage for a positive first visit. There can often be concern about what to say because suddenly the parents are having an open conversation about what is troubling them at home regarding their child.

At the first meeting between Winnicott and Gabrielle, he invited both parents and child into the consulting room, and instructed the mother, with whom Gabrielle sat, to do nothing. A mother who is familiar with the therapeutic process (as Gabrielle's mother seemed to have been) may interfere and attempt to steer the therapy in a particular direction. This may have been Winnicott's motive in suggesting that the mother do nothing, as he certainly was aware of how parents could be a hindrance to the therapeutic process. In *The Piggle* the parents appeared to see themselves as co-therapists and in a way this is how Winnicott treated them in regard to thinking about Gabrielle. Inevitably, there is a therapeutic component in enlisting parents to think alongside the therapist, but at the same time the parents also remain our clients. From my clinical perspective, when parents come into the consulting room with their child, they are not directed to do anything in particular, but the therapist simply observes and experiences how they naturally relate to each other and to their child.

When parents of younger children seek help, they often need it rather urgently. Normally, children are referred when the issues have become more complicated and when an external person or professional notices some difficulties. In terms of the Piggle, we can speculate about who instigated the referral and what was it that became so difficult for the parents to manage. A child can evoke powerful feelings for their parents, triggered from their own history. These feelings are often unprocessed and unbearable to hold, and therefore may in turn may be projected onto their child. Bearing in mind the strength of feeling the parents may be experiencing in such cases, a supportive professional has to work hard to contain parental feelings (of shame, feeling deskilled, anger, among potentially many others).

The goal of the first few meetings with the parents is to gather background historical information, carefully noting not only what is being included in the narrative, but equally what is being left out; how these dynamics are being conveyed is also significant. Somewhere along the line the family has become stuck and they need to learn to relate to one another differently. A therapist tries to understand the explicit and implicit dynamics and convey them in a more "digestible" form when the parents are ready to consider them. When the parents seem to be repeating their own unconscious model of relationships, the therapist works together with each of them to understand how their own experience links with their particular parenting style (and how it differs towards each child in the family). As Fraiberg, Adelson, and Shapiro (1975) discuss in the clinically invaluable paper, "Ghosts in the Nursery", these re-enactments of the negative way they were parented (ghosts) reappear uninvited and during the therapy there is an opportunity for them to be extinguished: "In each case, when our therapy has brought the parent to remember and re-experience his childhood anxiety and suffering, the ghosts depart and the afflicted parents become the protectors of their children against the repetition of their own conflicted past" (pp. 420–421).

These elements tend to be rather specific unconscious dynamics which can only be assessed in person. If Winnicott had taken a more detailed family history it would have indicated whether anything traumatic had been experienced by either of Gabrielle's parents or whether trauma had occurred even further back in the family history. It is extremely likely that a young child's symptomatology is linked to something in at least one of the parents. In *The Piggle*, we could hypothesise that Gabrielle had absorbed unresolved parental issues. For example, the recurring feelings about her sister may actually have belonged to her mother. We know from the mother's letter to Winnicott that she had a brother born only two years after her own birth: "My anxieties were very intense at the time of Susan's birth—I forget whether I told you that I have a brother, whom I greatly resented, who was born when I was almost exactly the same age as Gabrielle was when Susan was born" (p. 161).

Another therapeutic aim is to gauge the parents' capacity to self-reflect (Slade, 2005). Related to this is their capacity to empathise and mirror different mental affective states accurately to their child; for example, perceiving their child's sadness as just that and not as rejection or defiance towards them. In other words, we would be assessing whether the parents are able to differentiate between their own thoughts and feelings and those of their child, that is, whether they can really hold their child in mind. They may hold an unconscious image of the child and it may be difficult to separate that from who the "real" child is (Cramer, 1992). The hope is that eventually through self-reflection they can create a protective and containing way of being with their child, slowly letting go of any unhelpful narratives.

In the first session, Winnicott asked Gabrielle to attend on her own but she wanted her mother to join her; she entered his office hesitantly. Today a young child might also be seen on their own, but there may be some flexibility in that they might be seen together with the parents for some of the time if they were anxious about separation or if other factors suggested that conjoint therapy was indicated. What Winnicott highlighted in his many writings (e.g. 2006) and in *The Piggle* was that psychopathology can sometimes be located within the child (not purely as a result of parental projections) and therefore there are times that it is appropriate to work only with the child in the room. However, deciphering what is within the child and what is located within the family members is in no way straightforward even for an experienced clinician. For example, we would expect that during new situations or when feeling dysregulated, a child would tend to seek close proximity to the parents for safety. Although Winnicott was comfortable with Gabrielle's comings and goings with her father (who was sitting in the waiting room and sometimes joined her in the consulting room), the father did not take an active part in her play. Nowadays in conjoint therapy both parents would be encouraged to attend and a more active interaction between the child and each parent would be encouraged. The aim would be to observe the affective, behavioural, and verbal exchanges with the child and each parent. Schechter and Willheim (2009) remind us that "Central to the work is the observation of parent–child interaction—holding, communicating, feeding, grooming/diapering, dressing, and of course, playing" (p. 249) which all take place during unstructured interaction time.

Thus far the focus of this discussion has been about the richness of Gabrielle's parents' psychic lives and the possible influence on their child. This might have been a particularly salient dynamic in the case of *The Piggle* as she was the eldest child in the family. It is not clear whether parental consultations were considered by Winnicott (of course he offered many during his career) but in contemporary practice these are often an option, especially with younger children. Sometimes, family dynamics can alter via parental consultations, but in the case of *The Piggle*, Winnicott made the decision to work with Gabrielle directly. He seemed to have made the clinical judgement that the psychopathology was located within Gabrielle and not within her parents. Casting our minds back, one of the primary reasons Gabrielle was referred for treatment was related to her powerful feelings towards the birth of her sister. Although this is a very common issue that children grapple with, especially firstborn children, in contemporary work we would also try to understand the further impact of Gabrielle's mother's experience (she had stated that she "resented" (p. 161) her younger brother and she had the same gap with him as Gabrielle and her sister). This may have fuelled Gabrielle's intrapsychic conflict and as a result was replayed in her life. More contemporary writings discuss how siblings are more prominent in the formation of the self than previously considered in psychoanalysis (Coles, 2018; Mitchell, 2003). In such a case, the clinician has to consider whether it would be helpful to invite the whole family into the consulting room, including the sibling(s). As indicated earlier, the direct observation of sibling interaction can help us to decipher how much of the conflict is in the child's mind and how much it's fuelled by parental projections.

Play, language, and interpretations

One of the most significant aspects of learning in *The Piggle* is the role of therapeutic play. Winnicott (1971) believed passionately that play gave access to the fantasy and the imagination, and therefore that it was a valuable assessment and therapeutic tool which required continual inventiveness. He wrote that "The game is played and enjoyed" (1977, p. 175) before being understood and interpreted. He believed that the therapist should be an observer as well as an active participant who also gets enjoyment from the play. Through small enactments of Gabrielle's fears (for example, Winnicott enacting the role of the greedy baby), he made it tolerable for Gabrielle to experience her anxieties in the presence of a sensitive and regulated adult. In *The Piggle*, we get a taste of how Winnicott began to refine child analysis. He seemed to know instinctively that he needed to be at the child's physical level and he placed himself on the floor, which at that time would not have been common practice in psychoanalysis. Most therapists, nowadays, would agree that it is essential to be at the child's level, especially when working with younger children. Winnicott encouraged children to find whatever toy or object in the room could represent their emotional experience. He provided everyday objects, such as bits of wood, plastic strawberry boxes, a handle tied to some string, a stick, an Optrex eye solution cup, a little bottle, and some tangled string. It is evident that he was comfortable having a mixture of toys and non-toy items available. When he sensed Gabrielle's hesitancy to come into the room, he found a creative way of introducing Gabrielle to the toys, saying: "Bring teddy over here, I want to show him the toys" (p. 9). Here, Winnicott and Gabrielle shared a moment where they were both meeting the toys. We see how he took care building the therapeutic alliance, just as a clinician would in today's clinical practice.

Winnicott seemed to form a therapeutic alliance (via play) rather quickly with Gabrielle, because he grasped her communications and he was selective in what he chose to interpret. Some contemporary clinicians might try to encourage play more actively, but I would argue that it was only through Winnicott's patience that Gabrielle began to understand how to play (particularly the symbolism of play). A young child who is stuck in the same game and doesn't have the conceptualisation to express their emotions might be facilitated to communicate through play with the traditional mini figures and animals, very much as Winnicott did. A contemporary therapist might use a wider range of arts-based methods (such as drawing, puppets, play dough, or sand play to enable the child to enact an emotional state. However, I believe Winnicott provided the right balance with different materials and yet he did not flood the very young Gabrielle with too much choice. In a more contemporary way, I wonder if a clinician might use more age appropriate language to help the child process their feelings and think, such as: "Monkey is saying that sometimes he feels sad saying goodbye to mummy." The next step might be to make a link to the child: "Maybe monkey feels sad, like Gabrielle feels sometimes when she has to say goodnight to mummy." However, this depends on the child's readiness to receive such an intervention, otherwise the communication might have to remain in the metaphor of the play. There would be an accompanying open attitude, giving the child the opportunity to consider the feeling suggested by the therapist, agree or disagree with it, or even rename it.

Reading *The Piggle* closely we can find contradictions. Winnicott sometimes fell into the way therapy would have been thought of at that time, not dissimilar to adult psychoanalysis. There were moments when he interrupted spontaneous play and resorted to traditional interpretation, which we might now think of as having been too sophisticated (for example with themes of infantile sexuality). However, at times, he also interpreted the transference sparingly. In an example where he went about things in an exploratory way, gently questioning Gabrielle, rather than appearing the all-knowing adult, he stated:

> She was still joining up bits of trains and I said: "You could be joining up all the different times that you have seen me." Her reply: "Yes." Obviously, there are many interpretations to do with the joining of parts of trains, and one can use this according to the way one feels is most appropriate at the moment, or to convey one's own feelings. (pp. 77–78)

Overall, it was always important to Winnicott to retain fluidity through creative play and his playful choice of wording. We can see that he opened up the whole idea of there being different possibilities for understanding the dynamics at any one moment in a session of therapeutic play. Likewise, Anna Freud (1983) stated "Experimenting and guessing are the task of the analyst—we can't help that, there are no certainties" (p. 100). Winnicott believed making contact was the most important aspect of working with the child and it wasn't always through an interpretation. He was on the cusp of something new, moving away from dogmatic practice, placing more emphasis on play (and its unfolding) and the importance of the therapeutic relationship. Interestingly, in his later life he said "Psychoanalysis is not just a matter of interpreting the repressed unconscious; it is rather the provision of a professional setting for trust, in which such work may take place" (1990, pp. 114–115). He certainly did not always remain the "neutral" psychoanalyst. For example, when Gabrielle needed help cutting, he helped her with the scissors that were in his pocket. This has more of a contemporary component, acknowledging a real relationship with a child rather than responding with an interpretation of early anxieties and naming the transference.

Contemporary interpersonal psychoanalysts, such as Stern et al. (1998), have written extensively that the therapeutic relationship is of paramount importance and more important than interpretation. Stern also discussed different therapeutic interventions, such as addressing the parents in a session with a child, sometimes directed to the child, and finding moments of addressing the parents and the child together. Similarly, Brafman (2016) refers to the therapist as a "simultaneous interpreter" whose role is to understand the unconscious anxiety of the child but also those of the parents and what sense they are making of the child's distress. One might say something along the lines of: "Mummy [including the parent as much as possible], I am wondering what Gabrielle is doing with that car." This might get the child interested and to respond verbally or show something significant. This would be noted and the clinician may wait until there is further clarity before making a comment addressing the unconscious content more directly.

Once again departing from adult psychoanalysis, we know that younger children are not able to wait for containment. They sometimes need someone to think for them and cannot cope alone when distressed.

Gabrielle seemed stuck in a state of fear, and when it got too much she sought out her father in the waiting room. It was an important sign that she was able to look to her parent for regulation of her distress. However, we cannot assume that parents will be receptive to their child's stress signals, and when they are not we need to find ways to facilitate the parent to respond appropriately as soon as possible, before difficult dynamics are reinforced. We don't know how long it took Gabrielle to calm down at home, but the letters indicated that, at times, her distress was prolonged. It would have been helpful for Winnicott to have watched how Gabrielle behaved as well as observing the nature of her play in the presence of her mother. Research has shown that mothers of secure children will facilitate more exploration and seem comfortable to become involved in their child's play (Slade, 1988).

Furthermore, it has been shown that "Parents of insecure children do well enough when the going is good, but find it hard to cope with their children's negative affects" (Holmes & Slade, 2018, p. 27). We know that Winnicott fully comprehended toddlers' primitive feelings and as a result tolerated Gabrielle's intense feelings of rage and fear. This seemed therapeutic for her. However, in some types of contemporary therapy the aim would be to facilitate safe expression of these emotions in the presence of the parents too. One can speculate that Gabrielle could not express feelings of rage, fearing she would be rejected by her parents. Additionally, anyone working with a young child has at some point witnessed how the toddler's immature mind cannot process intense emotions and they are expressed via bodily disintegration. In order to redevelop safety and trust, the young child needs to be contained in close physical connection with the parents. If the therapist assesses that the parents are receptive to touch and cuddling this can be gently encouraged or introduced via play. This "co-regulation" of emotions by the parents is absolutely necessary and eventually facilitates the child's ability to self-regulate.

Psycho-education and developmental issues

As stated earlier, parenting is consciously and unconsciously informed by people's experiences of their own parenting. Alongside this exploration of their history, within the treatment setting, parents can often benefit from some psycho-education. For example, as Dowling (2019) suggests, "A frequent concern is the toddler's anxiety about separation from the mother, which may become particularly intense at bedtimes … the first child can feel rejected by the mother with the arrival of the next baby" (p. 46). It is helpful for the parents to hear how common these issues are and that they are likely to be more intense when children are at their most tired. This can help parents to understand their child's anxiety states better and to even anticipate them. It is extremely common for children of Gabrielle's age to have bedtime worries and it is often helpful to develop rituals to create safety. Predictable bedtime routines are crucial and one could spend time finding a safer way of preparing the child for saying goodnight. Talking parents through these emotional milestones might help them to understand whether their child's behaviour is age appropriate. Difficulties with a toddler are often the result of the parents viewing the toddler as capable of functioning at an older developmental level. The toddler usually feels the parental pressure (for example, to sit down or to go to sleep) but cannot fulfil the expectation and, as a result, goes into a meltdown. It can exacerbate behaviour issues if the parents misread the toddler's state as being defiant or naughty. In turn, the toddler feels unsafe because the adults do not understand their powerful impulses. A therapist can help break things down for both the child's and the parents' benefit in order to help the parents respond to the child's specific emotional/developmental level.

Due to her developmental stage, Gabrielle was grappling with a two-year-old's questions of what are her own self/body boundaries, what belongs inside her, what is located outside, and therefore what belongs to her mother. Gabrielle was wondering if she was a baby, a girl, or a mother who could bear children and with whom. These themes became further intensified with mother's pregnancy and the arrival of a sibling. Gabrielle used the word "babacar" repeatedly to communicate her state of confusion. She brought it to Winnicott from the beginning, such as in the second session (p. 24), where she asked Winnicott if he knew about the "babacar" and he responded, "It's the mother's inside where the baby is born from." In turn, she told him, "Yes, it's black inside" (p. 24). Winnicott facilitated fantasy play with Gabrielle which enabled her fears about the "babacar" to unfold. He concluded that the "babacar" image represented a sort of "baby car" or a type of container; in other words, her mother's womb. Winnicott also interpreted the related oedipal themes, such as her wish for daddy's attention and her fears that mummy would retaliate.

As shown by her rich vocabulary, Gabrielle seemed to possess advanced language skills but immature conceptualisation of her emotions. With such a child we need to communicate using language suited to the child's level of ability. Nowadays, as mentioned earlier, I wonder whether aside from the classical psychoanalytic themes (which undoubtedly were present, but perhaps at times were overemphasised by Winnicott), a clinician might tackle Gabrielle's fears with more developmentally appropriate language; such as that "Gabrielle is so sad not to be mummy's baby any more". Furthermore, "Sometimes you really want to be a grown-up girl and sometimes you want to be a baby again—and I think you want to be the only baby for mummy but it's scary that if you are a baby again you worry that mummy will get cross with you." Observing the child's words more closely can maximise parental empathy and support the child to feel psychologically validated. Another example of speaking simultaneously to the parent and the child might be something like: "Perhaps Gabrielle is telling us how going to sleep feels really scary," and saying to the child (in front of the parents), "We are going to help you go to bed safely."

Gabrielle was asking confusing questions, such as: "Am I the good one or the bad one?" With such questions, parents need to respond in a way that helps the child feel that they are not bad inside and that they will not anger others or be punished when trying to convey their feelings. The therapist can take the time to explain the nature of immature toddler logic; for example, taking the child's fears seriously and not being dismissive. Toddlers often imagine that their thoughts and wishes will actually happen and parents must be helped to distinguish this fantasy from reality. For example, young children often feel like they are really living with monsters. When toddlers are unable to rid themselves of these monsters and the fear associated with them, these metaphorical monsters need to be got rid of by the parents. Although we know that Gabrielle found it extremely difficult to separate from her parents, we don't know in detail what they did or said about this or their affective unconscious state related to their own separations. A contemporary therapist might encourage Gabrielle's mother to have some joint meetings with Gabrielle. The clinician could then explore how much Gabrielle's entrenched relationship with her mother was preventing her from age appropriate curiosity and exploration, including playing with other children. Developmentally, we would expect Gabrielle to be intrigued by other children and to seek out their company. Today we might wonder what it would have been like if Winnicott had facilitated a safe exploration for Gabrielle to come and go in relation to her mother. From the case account it is not clear how much Gabrielle's mother was involved emotionally, as the letters do not convey the quality of her emotion; of course, they were written at a particular historical and cultural time.

Winnicott learnt from experience that the baby has to be tolerated by the mother (and nowadays we would add the other parent/father too) in a rather special and intense way; the child's dependency on the mother is normal and necessary for later development. He stated: "The normal child enjoys a ruthless relation to his mother, mostly showing in play, and he needs his mother because only she can be expected to tolerate his ruthless relation to her even in play" (1945, p. 145). Through this powerful insight, Winnicott at sixty-eight years of age demonstrated his special gift in being able to think about young children. He tolerated Gabrielle's repetitive fears and anxieties in such an open way and he readily allowed her to make use of his thinking. He showed a great capacity in the way he took on the "different Winnicotts"; without being reactive he digested all her fluctuating primitive states, for example, when she became angry or when she engaged in comings and goings. I wonder if even nowadays therapists may find this too disruptive or threatening. By tolerating it, he actually modelled to the parents the need for them to tolerate Gabrielle's movement towards independence. After all, one of her main symptoms was her inability to say goodnight to her parents and therefore the constant leaving of Winnicott and his graceful reunion with her was an important experience for her. Parents may have an intellectual understanding of these matters but this is not the same as when emotional engagement and reflection take place. Supportive statements can encourage parental empathy with their child, such as stating: "It is really difficult at her age to understand why she doesn't have your sole attention anymore," or that she has rather "mixed feelings towards her sister and that is normal".

Treatment on demand

In today's society there is pressure to offer short-term therapeutic work due to financial pressures and long waiting lists for mental health services in the public sector. Some parents, who do not feel able to wait, may decide to go via the private referral routes. In today's world, if Gabrielle were to be seen in the public sector, it is likely she would receive about six sessions of treatment and that is only if the family were considered to be "at risk".

Winnicott was criticised for his "treatment on demand" (although, of course, he was not always able to offer Gabrielle a session when she requested it), questioning if he was providing psychoanalytic treatment at all. He also said himself that once-weekly work is of "doubtful value" (1977, p. 3). However, with busy lifestyles and both parents working, these days it is often difficult to see children more than once weekly. Moreover, most therapists (i.e. not psychoanalysts) believe that once-weekly work can be effective. However, even within psychoanalysis, more contemporary writers, such as Stern (2009) and Bass (2007) have challenged orthodoxy, suggesting that the less frequent psychoanalytic venture can still contain the essential elements of treatment as long as the therapist has undergone sufficient analytic training. The pioneering way that Winnicott conducted therapy with Gabrielle highlights the rationale for widening psychoanalytic parameters. He did not seem to sacrifice the psychoanalytic values of direct contact, engagement, authenticity, curiosity, and playfulness in his work with Gabrielle. Of course, at times, intensive work is necessary and extremely beneficial for some children. However, logistics can be difficult, working with nannies or other caregivers has its unique issues, and therefore sometimes we have to compromise on the frequency of sessions in order to ensure that the family maintains contact with us.

Even though Gabrielle was not seen frequently, one element of the treatment which appears to have been beneficial was having Winnicott's involvement over a prolonged period of time. The way Gabrielle's treatment unfolded was almost by chance and there is a question regarding whether Winnicott expected to be involved for as long as he was. In therapeutic work with young children, sometimes letting the family have space from treatment is important. There are two reasons for this: first, it gives us an opportunity to assess whether the child's maturational processes can come into play and take care of a certain amount of recovery. Winnicott stated that with caution that "It is possible for the treatment of a child actually to interfere with a very valuable thing which is the ability of the child's home to tolerate and to cope with the child's clinical states that indicate emotional strain and temporary holdups in emotional development, or even the fact of development itself" (p. 2). Furthermore, "It becomes very difficult to distinguish between clinical improvement and emotional development, between work done in the treatment and the maturational processes that have now become freed" (p. 2). Second, space away from therapy can be beneficial for the parents. As mentioned earlier, we cannot underestimate how parents of young children are steeped in their own primitive developmental process, triggered through their children's developmental processes. Consequently, for some more well-functioning families, after learning how their own unconscious processes have interfered in their parenting, having some space might also be a way that they can explore new and different ways of parenting and communicating with each other and with their child and begin to trust in their parenting skills again.

Cultural and racial issues

On re-examining *The Piggle,* one might wonder if nowadays we might tackle the material in a broader way. Racial and cultural factors are very much part of our multicultural society and they inevitably enter therapeutic work (Eleftheriadou, 2010). For example, right from the outset when Winnicott met Gabrielle's mother, he heard that there was a particular German song with made-up English words which made Gabrielle cry (see p. 13). During the interview with Gabrielle's mother (p. 13) she told Winnicott that Gabrielle associated (often, tearfully) this song with babyhood. When they had sung the same song to her at a later time, with new words, Gabrielle cried and wanted it to stop. We can speculate that the song may have been a reminder of the intimacy she had lost with her mother. Asking for the singing to stop may have been a way of retaining some control and gaining mastery over the situation that felt out of control for her. We also don't know what meaning this song had for her mother and whether it held feelings regarding her own family relationships, or even to separation from her own family, mother tongue, and country (since it was referred to as a "parting song"; p. 15). Mother's meaning may have been transferred to Gabrielle which made it even more upsetting. This is in contrast to humming a song with Winnicott, which Gabrielle took part in. This song was apparently familiar to Gabrielle as it was taught to her by her English father. Clearly, the emotional association of the English language was linked with her relationship to her father and had a positive valence. Interestingly, Winnicott referred to Gabrielle as "deeply attached to her father" (p. 12) and her mother stated that "From the age of six months, she adored her father" (p. 14).

As mentioned in an earlier section, with the arrival of her sister Gabrielle presented with intriguing vocabulary, such as that the "babacar" is "black inside" or referring to the "black mummy". Although at first Winnicott was confused by these references, he took a risk and interpreted them as representing her mother's body. His interpretation of these frightening primitive thoughts opened up her associations to "good" and "bad". Gabrielle had split her mother into the good and bad mother and she feared that the bad mummy could retaliate and spoil everything (especially at night which prevented her from going to sleep). Repeatedly, she seemed to equate "black" for badness; at times, this was projected into her mother but she also feared that it was inside her or would intrude (for example, "the dark will make her black", p. 50). In his notes, Winnicott added that "black" is "linked with a sense of guilt" (p. 36) in relation to her aggression and (occasional) physical attacks on her sister. This was also linked to her overwhelming fury and disillusionment with her mother since she gave birth to her sister. We can not exclude the fact that her meaning of the word "black" may have also been derived partly from parental meanings, although this became her distinct vocabulary for her distress.

Gabrielle's wording was unusually rich and her use of the colour black was very interesting. In some contexts, one might wonder if a child's equating blackness with badness might come not only from internal fantasy but also from sociocultural values absorbed from parental attitudes or from the larger culture. However, there is insufficient evidence in the case of The Piggle that her use of the colour black derived from such sources or had such meanings. However, nowadays in our multicultural and multiracial world, a clinician would certainly be interested in the usage of these words and would consider the possibility that they held a racial meaning. In such cases it might therefore be helpful for a child to have access to a range of racial/cultural play figures, where, like Gabrielle, she could play out her fears, such as separations and sibling rivalry. When our clients (children or adults) bring cultural or racial references it is important to explore potential intrapsychic as well as interpersonal meanings. Racial or cultural references would have been viewed as being "external" to the therapeutic process in traditional psychoanalysis (and are still underestimated by some psychoanalytic schools today). In general, it is essential not to view racial or cultural issues concretely and to understand the multiple meanings they hold. Younger children may need help in separating parental or societal meanings which they have adopted but they simply do not comprehend.

Conclusion

This chapter provided a re-examination of Winnicott's case of *The Piggle* with some therapeutic aspects questioned and others praised. One of the main points of difference between Donald Winnicott's handling of the case and contemporary practice is that today, Gabrielle's parents would have been more involved, initially invited to come in on their own, in order to understand their relationship and individual psycho-histories. Then, if it was still thought to be necessary, Gabrielle would have been invited to attend a subsequent session with them. Gabrielle's intrapsychic images of her family would have been explored as well as their interplay with parental or intergenerational issues. Moreover, the therapist would actively facilitate ways that Gabrielle's parents could provide a sense of safety as early as possible.

We will never really know exactly what it was like for Winnicott to be Gabrielle's therapist. However, from the information which we have available, Winnicott creatively managed to find the right words to convey his understanding. He managed to get the key therapeutic ingredients right, such as how he engaged authentically and directly and validated Gabrielle's intrapsychic reality. Undoubtedly, Winnicott started to carve out a different model from what was common practice at that time; he utilised creative play, he emphasised the significance of the therapeutic relationship, and he did not hide behind technique. Although Winnicott did not see Gabrielle together with her parents (which may still occur in some current psychoanalytic practice) what differs from contemporary practice is that he did not meet with them regularly. However, he maintained a close relationship with them via letters, unlike other psychoanalysts of that time. There is a real feeling of his having "held" both the parents and the child in this family. Despite making a variety of traditional interpretations, Winnicott demonstrated an openness to Gabrielle's material and waited to see how much Gabrielle gained from his therapeutic interventions. At the same time he also acknowledged the importance of letting the maturational processes unfold. Overall, Winnicott managed to capture something substantial of Gabrielle's unconscious experience which helped her to progress emotionally. There were many clinical issues raised by this case study, such as the nature of contact with parents, the use of play, and the timing and nature of interpretations. Today, these continue to be ongoing themes for consideration in psychoanalytic therapy with younger children. The hope is that detailed case studies such as *The Piggle* will stimulate discussion and an appreciation of young children's rich psychological worlds.

References

Bass, A. (2007). When the frame doesn't fit the picture. *Psychoanalytic Dialogues, 17*: 1–27.

Beebe, B. (2005). Mother–infant research informs mother–infant treatment. *Psychoanalytic Study of the Child, 60*: 6–46.

Brafman, A. H. (2016). *The Language of Distress*. London: Karnac.

Coles, P. (2018). *The Importance of Siblings in Psychoanalysis*. Abingdon, UK: Routledge.

Cramer, B. G. (1992). *The Importance of Being Baby*. Wokingham, UK: Addison-Wesley.

Dowling, D. (2019). *An Independent Practitioner's Introduction to Child and Adolescent Psychotherapy: Playing with Ideas*. London: Routledge.

Eleftheriadou, Z. (2010). *Psychotherapy and Culture: Weaving Inner and Outer Worlds*. London: Karnac.

Fraiberg, S., Adelson, E., & Shapiro, V. (1975). Ghosts in the nursery: A psychoanalytic approach to the problems of impaired infant–mother relationships. *Journal of the American Academy of Child Psychiatry, 14*(3): 387–421.

Freud, A. (1983). Excerpts from seminars and meetings: The technique of child analysis. *Bulletin of the Hampstead Clinic, 6*: 115–128.

Holmes, J., & Slade, A. (2018). *Attachment in Therapeutic Practice*. London: Sage.

Mitchell, J. (2003). *Siblings*. Cambridge: Polity.

Schechter, M. A., & Willheim, E. (2009). When parenting becomes unthinkable: Intervening with traumatized patients and their toddlers. *Journal of the American Academic Child and Adolescent Psychiatry*, 48(3): 249–253.

Slade, A. (1988). The quality of attachment and early symbolic play. *Developmental Psychology*, 23(1): 78–85.

Slade, A. (2005). Parental reflective functioning: An introduction. *Attachment and Human Development*, 7(3): 269–281.

Stern, D., Sander, L., Nahum, J. P., Harrison A. M., Lyons-Ruth, K., Morgan, A. C., Bruschweilerstern, N., & Tronick, E. Z. (1998). Non-interpretive mechanisms in psychoanalytic therapy: The 'something more' than interpretation. *International Journal of Psychoanalysis*, 79(5): 903–921.

Stern, S. (2009). Session frequency and the definition of psychoanalysis. *Psychoanalytic Dialogues*, 19: 639–655.

Winnicott, D. W. (1945). Primitive emotional development. In: *Through Paediatrics to Psychoanalysis* (pp. 145–156). London: Karnac.

Winnicott, D. W. (1964). *The Child, the Family and the Outside World*. London: Penguin.

Winnicott, D. W. (1971). *Playing and Reality*. London: Routledge.

Winnicott, D. W. (1977). *The Piggle*. London: Penguin.

Winnicott, D. W. (1990). *Home Is Where We Start From: Essays by a Psychoanalyst*. C. W. Winnicott, R. Shepherd, & M. Davis (Eds.). London: Penguin.

Winnicott, D. W. (2006). *The Family and Individual Development*. London: Routledge.

Final thoughts

Corinne Masur

*T*he *Piggle* is a case study with no peer. It lends us insight not only to the inner world of the very young child but also into the thought processes of the analyst treating the young child. More-over, Winnicott's write-up of the case lends credence to the belief that the young child *has* an inner life, a belief that is in short supply in these days of "evidence based" treatments. In a time when we are increasingly looking at people as mere products of their environments and as collec-tions of behaviours that can be easily and quickly changed via manual-ised treatments, it is more important than ever to read and reread *The Piggle* and child case studies like it (those of Klein, Kramer, Luepnitz, and Smolen come to mind). We need to hold tightly to our belief in the importance of the child's fantasy life and the ways that the child's own particular understanding of relationships and events influences her cur-rent reality, her sense of self, her character development, and her inter-nal object relations.

In her foreword, Angela Joyce states that in this volume Donald Winnicott's most famous case receives creative and critical engagement. For all the authors, this engagement was pure pleasure. Playing with Winnicott's case formulations and technique was an exercise in getting to know him and an opportunity to play with him—if only by proxy. It was a privilege that those of us who never had a chance to know him or to engage with him in person did, at least, have an opportunity to meet with his ideas.

If this volume has, in any way, brought new life to Donald Winnicott's wonderful work, then its best purpose will have been served. If it comes close to extending our thinking not only about this fascinating case but also about psychoanalysis, the internal lives of children, the role of the external world in the inner reality of the child, and the development of psychoanalytic theory and child analytic technique, then it will have served its intended purpose.

Corinne Masur
Chester Springs,
Pennsylvania, USA

Index

9781912691630